A GIRLHOOD

A GIRLHOOD

LETTER TO
MY TRANSGENDER
DAUGHTER

Carolyn Hays

— BLAIR —

Printed in the United States of America
Cover design by Mel Four, Picador art department
Interior design by April Leidig

Blair is an imprint of Carolina Wren Press.

The mission of Blair/Carolina Wren Press is to seek out, nurture, and promote literary work by new and underrepresented writers.

We gratefully acknowledge the ongoing support of
general operations by the Durham Arts Council's United Arts Fund
and the North Carolina Arts Council.

Library of Congress Cataloging-in-Publication Data
Names: Hays, Carolyn, author.
Title: A girlhood : letter to my transgender daughter / Carolyn Hays.
Description: [Durham] : Blair, [2022]
Identifiers: LCCN 2022011030 (print) | LCCN 2022011031 (ebook) |
ISBN 9781949467901 (hardcover) | ISBN 9781949467918 (ebook)
Subjects: LCSH: Parents of transgender children. | Transgender children.
Classification: LCC HQ759.9147 .H39 2022 (print) | LCC HQ759.9147 (ebook) |
DDC 306.874086/7—dc23/eng/20220421
LC record available at https://lccn.loc.gov/2022011030
LC ebook record available at https://lccn.loc.gov/2022011031

AUTHOR'S NOTE

I've changed the names of people and
obfuscated the names of places in this book.
I wrote this for my daughter, and she's
allowing me to share it.

FIRST . . .

THIS IS NOT A TRAGEDY.

But it started the way so many tragedies do—in a quiet and awful way, a common occurrence, a weary dailiness to it. It started with a knock at the front door.

I didn't hear the knock. I was writing in the mother-in-law suite connected to the house by what we called the breezelessway.

Your older sister answered the knock and then came to get me.

This moment, this knock, changed our lives forever. It created fissures that remain: This was our lives before it. This was our lives after. Everything changed. There was panic and loss and a kind of fear that never really goes away.

You were at its center, but we protected you from it—your father and I, your older sister, and your two older brothers. It was a story that I finally told you when you were nine years old. We'd left that house by then. We'd left that southern state. We'd moved more than a thousand miles away, due north. But I worried that the story might pop up in conversation, unexpectedly—from an aunt, a friend, someone assuming you knew about it because it was about you. I didn't want you to hear it from someone else.

I told you a pared-down version of it, sitting on a sunny sofa in our living room. We've moved so many times that the sunny sofa blurs in my mind from one living room to the next, like each living room is a train car zipping past. The story went like this. A man was at the door, sent from the Department of Children and Families. He was there to investigate us, as parents. There had been a complaint. The complaint was about you being transgender, and we quickly learned that in this southern state with Republican-appointed judges, we could lose custody. We could lose you. This was what I tried to explain—the knock at the door and what happened in the days and weeks and months that followed. When I was finished, you didn't have any questions, and you never asked to hear the story again.

But I think you deserve to have it in full. It belongs to you. I'm committed to telling you the brutal truths of this story, your story. For a long time, I haven't known how. But now I do. I'll also tell you the beautiful truths. This is how it should be. This is how we should prepare children for the world. (I don't know how to prepare children for this world.)

What happened upended us, and yet it oriented us. Before the knock at the door, our idea of family—of what we would do for each other in crisis—was theoretical. It became manifest.

What happened to us shouldn't happen to anyone. But it did, and it keeps happening, especially to families like ours.

How we responded made us understand who we are. What we did for you, we suddenly understood that we would do for any of us.

In the end, though, this is just one part of your larger story, and it doesn't define you.

Part I

BEFORE THE KNOCK

AS I SET OUT to write this, you've recently had your thirteenth birthday. I remember it this way. You're sitting in a spindle chair that's been transformed into a flowering throne. It's morning, and you're still in your pajamas. The night before, while you were sleeping, your father and I cut some of the low-hanging boughs of the massive tulip magnolia tree in our backyard and taped them to the chair in such a way that they curve and fan out over your head. The petals are thick, the blooms heavy, white with flushes of purple and pink. In my memory, they're luminous. You're smiling. You look up to see the blooms bobbing over your head, and I wonder what it looks like from your perspective—the structure of branches, the petals surrounded by waxy green leaves.

Throughout your life, I've tried to imagine what things must look like from your perspective. I can't ever really know this. And so much of what I have to tell you happened before you could form memories of your own. But I took notes. I paid attention. What I can offer you is what I saw, what caught my attention, what sometimes astounded me, and this telling is my attempt to put it together for you. Imperfect, limited, and awash in love.

I could start where so many of these stories begin, with a label. But that wasn't the beginning.

This was: Your brain, a small blushing bud. It unfurled, as all of our brains do, with the ticking of some internal clock. On cue, certain areas began their quiet work of becoming. Neurons fired away—those brilliant pistons. Within the exquisite architecture of your brain, there is a small area tucked away, like a pearl. This one region grew, yes. But in a "typical boy," it would be double in size. Yours is the size one would find in a "typical girl." (Apologies for using the word *typical* here, in its more limited medical way, especially as I'm trying to broaden experiences, not narrow them down. You will never be a "typical" girl, but neither was I. Neither was your sister. Neither were your grandmothers or great-grandmothers or any of your ancestors. I don't actually believe that *typical* exists.)

This area is known as the central region of the bed nucleus of the stria terminalis. I think: *Bed*, like a garden, lush flowers, heavy-headed, nodding in a breeze. *Nucleus*, like a lit globe, a fiery hub. And *stria terminalis* reminds me of the last train stop in Rome, where I once spent Christmas in my early twenties. This is how my own brain works—trying to collect what I remember and hitch it to what I hope to understand.

(And I love the human brain. There is a long and brutal history of pathologizing trans people. But I'm not doing that. I'm awed by how neurologically diverse we all are, how intricately wired, all of the vast and stunning individual structures within each of us.)

Meanwhile, your genes, the double helix that expresses so much about you (but not all, not even close) were twinning within. I think of them as two hummingbirds, locked together, spiraling in flight. More than one hundred genes—that we know of so far—are part of the process that created your gender identity; I would say your *girliness*, but that presumes so much frill and pink (though you love frill and pink). So I will restate it this way: More than one hundred genes—so far—are known to be part of the process of creating your *girlness*, a tough knot of self-knowledge that exists within a larger framework: your *girlhood*.

For a long time, we thought that a child's chromosomes were either XX or XY. (We once thought so many things—before microscopes made the invisible visible, before telescopes exposed us to a vast universe, before MRIs and fMRIs lit up our brains—which are vast universes in and of themselves.) Now we know there are XXX and XXY and XYY . . . and one out of every one hundred infants is born with deviations from the "typical" male and female anatomy. One in every two thousand is so diverse that a specialist has to come in for a consult, and some of these infants are considered to be intersex. Your chromosomes were never questioned—a simple XY. No doctors were called in for a consult. All of the exteriors and blunt frameworks were clear. But within?

We can barely begin to explain the interiors of each of our unique neural networks, the synchronicity of all of our functions, from our ticking hearts to our ability to form language.

For example, my own thoughts, in the form of these words, are appearing in my brain, one after the other, as they transfer almost automatically through my fingers to be collected and passed on to you—in the moment where you find yourself in the middle of your life, into your brain where they arrive as ideas and images (and love).

Let me say the word *storm* and then *garden* and then *girl in a stormy garden.* . . . See what happens in your mind? See the girl in the stormy garden, rain and wind, her face—surprised or scared or happy? Is it day or night? Does she lift her face to the sky?

With you—my fourth baby, whom I believed to be my last—I felt so in sync. The pregnancy, after three kids in quick succession and then a seven-year gap, seemed brazen. I strode down hallways at work, carving a wide berth. I loved the swell and arch. I loved the way my stomach found the old pleats and started filling them, found the old stretch marks and brightened them with streaks like lightning.

We were a big, loud East Coast family, new to the Bible Belt. We moved here because of my job. My academic career was going very well. But this made it even more confusing to my fellow academics that I'd insisted on having children. One? *Okay.* Two? *Fine.* Three? *A strange personal choice.* But four? *My God.* I came from a big Irish Catholic herd that believed in herds. My definition of a happy family was *rowdy.*

A colleague of mine in gender studies, a staunch communist, tried to joke with me in the elevator. "You know how these things happen, right?"

I laughed. "I'm starting to catch on." But my tone was a little steely, and she didn't bring up anything about my pregnancy again. This was how I preferred it. Whenever any of my colleagues mentioned the pregnancy, I responded with some variation of "Oh this?" and moved on. In my office, there were no pictures of my kids. No little-kid art, either. Students walked in for office hours and made comments like, "This is very . . . Spartan chic?"

"You know how these things happen, right?"

This was how.

Your father and I are crazy about each other. It's embarrassing, I know. It's implausible if you sort through our cultural baggage of depictions of marriage. We'd constructed a life where we spent the bulk of our days together. I was the stay-at-home parent for the first six years of our marriage when the first three kids were born.

But then my career shifted into gear, and by the time I was pregnant with you, Jeff was the primary caregiver and I was the primary breadwinner, but I worked at home a good bit. Even though we were together almost all the time, we usually had too much to say and couldn't get it all in.

Some friends of ours once said that you should never invite a couple newly in love to dinner because they're the most boring guests—they're only interested in each other. Sometimes we're still this couple. At parties, we force ourselves to go in separate directions so we can swap the stories we collect at the end of the night, like so much Halloween candy.

What did we look like back then? Jeff was a fit soccer coach, permanently sunburned, with that disarming sense of humor, that way of making everyone feel like they had something important to say. I was a very pale Floridian, avoiding the sun. I wore my dark hair back in ponytails or messy buns, always a little rushed and disheveled.

Jeff loved raising kids. How else would I be able to have such a strong career while raising so many? While it could strain other couples, raising all of you has been galvanizing for us. This wily brood consumes us, in the best ways. If raising children is overwhelming—and it can be—we have made a life of being overwhelmed together, as if in an ocean, pulled under and whisked from shore, but always by the same riptide.

My academic office might have come off as Spartan and impersonal, but not our home. Walking in, you were likely met by barking dogs, an enormous puppet made out of papier-mâché on the dining room table, and a few kids making a spy movie with a GoPro with an occasional shout of "Quiet on set!" A scaled-down soccer match in the kitchen might have respectfully called a time-out. The agony of a violin practice might have gone silent for a few minutes. We are a family that takes our projects very seriously.

In the fall of 2006, leading up to your birth the upcoming spring, Tate was six-about-to-turn-seven. He didn't remember living in the North. He was a small but muscular kid with blue eyes and a bowl cut. He'd become more quintessentially southern. When friends went to a monster truck rally, he begged to go along and loved it. He wanted us to turn the radio to country music. He loved riding on the John Deere Gator on our friends' family farm. He borrowed our neighbor's ghillie suit and made films with Isaac about swamp monsters. His friendship with the wild sons of a minister struck me as stereotypically southern. It was at their house that a neighbor almost put Tate's eye out with a BB gun. Tate showed me his baby photos one day and said, "Look, there!" I leaned in close, not sure what he wanted me to see. In the photo, he was about three months old, asleep in a car seat, in profile. The photo is mostly of the back of his head. "I was born with a mullet," he said, proud that he'd found what he saw as proof of his southern roots.

Isaac was ten, with a round face and a head of curly brown hair. His kindergarten nickname was The Mayor because the other kids would shout to him when he arrived and at the end of the day, and he'd wave magnanimously. This never really changed. He's a beloved type and very funny—funny beyond his years. One afternoon, he got in the car after school and told me that they were talking about unhealthy eating habits and why smoking was deadly. He really went off on why it was all terrible, really deadly. And then, having set up the joke, he went quiet, really gave it a beat, and then said, "God, I want to smoke." This was funny. But he was just getting started. "I want a smoke and a Big Mac." He sighed and then went on, heated up now. "I want to cut a hole in a Big Mac, shove a cigarette in it, and smoke the Big Mac that I'm eating." And, trust me, he knew it was funny because he was just a kid in a minivan. This was Isaac.

Sophie? She was a tree climber who would join an all-boys teen youth soccer team and become captain. She was fierce, with long, straight, light-red hair. At around age ten, she was putting on her boots one morning when I asked her where she was going. "To borrow the neighbor's blowtorch." She hadn't asked permission, but the answer was no. She loved projects—art, sewing, building. When I became pregnant with you, she was twelve and didn't appreciate middle school politics, at all. But she threw herself into advocacy for turtle migration and ended up on the local news, explaining why we should protect turtles. She was very tough and, to be honest, a little intimidating. She always had a grown-up nature. Your dad is a middle child, and I'm the baby of my family; so when your sister was born, she took charge as the oldest child among us. When Jeff and I aren't sure what to do, one of us will usually suggest that we consult with her. And she always has an opinion. Always. And she has saved a lot of turtles.

With the kids' curiosity, I sometimes felt like being pregnant with you was strangely scientific—you and I were the experiment itself. Their interest came and went. But sometimes I would see one of them eyeing me suspiciously as if wondering if it was still me. It wasn't. It was *us*.

There was also politicking—each kid took up lobbying efforts over your name. Meanwhile, a nickname appeared. We were so used to rattling off the concise litany of your sister and brothers' names that we felt there should be a dramatic pause before yours. "This is Sophie, Isaac, Tate . . . and then there's Maude." It was from the refrain of the theme song of the 1970s TV show *Maude*. The song played over images of a frazzled, dour Bea Arthur, trying to navigate her life as a liberated woman. The song nodded to Lady Godiva, Joan of Arc, Isadora Duncan, and Betsy Ross. *And then there's Maude!* Before we'd seen the ultrasound that would distinguish body parts, we were saying, "And then there's Maude!"

Isaac, for example, was eating peanut butter sandwiches with a neighborhood friend while camping out under the dining room table. "Yeah," I heard him say, "my mom sometimes feels queasy and lies down. Because . . . *there's Maude!*"

Of all the kids, Sophie was the most fascinated by my pregnancy. She insisted on coming with Jeff and me to the ultrasound that would reveal the blunt framework of gender.

The room was small and stuffy. The technician showed us the screen.

Sophie was the one to make the announcement. She said flatly, "It's a boy." With two brothers, she'd been hoping for a sister.

I didn't care one way or another. With my first pregnancy, I dreamed I was having a boy and was convinced I was prescient. How could I not know something so obvious about the person living inside of my own body? I was wrong. With my second, I had a gut instinct that I was having another girl.

I think that my reasoning was simple and idiotic. "It's a girl because I have girls." I had exactly one data point and irrationally assumed things. I was wrong.

With my third, I realized that I don't actually know the gender of the fetuses inside of me. (There is a larger metaphor here.)

———

Preconsciousness, in utero, we all start out with only the chromosomes traditionally thought of as "female" having an active part in our development. The Y chromosomes in "typical" male fetuses don't have any role until after the first five or six weeks of development, when a certain gene on the Y chromosome is activated. When that Y chromosome sets to work, it blocks some of the features of the X chromosome.

The formation of nipples, for example, occurs during those early weeks, which is why we all have them.

———

And let's not forget about the environs—my womb, the place where your cells divided and multiplied, where you were being bathed and steeped, suspended in amniotic fluid, awash in hormones. My thyroid—that thug in my throat—wasn't doing what it should. A butterfly-shaped organ, you'd think it would flit, but mine lumbered. My endocrinologist was supposed to be vigilant, upping my meds, but there was a delay that perhaps overlaps with the beginnings of your development of gender identity. Years later, I would mention this to doctors. Each one told me that there was no correlation. Why did I want to find some root cause?

———

It was also possible that there was this little receptor gene of yours—one that helped take in testosterone in utero—that maybe didn't take in as much as usual. You can see how much I've fallen into research, a well of wanting to know what can't really be known. Scientists have done the research and found that this phenomenon can result in what they've called a more "feminine brain."

Nothing good can come of the term *feminine brain*. What could it even mean? It will be used against women. I can feel the nineteenth-century claws of it. Like a chorus of ancient phrenologists has a new way of doing old, terrible things, and they break out in a *Hurrah!*

The term is dangerous.

But all of this is dangerous.

2

MONTHS PASSED AND I became hugely pregnant—overdue, in fact. Your great-grandmother was in a hospice facility. My parents moved down for the winter months, and she came with them. We maneuver intergenerationally this way.

My grandmother was a Marilyn Monroe beauty in her forties. An agoraphobic in her fifties, she gained weight and now had the regal air of an ample, aging southern belle. Into her eighties and nineties, she would be stopped by strangers who told her how beautiful she was. She demanded this kind of attention. And, as a stunning matriarch, she insisted on dying naked. She wore only a light sheet—as light as her muumuus had been—and was surrounded by family who had poured in from all over the country. A queen, she directed one of us to hold one of her hands, the second to hold the other. The next two could rub her feet. The fifth was charged with positioning a mini fan from the dollar store up to her face.

For weeks, I'd been having night labor. My contractions lined up, five minutes apart, but never progressed. In the morning, they faded but never completely disappeared.

I pulled a chair to the side of her bed, as close as I could get, and she put her hand on my belly to feel you kick, with fingers swollen at the knuckles and constricted by arthritis. You were outgrowing me. Head down, your heels were little knobs poking up at the top of my belly. Your movements were strong and powerful.

The two of you—across a multigenerational divide—were locked in a life-and-death exchange. The whole family needed you to be born before she died—or at least that's how I felt. I sat there like I'd swallowed a giant ticking clock. Sometimes she got tired of waiting. She went through phases when she'd call out, "Take me now, Jesus! Take me now!" But she would always demure, adding in a quiet voice, ". . . But not today."

(This has become an ongoing joke. Whenever someone in the family is mouthing off about what they're going to do about some situation when they probably won't do anything, someone will mutter, ". . . But not today.")

One evening, at the end of a visit, your dad and I were saying our good-byes, always a slow process. As we moved toward the door, your great-grandmother said in a hushed voice, "I know what you should name that baby."

We had a name picked out that we weren't sharing, but this moment felt holy. We rushed back to her bedside. "What?" we asked. "What should we name the baby?"

She held the quiet, dramatically, and then finally said, "Jackass! Because that baby is jack-assing around in there!"

Your first label wasn't girl or boy. It was jackass.

Eventually, you would be born, and your great-grandmother wouldn't die naked in this hospice bed. Jesus wouldn't take her for some time—*not today* and not the next. She was lovingly kicked out of hospice. At great expense, my parents chartered a private plane that allowed her to fly with oxygen, back to where they lived in the Northeast.

"A private plane," my grandmother said to the orderlies as they wheeled her out. "I feel like Marilyn Monroe."

She lived for two more years when, one day in March, Jesus finally relented.

Sophie went to as many of my appointments with the obstetrician as possible. She has a keenly scientific mind. She was astonished by this wild act of making a human being that was so strangely being taken in stride, being seen as ordinary. It was not ordinary to her.

While my body was going through pregnancy, she was also going through puberty, and her great-grandmother was supposedly dying as you were preparing to be born. The four of us—you and her, my grandmother and me— were all going through dynamic shifts, ones that expanded Sophie's understanding of what bodies could do and how our bodies betrayed us. She wanted to be there for the birth, but things shifted and I had to have a C-section. She wasn't allowed in.

On the day of the C-section, she was pacing with my parents in the waiting room. Your aunt was there, and Tate. I'd given the kids the option of not going to school. Isaac was the only one who chose to go because he didn't want to miss a fishing field trip.

Your father was told to suit up for surgery so he could be with me. He was led to a room and given scrubs to change into. This was what he'd been waiting for. Sophie was born via C-section, but the boys weren't. He knew his goals and was reminding himself of them. "Stay by her head. Don't look for the baby. Wait. Whisper good things. Don't pass out. Don't pass out. Whatever you do, don't pass out."

He hadn't passed out during the previous births, but when someone labors for days on end, partners are bound to hear story after story of fathers passing out.

He was told that someone would come to get him, and he waited there for longer than he thought was right.

A nurse walked into the room. "Who are you?" she asked.

"I'm the father!" he said. "I'm the dad!"

"Of who?" she said. He told her, and she said, "Huh." The nurse didn't recognize his name and didn't know what to do with lost fathers.

Meanwhile, in the operating room, the doctor asked me if we should wait for the father. The doctor was a small woman with an intense gaze.

If it had been my first—or second or third—maybe I'd have chosen to wait. But this was work. I wasn't a curiosity or a science experiment. This was birth and major surgery. I'd been in labor for weeks by now, with labor that wouldn't progress.

"No," I said. "Let's go."

The petite doctor climbed up on a step stool and began.

One of the first doctors on record to perform a cesarean in which both the mother and the baby lived was Dr. James Barry, assigned female at birth in Ireland in 1789. His private anatomy was discovered only after his death. No one would have known, in fact, if the charwoman who'd attended to the body hadn't taken the story to the offices of Barry's attending physician, telling him he'd gotten the gender wrong on the death certificate.

"The woman seemed to think she had become acquainted with a great secret and wished to be paid for keeping it," the attending physician wrote in a letter. He refused to pay her. "But whether Barry was a male, female, or hermaphrodite I do not know, nor had I any purpose in making the discovery as I could positively swear to the identity of the body as being that of a person whom I had been acquainted with as Inspector-General of Hospitals for a period of years."

the identity of the body as being that of a person

a person whom I had been acquainted with

You, my sweet person, were lifted up from me. You were full and round—a light blush of reddish-blond hair—and then you were whisked away.

We would become acquainted.

―――――――

On your chart, someone marked down *male.*

Here is a quick breakdown of a possible evolution when it comes to gender:

1. Two boxes. One labeled F and one labeled M. You check a box.
2. A slider scale—at one end there's feminine and at the other there's masculine. You move the slider wherever you want, as many times as you need. (Neuroscientist Dr. Baudewijntje Kreukels doesn't believe in a male or female brain. "It's more of a continuum.")
3. Or forget the slider scale. Instead imagine a multidimensional structure—3D isn't quite enough to hold it. And this structure is informed by the brain, the body, its hormones, its in-utero development, its chromosomes, its neurology, its inner complexities that do not yet have names, and culture and society and family and history (and your moment in it). . . .

―――――――

Shortly after your birth, you were on your belly, being attended to by a nurse, and you did a full push-up and turned your head to the other side, which is remarkable for a newborn.

"Did you see that?" the nurse said.

I was in recovery. She was talking to the big family that had shown up and circled around you. Grandparents, an aunt, your father, and all three siblings (your big brother now back from his fishing trip).

"I've never seen a baby do something like that!" the nurse remarked.

I would later think of it as a sign of your strength, yes, but also the sheer force of your curiosity. You wanted to see more.

What was on the other side of your vision that drew your attention?

It might have been your father. Newborns recognize voices from their time in the womb. Maybe you were drawn to his bass.

Or maybe it was your sister, Sophie—her voice.

———

Sophie is now in graduate school. On a recent call, she told me about the first episode of a Netflix special called *Babies*. She explained that they've taken tests on the primary caregivers of infants and found that whether moms or dads, gay or straight, biological or adoptive, the primary caregivers' bodies change—the ones who hold, tend to, and take care of the baby. "And the amygdala opens up—that part of the brain that is fight, flight, or freeze," she told me. "I think mine opened. I held her so much."

I thought of the extended amygdala, the bed nucleus of the stria terminalis. Yours is likely the size of a "typical" girl's. I've since learned that the amygdala grows more than it opens, but I prefer the term Sophie used. Maybe hers, as a girl, *opened* because she took care of you, helped give you baths, rocked you. All of the associations I've made around the words *bed nucleus of the stria terminalis* flood back to me—the garden, the lit globe nucleus, the last train stop in Rome. "What happens when that part of the amygdala opens?" I asked her.

"You worry about that child. You have the instinct to protect that child at all costs."

I imagined the moment when my own amygdala may have suddenly grown. It was shortly after Sophie's birth. The nurse was moving her newborn body around too quickly and roughly, swaddling and swapping her from one arm to the other. I didn't like the casualness. I read it as reckless. And I felt this heat rise up inside of me, fiery and quick. "I'll take her," I said, but what I meant was *Never touch my baby again.*

Your brothers were very excited to have a baby in the house. They adored you and argued over who got to hold you. Once you were old enough to laugh, they excelled at making faces and weird noises to get you going.

Sophie's attachment ran deeper. "I was obsessed with her breathing," she told me on that same phone call. "And when she was sleeping, I'd put my finger under her nose and keep it there to make sure she kept breathing."

I'd never heard this story, but it's so *her*.

What I do remember is waking up one morning a few days after your birth to Sophie's face bobbing in front of mine. She was ready for school. She said, "I got the baby dressed and picked out two outfits in case there's need for spares. They're on the changing table." Leaving you wasn't easy for her, and she wanted to make sure all went to plan.

"Once the amygdala opens up, it never closes," she told me. She has always been a sisterly presence and a maternal presence, her love for you swinging between these two states. She wanted to protect you, fiercely, from the amygdala out.

We all did. And eventually all of our collective protectiveness would kick in. That's where this story is headed.

MOST PLANTS HAVE PERFECT flowers. And here the term *perfect* isn't subjective—botanists use it to relay when male and female structures exist within the same flower. Imperfect flowers are called *dioecious*, which is Greek for "two houses." They are *imperfect* because their flowers are only either male or female, not both.

When we first moved to the South, I wanted a blueberry bush. We soon learned that blueberry bushes need to be bought in male and female pairs, if you want good fruit. The same is true of bayberry, juniper, and the yew, though its berries are poisonous, so it's usually chosen for its shape.

I'm not bringing up this idea of perfection because it shifts gender expectations.

I bring it up because some people claim to be able to tell a male holly from a female by looking at the leaves. A good botanist will explain that this isn't true. The only way to know the gender of a holly plant is to be there when it flowers.

———————

You were three years old, amid all of your brothers' very boyish toys and wearing their hand-me-down clothes, when you began to tell your father and me that you were a girl.

You heard me talking on the phone to my mother about you: ". . . He's in the playroom . . ."

You shouted, "She! She is in the playroom!"

You told your preschool teachers and the other kids in your class that you were a girl.

A teacher was driving back to school after a field trip, and she heard an argument in the back seat. You were soft-spoken, but you held your ground. "I'm a girl," you told the other kid. "I am."

You came home from school one day and told me that during snack time, one little girl whispered loudly to another little girl that you were a boy.

"What did you do?" You did nothing.

So the little girl turned to you and said, "Did you hear what I said?"

"Yes," you told her, and then you corrected her. "I'm a very nice girl." The subtext was clear: the other girl was not a nice girl.

Your father and I were in bed one night. One of those gusty southern storms had just passed through. We stared at the ceiling.

"I thought I had it figured out," he said.

"What did you have figured out?"

"Parenting," he said.

"I don't know if that's something anyone ever really figures out."

"I just thought maybe there's some future where it's all a lot easier and I take up golf."

Even though we knew that there is no more humbling act than raising children, we were cocky like this.

"What if this kid learned to talk just to let us know that we've gotten it wrong?" he said.

"You mean, what if she's a girl?"

"That's exactly what I mean."

This was a kind of flowering, a bloom of language. You were telling us who you were.

I remember you dressed for the three-year-olds' school program, wearing khaki shorts and a short-sleeved shirt, another hand-me-down from your brothers. But you had also collected five discarded pocketbooks that once belonged to your sister and me. A clutch, two over-the-shoulder bags, a third cross-body bag, and a fanny pack (that your sister had only worn iron-ically). You picked out a Dora the Explorer backpack. Empty, it was strapped to your back. With blond curls puffed on top of your head, you were smiling, bright and wide.

I can't help thinking of the pocketbooks as a kind of armor, an assortment of spotty and useless shields.

I can't help thinking of the pocketbooks as targets, a series of ever-tightening red circles.

Anyone who believes in binaries hasn't been paying attention to medicine and science and exploration. We never send someone out on a mission to discover what's beyond us or the vastness of what's within us and have them return to report, "Actually, we found less." They never come back and reduce. There's always more. Two boxes, one labeled F and one labeled M? The person who wants binaries—not just in gender but in life—is bound to be frustrated if not angry at the multiplicities of life.

Over the years, we've learned that if you'd been an identical twin, your twin would have had a higher likelihood of being transgender than if you'd been fraternal twins.

And that a woman in Australia found out in her forties—while pregnant with her third child—that she had male and female chromosomal makeups. The news came from a routine amniocentesis. The baby's test came back as expected. But her own body's genetic makeup was very unusual. It's possible that she had once shared her mother's womb with a twin who had XY chromosomes. Her twin didn't continue to develop, and the two embryos merged. She had both her own XX chromosomes as well as the twin's XY chromosomes, known as a *chimera* in medicine.

And how in the village of Salinas in the Dominican Republic, it's not unusual for a child to be labeled a girl at birth but then develop a penis during puberty.

Eventually, your father and I would learn about trans people throughout history.

But at this point, all we really knew was you. More powerful than that, you knew yourself. And I had an inkling that to watch you demand your selfhood would change us.

As much as I'm drawn to understanding biology, genetics, neurology, and endocrinology, none of it really matters. People will think that your body—when reduced to a blunt framework—is a curiosity, something open for debate and conversation. It isn't. You, like all of us, are more than that. As you started to tell us you're a girl, you didn't know anything about the brain and body. On the gay and lesbian front, the debate has raged for years about whether someone is "born this way" or not. (You will think for many years that Lady Gaga's song "Born This Way" is a birthday song. "Baby, you were born this day! Baby, you were born this day!") The argument is moot. It was never important. Because being lesbian or gay or bisexual or transgender or queer or straight or cisgender, doesn't hurt anyone. These states of being cause no harm. Being who you are causes no harm.

I also could sense what was coming, but in the most general way. I didn't know it would start with a simple knock on the door and upend our lives in an instant, but I knew what the world demands of mothers. It forces us to hand over our children. And I had fears. I wondered if watching you grow up would be like trying to create a bulletproof vest with the intelligence to know which bullets should graze you—so you can understand bullets, so you can one day grow your own bulletproof skin, an exoskeleton that can protect your body, your heart, the divinity of your soul. But I wasn't just creating that bulletproof vest. I was trying to *be* that bulletproof vest. It's a brutal metaphor at this time in American history, but this was how my fear was taking shape.

———

Your father and I were at a conference with your two pre-K teachers. We gathered around a tiny table, sitting in tiny chairs, to discuss your progress.

Both teachers agreed that you were a delight—funny and smart and sweet.

One was worried about how soft-spoken you were.

"We need to work on that big voice!"

But the veteran teacher drove to the point—that you had continued telling the other kids that you were a girl. The teachers exchanged worried glances. "I've had kids say they were a dinosaur," the veteran teacher said. "So maybe it's just a phase."

"It doesn't feel like a phase," your dad said.

I didn't have the language yet to explain that this was deeper, this was a sense of self, a sense of gender, truly a sense, *as in one of the senses.* "Jeff's right," I said. "It feels a lot deeper and more important than saying you're a dinosaur."

The teacher came at it a different way. "She's probably just emulating her big sister! Sophie is a great role model."

This was supposed to be a compliment to Sophie, but it felt like misplaced blame. And it also made no sense. Lots of kids have wonderful older siblings of a different gender.

We didn't buy it, and she quickly begged off. She knew that this was un-charted territory. We sat staring at each other for a moment. She was wear-ing a piece of chunky jewelry that you had made for her out of Styrofoam, duct tape, and string. "What do we do?" she asked.

We didn't know what to advise. "Stall." That was our suggestion. "Stall and distract."

Jeff and I didn't consider the term *transgender*. In a few years, the word would be everywhere, as would terms like *transgender youth* and *transgen-der students*. But this was 2010, years before Laverne Cox would appear on the cover of *Time* magazine and Jazz Jennings would have a reality TV show about her life as a trans girl. The term *transgender* made no sense to us. We had rigid notions of what it meant to be transgender. At the time, I thought these notions were based on approximately nothing. But this wasn't true. Jeff and I didn't know it, but we'd been inundated with stereotypes of trans people in film and television our entire lives—the trans person as someone to fear or to ridicule, the target of the cheap joke. It would take a long time to even begin to see how those rigid notions had been formed.

We quickly learned LGBTQ+ basics: sexual orientation is who you are at-tracted to; gender identity is your understanding of who you are, male or female, a fluidity between the two, or neither. We got rid of the idea that be-ing transgender had to do with taking hormones and having surgery. Those were choices way off in the future. But the outside world still wants to make this a central part of a trans person's story.

The main issue for us was that we didn't understand how a child who'd been clearly labeled a boy at birth could insist on being a girl. Surely a little kid couldn't know this.

But then we found the American Academy of Pediatrics' timeline for chil-dren to understand gender identity. These were the major takeaways:

By age two or so, kids understand the physical difference between girls and boys.

By three, they can easily label themselves a boy or a girl.

By four, most are pretty stable in their gender identity.

This is true of "typical"/cisgender kids, and so it is also true for transgender

kids but simply not in the expected gender. There is much to say about people who don't realize their identity until much later and much to say about
those who are gender fluid; this timeline doesn't address these complexities. But, according to the chart, you were ordinary but in an unordinary
way. By three, you easily labeled yourself a girl, regardless of the people who
seemed bent on saying the opposite.

I would eventually read accounts and hear stories of trans people who
would explain that their earliest childhood memories were often connected
to gender, sometimes in relation to a toy or a piece of clothing that had been
denied them or one that they knew they couldn't even ask for—an object
that they were excluded from because of others' ideas of gender. Jan Morris,
who was assigned male at birth in 1926, was three or four when she understood that she was truly a girl. She "cherished it as a secret," stating that the
"conviction of mistaken sex . . . [was] no more than a blur, tucked away at the
back of my mind." She wrote that she felt "a yearning for I knew not what,
as though there were a piece missing from the pattern, or some element
in me that should be hard and permanent, but was instead soluble and
diffuse."

You refused the secret. You pulled what could have remained a below-
the-surface blur up into the open air. You made sure the blur had edges and
was visible in stark relief. You didn't tuck this knowledge away as Morris
likely had to in her own childhood nearly a century ago. You didn't seem to
know that this was an option. You knew the piece in the pattern; it was not
missing. It was right here. There was nothing soluble about your gender—it
would not dissolve. And there was nothing diffuse. It held weight and den-
sity. This was the advantage of your moment in history, yes, but also of you
being you.

Still, your young age would sound alarms. It would be made clear to me
exactly how dangerous your understanding at this young age still was in our
current culture. It would become a mark against us, and it would be terrifying. I wanted to avoid noting your age altogether. I still obfuscate your age
when telling this story. When I do, it should only be read in one way: little
glimpses of *trauma*. Mine, not yours.

———

The Aztecs and the Mayans were accepting of transgender people. The Incans and the Moche who came before them elevated the status of those in the third gender. The Inca Empire revered their third-gender shamans. The Zapotec of Oaxaca had a third gender before the Spanish colonization; this gender endures in that part of Mexico, and its members are now called *muxes*—*vestidas* are feminine and *pintadas* are masculine.

———————

I found a piece published by NPR that looked at two sets of parents dealing with gender-nonconforming children. One father recalled his wife telling a gender specialist, "something to the effect of, like, you know, 'I'd be okay if Jonah was gay, I just don't want . . . him to be transgender.' And the therapist just laughed. She said, 'You know, fifteen years ago, I had people on this couch saying, 'I don't mind him being a little effeminate, as long he's not gay.' "

I was part of a history of parents, a moment in time, one that would shift. I've begun to hope that if some people in this generation, and definitely those a generation or two from now, read this, they'll think that I was awful. (Just as some people might read this and think I'm awful right now but for opposite reasons.) I hope all of this already will seem backward like some absurd old text that no longer makes sense, that this is a document that disintegrates. I hope that one day, human beings become so much more self-aware that the things I can't even see—the things that I'm blind to—will be doused with bright light; that human beings will be so much more enlightened that the wattage of my words is reduced to a dim hollow bulb that flickers, then pops, then goes out.

———————

The older women who marched at the height of women's liberation in the 1970s are protesting again, with signs that read *I can't believe I still have to protest this shit.*

So I also worry that what I have to say, or some of it at least, will continue to matter. That it won't all flicker and pop.

Again, this was 2010. I had no idea what was coming politically—the hostile contraction of the American heart, how violent it would be and how so much hate would be directed at trans people.

At this moment, Barack Obama was president and, amid all of my fear and ignorance, there was reason to hope.

That hope wouldn't hold.

We found an expert who worked for one of the leaders in the field of transgender youth. Jeff and I took the call in the mother-in-law suite of our house, in the corner that passed for my office. The phone was on speaker.

We expected data, hard research, but instead everything felt anecdotal. The expert explained how she got to where she was. As the mother of a gay son, she still shouldered some guilt. She listened to us too, and in the end, she told us that we were statistically most likely raising a gay son as well.

The expert told us that about one-third of gay men reported that in their youths, they'd been highly effeminate. One-third fell into the camp of no-one-would-have-ever-guessed; they were tough guys, jocks. The remaining third fell somewhere in between. She told us that being transgender was very rare, and she was not surprised by how young you were.

The expert had one piece of advice. "Tell your child that he's a boy who likes girl things and that there's nothing wrong with that!"

We dutifully wrote that down.

A boy who likes girl things.

And this was what we did. I found one of those moments when you were correcting my pronouns. We were in the car. We seemed to always be driving someone to some practice field or rehearsal.

I said, in a chipper voice, "You're a boy who likes girl things, and there's nothing wrong with that!" I looked at you through the rearview mirror.

You stared at me, wide-eyed. "I'm not a boy. I'm a girl."

Your father told me the same story. "It didn't work. I tried, and it was a hard pass."

But this was advice from an expert, so we kept trotting it out.

You kept correcting us.

As this was going on, you didn't know that transgender people existed. You knew girls existed and that you were one. Your flowering with language had begun. You had the ability to tell us who you truly were. We didn't know anything about the transgender experience; we weren't even botanists. If we had been, perhaps we would have had access to better metaphors.

The one thing we did—or were beginning to do—was this: recognize flowering when we saw it and know to be astonished by it. We knew it was essential, divine.

YOU MADE WISHES BY blowing out candles. Not just on your birthday, no. Anytime you saw a candle, you asked to make a wish. You said your wishes out loud. You wanted to be a girl.

You started asking for candles at dinner, candles at lunch. Our next-door neighbor invited you over for a craft that included tea-lights and jars. You made as many as you could.

I lighted the tea-lights in their decorated jars.

You made the same wish over and over. Girl, girl, girl.

We were standing in the corner of the front yard where our wildflower garden ended, where a pumpkin vine had started to grow.

How did the topic of puberty come up? Was it because of the wishes? Was it because Isaac and Sophie were both going through puberty? Sophie and her friends suddenly seemed like women; some were already driving cars. Isaac's voice had started to deepen. I don't know what started it, but I found myself explaining what happens to girls—womanhood. And what happens to boys—manhood. (These were my limited definitions at the time.)

You asked what would happen to you.

"You're like Isaac. You'll change the way he's changing."

Your face tightened. You started to cry. I picked you up and carried you inside. I knew I'd done the wrong thing and that I couldn't undo it. I didn't know what else to say. I'd spoken the truth, right?

I hadn't spoken your truth. I was still stuck on a boy-who-likes-girl-things.

Throughout that day and for a few days that followed, you would suddenly burst into tears while playing your favorite games: vacuuming, flight attendant, and matchbox cars. (Your father bought you so many matchbox cars in those days.)

I was stuck. You weren't.

I brought you to work, and one of my colleagues asked you what you wanted to be when you grew up.

You said, "Woman."

I have no memory of my colleague's reaction. I was focused on you. You looked at me.

What did my face say? Did it say, *I see you. I'm getting there. I will meet you.* Was I starting to make a promise?

While playing with your matchbox cars, you whispered in their different voices.

"What's the story? What are you playing?" I asked you one day.

"Sisters!" you said.

When you played with your brothers' dump truck, I didn't have to ask any questions. The dump truck was wearing one of Sophie's brightly colored headbands.

A friend of the family brought back a beautiful gift for Sophie from Hawaii, a complete authentic Polynesian hula dance costume. You were there wearing your flight attendant jacket, as you often did; it was part of your cousin's pastel yellow hand-me-down Easter suits. Your father started to pin one of the flowers to your lapel, like a man's boutonniere.

"No," you told him. You took the flower and put it over your ear, knowing just where it was supposed to go.

One morning, you sang us a song in the kitchen, one you'd made up.

"We should record that and send it to the grandparents," your dad said.

"It's really beautiful!" I told you.

"No," you said. "It's a man-voice. I want to cut out this man-voice!"

You turned and ran away. We heard your feet running up the stairs.

This scared us.

"I'll go," I said, and I headed toward the stairs.

"I'll think of something fun for us to do," your father said.

Upstairs, you were in bed, curled away from the door.

I sat down and rubbed a small circle on your back. Your t-shirt was damp with sweat. "It's going to be okay," I told you. "We'll figure it out. Dad and I are working on it. We're going to make it okay."

I didn't know what this meant. I didn't know how we would figure this out. But I knew that your breathing calmed, and soon you sat up and wanted to talk about the anthills in our driveway. You didn't like fire ants.

"I don't like the fire ants!"

"We can work on that too," I said.

The brain is full of maps. We used to think that body maps developed solely in the brain over time through usage, wiring. But then there was the case of a woman in India. She was born without arms, and yet she was vividly aware of her phantom arms. In fact, they were very expressive hands, she explained to her doctor. They gesticulated wildly while she spoke. She could sense them moving through the air. They were different than average arms, however—her arms were shorter by about six to eight inches. When sized for prosthetics, she asked the designer for shorter arms, ones that matched the body map in her brain. He told her that they would look strange, but she insisted. They compromised, making her prosthetic arms a little shorter than someone of her stature, but not too noticeably.

(Why did she have to compromise? Why would the doctor get to weigh in on how she wanted to feel in her body and be seen? Why was this not her call completely? This is an example of the dominant culture making decisions for those who don't fit into the sanctioned views of what a body should look like. The dominant culture thinks this is its right—to make you fit in. At a young age, you understood what was expected of you, and you started working against this fitting in without knowing how dominant that dominant culture was.)

Since this woman was born without arms, this means that her internal map was formed in her brain, likely in utero, when these portions of the brain develop naturally. This makes sense to me. It means that your body—the map of it that resides in your mind—was developed in your brain and you were born with it intact. Yours developed as mine did: For a girl's body and for the eventuality of a woman's body. The idea of puberty turning you into a man was as terrifying for you as it would have been for me as a little girl.

You have a body. And your body is good and beautiful and healthy. You've told us that the phrase "trapped in the wrong body" doesn't resonate with you, but I understand why this phrase is used to explain what it feels like to be transgender for many trans people. I think that being embodied is the most natural and foreign thing about the human experience, for all of us. Our consciousness tells us *we are here*, tries to tell us what *here* is, and who *we* are—gives us a sense of the verb *to be*, which, in and of itself, is not yet understood. Our *being* is not understood.

First, you exist.

Second, that existence is complex, as it should be for all of us.

Third, the larger world that exists around you isn't always healthy. You exist in a body that is good, yet some people will think they can say things about your body, ask you intimate questions about it. They might think that your body—because the transgender body is part of the public discourse, because it is "other"—belongs to the public, belongs to them. They might devalue your body. They might try to dehumanize you. They might try to sexualize your body. They might misinterpret your very basic human right to be seen for who you are as an invitation for them to accept or decline. They might think that commenting on your body is wanted. They might think you need their approval. They might think that they are the arbiters of whether or not your existence is real. Some people are capable of terrible acts.

Mainly, what I want you to know is that beauty is not in the eye of the beholder. That's a myth that transfers power from you, yourself, to the person looking at you. It's an act of thievery. Your beauty is in your own eye. Your beauty is your own.

WE WERE IN IRELAND, the six of us plus your twelve-year-old cousin. It was summer. We were renting a small row house in Blackrock, outside of Dublin. Here, visiting our cousins, I realized for the first time the beauty of staying. We were visiting my father's relatives, listening to the stories of the ancestors who remained, who chose family, who decided to fight through famine and violence to rebuild what was lost, those who could be described as the loyal ones. It ran counter to the American story I'd been raised on— the bold immigrant, the risk taker.

These two narratives would become important in a very immediate way.

But what happened here in this sweet row house was quietly astonishing. You were upstairs with your sister and your cousin, playing dress-up. Your cousin called to your dad and me to get ready.

"Ready for what?" your dad asked. "Are you putting on a show?"

She told us to gather at the foot of the stairs.

After a few minutes, they were ready.

Your sister shouted, "Now presenting—Olivia!"

And you appeared at the top of the stairs wearing your new name and a dress fashioned from one of their shirts. It was lime green. They'd gelled your curls and pinned your hair back with a glittery barrette. Your toes were jammed into American Girl doll–sized shoes. You descended the staircase like someone who'd spent her life elegantly descending staircases.

You smiled so brightly. You waved like we were adoring fans. (We were.) There was an assumption of paparazzi.

I wonder how this true gaze of ours reverberated through your body. All that connectivity was visceral. I imagine the lime-green t-shirt as a dress being a way to stitch your body into your true being. I imagine how it must have felt to be fastened into this world through the fiery bursts of neurons as all of these connections were made—brain to body, and from our gaze to your brain and back again—all of these new pathways being forged. Your brain a full field, popping open with a frenzy of wildflowers.

I thought of your heart as it pounded with your own story of being, ticking across your wrists, beating in your ears, flooding your cheeks.

A small body brimming with being.

Your father took pictures. We clapped and waved. But did we really get it? Did we understand what was happening? Was it only in retrospect that this would be a watershed? When we look at the pictures in the future, it will be so vivid and clear. There you are, showing up.

When would we?

It was one thing in Ireland where we were foreigners and no one cared what you wore or how you did your hair. No one knew you as a boy or a girl. No one knew us. What about when we returned to our southern city? It was a complex place, with its liberal universities and its high crime rate, its gentility and open racism and poverty. We were worried but also not worried. (Not in the ways that we should have been.) Like so many college towns in the South, this city was a blue dot in a predominantly red state. Our county always voted Democrat. We felt protected.

The blue bubble was imaginary, though—a fabrication, part of some collective bedtime story that we'd been told and believed.

Around this time, before we were using the right pronouns but as you were starting to choose the frillier bits of your wardrobe—brighter colors, your sister's headband, and some pocketbooks—we went to an annual checkup. It hit me in the waiting room that I wasn't prepared to talk to the pediatrician about this. I'd come to admire this pediatrician. He was very calm and didn't throw antibiotics at everything as a matter of course. I nervously tried to prepare a speech.

But when he appeared in the examination room, I forgot everything. I kept it short and probably a little defensive. I simply said that this was how you liked to dress.

The pediatrician smiled and said, "Nature loves diversity."

And that was that. Nothing more.

———————

Nature does, in fact, love diversity. It's how we adapt and survive. Some folks will deny it, but if someone believes that God created the planet, our existence, nature, then this is another way of saying that God loves diversity.

Still, I wanted proof. Of what? I didn't know. I wanted to understand how gender works, how it forms.

I wandered into dangerous territory. I read a lot and I read weirdly. I found this old theory—now thoroughly debunked—that the more sons a woman has, the more likely the younger sons will be gay. It's called the Older Brother Effect. At this point, we still thought that maybe we were raising an effeminate son, one who would likely grow up to be a gay man. The theories around the Older Brother Effect are interesting. One is that the woman's body builds up an intolerance to the male fetus, which could result in her body's restriction of testosterone in utero. As someone with an Rh-negative blood type, I understood how an infant's different blood type to my own could be seen as a foreign body. As a result, antibodies build in the woman. In the case of different blood types, this can eventually result in miscarriage. I'd gotten RhoGAM shots to prevent this build-up after giving birth. Studies show that there's a higher birth rate of girls during times of famine and war and a higher birth rate of girls born to mothers in poverty. Many researchers have speculated about various evolutionary upsides of having daughters during crisis. And new research about the evolutionary benefits of same-sex attraction and how it creates prosocial behaviors, which are good for building community, is really interesting and compelling.

One thing that parents who join support groups for raising transgender kids often note is what seems to be a disproportionately high number of children who are adopted. People have speculated that maybe the unintended pregnancy causes more stress hormone to be released, but there's also speculation that parents who are raising adopted children are more likely to see their child's differences more objectively, not as a reflection of themselves, and therefore more likely to take their children seriously. Also, parents of adopted children might simply be more likely to seek all kinds of supports for their children.

Had I been stressed during the pregnancy? Had I sent signals that we were in crisis? I didn't think so. Because we weren't in crisis at all. Busy, yes, with three kids. But not in crisis.

I knew that none of this was good. These were the kinds of studies digging around for root causes, digging for blame.

I became overly invested. I read studies from Denmark. I tracked down researchers who lacked independent variables and told them that they lacked independent variables. I wrote fan mail to scientists. They often wrote back. They don't get a flood of fan mail.

I didn't worry about protocols for hormones and surgeries. Any research that I did in this area would be wasted. Science and medicine were changing at such an incredible rate that any research would be completely outdated by the time you might need it.

The studies really weren't helpful. Most of my questions weren't answerable. What I really wanted to know was the future. What was next? How should I prepare for that future?

What was helpful?

You. Here's an example. While looking at various personal stories and organizations that support trans kids internationally, I came across a recurring theme—that transgender girls are often drawn to mermaids. The idea is that mermaids are clearly girls from the waist up, while the waist down is invisible to all.

We were at a department store and came across a display of mermaids. "Do you like mermaids?" I asked.

You shook your head, sadly. "No," you told me. "I feel bad for them."

"Why?"

"They can't wear high heels."

You were so clearly yourself.

What was also helpful?

You weren't my firstborn. By the time you were born, your dad and I had twelve years of hands-on experience. We'd gotten over the idea that our kids would be mini versions of us or *idealized* versions of us, or a misplaced hope for some personal redemption. We'd suffered our failed attempts at perfect parenting. Raising kids isn't about your grievances. It's about the child who is right in front of you. It took us a while, but it had dawned on us that each child teaches you how to raise them. You have to know how to adjust. You can't condescend. If you do it right, it should be humbling.

We weren't new to raising kids, but you were definitely new to us. And we understood that this was uncharted territory for us. But, to be clear, for all of my obsessive research, you weren't, in fact, my sole concern. This was a good thing. These were really busy years. We were in full sprint, every day. You were part of the mix and you mixed it up; you held your ground.

What helped most of all? Having conversations with your father at this dim little Italian place in our favorite corner booth. One night, we were eating bruschetta and having drinks, just to get out of the house. A Canadian couple had recently created a stir because they left their baby's gender off of the birth announcement, which they felt was too premature to call.

I told Jeff, "I don't like it. It's a stunt."

"But they're forwarding the conversation, right?"

"Yeah, except everything on a birth announcement is subject to change. We don't expect someone to remain twenty-two inches long, weighing seven pounds." Knowing the gender of the child—if it's obvious—feels simple. It doesn't mean it's not going to get complex.

Years later, at another favorite restaurant in another town where we lived, I'd say to your dad, "Remember that Canadian couple who seemed so progressive and avant-garde because they left their baby's gender off of the birth announcement?"

"Vaguely," he'd say. "You didn't like it."

"I just read that before colonization, the Yoruba and Igbo didn't categorize people into genders until they reached the age of five."

"Interesting."

"And the Mbuti people of the Democratic Republic of Congo assigned gender only after someone has gone through puberty. And—"

"I thought there might be more."

"The Dagaaba people, who inhabited what is now Ghana, assigned genders based on a person's energy, not their anatomy at birth."

"Your point?"

"That Canadian couple wasn't doing anything avant-garde. There is nothing new. Transgender people exist and have always existed."

What I was starting to understand was that gender variations were everywhere and always had been. I just hadn't been paying close enough attention.

Back to the night in this Italian place in this southern town, at the dawning of my understanding: I said, "So, growing up, I was girlish—or girlish *enough*—in the World of Girls and attracted to boys—who were boyish enough—in the World of Boys," I said to Jeff.

"Okay," Jeff said, not sure where I was headed.

"And I didn't see the edges of those worlds, the edges where genders blurred and overlapped or flipped. Did you?"

"I think I was actively taught to focus on the basics. Girl/boy. I mean, how else would they line us up in gym?" he joked. "A line without boys or girls? Mayhem. Chaos. New Hampshire would have imploded, I guess."

"I grew up next door to two women—my entire childhood—two women who were obviously in a long marriage. But we just never talked about it? They were just *professors*? Like that was all the code we needed."

"I think that might have been all the code you needed. I mean, wasn't it?"

"I can't remember the moment when I realized they were a couple. Maybe there was no moment, only a slow dawning."

"I don't know when I first knew trans people existed," he says. "I mean, I knew Provincetown existed. I knew men dressed as women, but I had no language for any of that."

"But they were there," I said. "There were tomboys. I mean I was a little tomboyish. I was a tree climber, a sprinter, a high school athlete, but then I also wore eyeliner and dresses and had that hair-sprayed puff of bangs."

"And there were always feminine guys I grew up with."

I saw them in my mind, with big gestures and soft voices and timid glances, sometimes wearing eyeliner too. "There was Jack." My uncle had been gay, and when exhausted some evenings after working at the bank, he put on a silk kimono and excelled at *Jeopardy!* My parents had helped raise his daughter when he needed support. He'd come to our wedding but died a few months later of complications from HIV.

"Yes, Jack," he said.

And I told Jeff about this image I remembered from living one summer in New York City in the late '80s—a young man, rail-thin, dying, in fact. He stopped to look at his face in the long side mirror of a mail truck parked on the street. I only saw him from behind and then his face in that mirror. His face, marked by a lesion, was still so beautiful, reflected and held for a brief moment, bodiless.

Throughout my life, gender and sexuality were there, in all of their stunning intricacies and brilliant blurs. "We missed so much," I said to Jeff. "We can't even begin to know what we missed."

"It's like we've been staring straight ahead our entire lives," he said. "And we didn't know we could be like owls and look all around."

We were new owls.

And this—owls will greet you with a bobbing motion of their heads. This is because their eyes are fixed, and by moving their heads, they can build a kind of composite of what they're seeing, contextualizing it all. They are trying to see—you and everything that is taking shape around you—until they have a whole.

ONE NIGHT THE FAMILY was getting ready to go to dinner with my parents. You dressed yourself. You walked into the living room ready to go. Both of your legs were in one pant leg of your shorts, having invented a skirt.

Jeff and I exchanged a glance. We didn't have a skirt for you to wear.

"I've got an idea," I said. You and I talked through another outfit, adding a bead necklace. You looked in the mirror. The necklace worked.

I was keeping something from your father. A statistic. As I was the researcher of the two of us, I was the one who'd come across it. But it's one that finds almost every parent of a transgender child, one way or another.

The suicide attempt rate. At the time, the stat was that 46 percent of trans people had attempted suicide at some point in their lives. For the general population, that rate is less than 2 percent. I've kept my eye on this stat over the years. I've seen it range from 41 percent to 47 percent, and when broken down, I've seen it as high as 51 percent for trans boys and men.

Now there is really clear research that explains how to bring that statistic down to the below 2 percent of the general population. It's this: acceptance, support. If parents, schools, faith communities, neighbors, and relatives shift pronouns, let the kid decide how they need to present themselves to the world—hair, clothes, name—the risk of suicide for that child plummets.

I was terrified of this stat. Rightfully so.

That night, I was changing into one of your dad's t-shirts to sleep in, and he was reading in bed. He put down his book and said, "When kids are playing soccer early on and the game gets too fast-paced for them, they'll get the ball and then, instinctively, put their cleat on it to hold it in place. They're just trying to slow it all down," he said. "I know that's what I'm doing. And I know the game is going to go on with or without me."

We'd been putting off letting you roam both the girls' and boys' sections because we were afraid of how it would bring up the inevitable question: Where would you wear your girl clothes? At home, sure. But where else? We were moving past this now. "There's this stat I found." It was time to tell your father. "I can't stop thinking about that 46 percent."

"My God."

"So, according to psychologists, this is a disorder." I was referencing the DSM-IV, which had replaced *transsexualism* with *gender identity disorder*, an attempt to destigmatize it. (In three years, it would change to *gender identity dysphoria*, so that the person themselves isn't the focus but the distress they might feel.) "What's a disorder that's not a problem when you're at home with the people you love but only a disorder when you step out of that house into society? I mean, society has the disorder in that case, right?"

"You should write that down," Jeff said.

"I will," I said. Why was I writing things down? Who would these things be for one day? I had no idea.

"We'll take her shopping," he said.

We took you to a few stores, letting you choose whatever you wanted. You delighted in the girls' sections. You picked a dress with cupcakes on it and a jean skirt and a ruffled shirt.

That afternoon, you put on a fashion show for the family, beaming.

The evening after you'd worn the ruffled shirt and skirt to school, I was reading to you in your room. You interrupted and told me that the dress was uncomfortable.

I was a little annoyed because you hail from a family who despises tags and seams and collars, a family who wears their socks and pajamas inside out. "I asked you a bunch of times in the store if it was comfy, and you said yes."

Then you stood up on the bed and started jumping. You said, "It's not comfortable because . . . what's the word?"

I waited.

"Because . . . man."

"What do you mean?"

"I'm a girl on the inside!" Jumping, jumping.

"And outside?" Jumping.

"I'm a boy." Jumping, jumping.

I had three questions. The first one: "Do you feel comfortable or uncomfortable wearing the dress at home?"

"Comfortable!" Jumping.

The second: "Do you feel comfortable or uncomfortable wearing the dress at school?"

"Both!" Jumping. "Comfortable and uncomfortable."

The third: "Do you feel comfortable or uncomfortable wearing the dress at the grocery store?"

"Uncomfortable!" Jumping.

"Got it. That makes sense. I'll put it in your drawer, and you wear it when you want."

I wrote all of this down in a journal:

Basically, we might be entering a new phase. (The road here is a long one, in general. These, we well know, are the easy years. But also what groundwork we lay here could make the road ahead a lot smoother.) The conversation about the differences between a very caring and open home, a wonderful safe school, and the world of the grocery store are perfectly delineated. That's it—in a nutshell.

Did I believe that any of this could really fit in a nutshell?

At home, you were safe. In the environments we chose for you, like school, you felt relatively safe. The outside world of the grocery store? No guarantees. The wilderness.

It was astonishing that you already intuited this.

In one of the specials we watched on transgender kids, a mother said, "There's a big difference between I want to be a girl and I am a girl." I was wondering if we were moving swiftly into the second category. "I'm a girl on the inside" is classic language for transgender kids.

Five days after I wrote about this in the journal, I followed up. You wore the jean skirt to school and the cupcake dress to a birthday party. You added your own flair by covering your fingers with a bunch of tape.

"What's with the tape?" I asked.

"Like Beyoncé," you said.

Of course. How could I have missed it? It was a shout-out to Beyoncé's robotic hand, shown off at the end of "All the Single Ladies." You held the pose, closed your hand, one finger at a time, then smiled.

———

This was a story that I didn't yet know.

There are several different versions of "The Crane Wife," a story from Japanese folklore. In one, a man saves a crane from being shot by hunters. Later, the crane takes the form of a beautiful woman and shows up at his house. She wants to be his wife. He can't afford a wife, but she has a plan. She locks herself in a room and weaves fabric that he takes to the village and sells.

In another version, she takes on her form as a crane in the locked room. She plucks her feathers in order to make the stunning brocade.

In another, she isn't a weaver. She stays up all night plucking her feathers so he doesn't know she's a crane. It's exhausting. Author C. J. Hauser puts it this way: "To keep becoming a woman is so much self-erasing work."

It can also be self-generating, a life force, an assertion of your existence.

In the version where the crane weaves the fabric, she has one rule for the husband. He must never enter this room while she's working. The sale of her fabric is how they sustain themselves. But each time she has to weave more fabric, she's skinnier and weaker. She pays.

One day, the man peeks in on her while she's weaving, and he finds the crane he saved from the hunters. He knows who she truly is, and so she has to leave. She flies away.

Of course, you won't need a romantic relationship to save you. But this doesn't mean you need to go it alone. There will be hunters. They will have arrows. This is life. Good friends can save each other.

The writer in me—the one you know well, who locks herself in a room and weaves—wants to tell you that you won't pay for your creations. But sometimes you do. Sometimes there is a cost.

The mother in me wants to tell you that you never have to become someone else to please others. But you are teaching me this.

You may think that I'm bringing this up because the crane wife is a metaphor for the trans experience. She is the crane *disguised* as a woman. No. "The Crane Wife" can be a metaphor for all of us when we are afraid to be who we are—all of us in all of our various disguises. Our lies to ourselves and others, our inauthenticities. They wear us down; we grow weak. We give too much. We hide too much.

But more than that, it doesn't matter if the truth is one's crane-ness or one's woman-ness. If we aren't seen for who we are, we aren't seen. If we aren't seen, we exist a little less and then a little less and then a little less.

But this isn't just about folklore. There is also the science of seeing and being seen.

Shortly after birth, you and I locked eyes. Healthy newborns focus on faces. Their vision, although blurry, has the ability to clearly see most objects that are eight to fifteen inches away, designed to see the face of the human being holding them. After one to three days, they can recognize faces even when rotated by forty-five degrees, and at two days old, they can mimic the expressions of those gazing at them. By four months, their ability to understand faces is nearly to the level of adults.

We gazed at you. You gazed back. You were surrounded by love-struck faces—mine and your dad's, your brothers', your sister's, your grandparents', our extended families', our friends'. . . . There was so much gazing.

What does all of this gazing do? An infant can't gauge all of the dangers of the world. This takes trial and error and experience, which they haven't amassed much of. And so they rely on the faces around them—their mother's, traditionally—to test the world. If they learn to read fear and delight on her face, they have a tool to understand the world around them, its dangers and joys.

But it's more than that. We need to see and be seen, to know and be known.

More than twenty years ago, a psychologist named Dr. Arthur Arons famously designed an experiment intended to fast-track falling in love. He and his team designed thirty-six intimacy-building questions that a couple is supposed to ask each other. After the questions have been answered, the two are supposed to stare directly into each other's eyes for four minutes. (Results may vary.) Gazing is part of how we fall in love; a channel between two people, seeing and being seen, flickers open.

We don't know if the man, after seeing the crane he'd known as a beautiful woman, wants her to stay. It's possible that he begs her not to fly away. It's possible that he's torn, and it's possible that he's bereft.

We do know that the Crane Wife flew away—with her beautiful, massive, powerful wings. She flies away because she can. What I want all of my children to believe is that love is abundant. You are loved—get used to this love, soak it up, become rich and spoiled in love so that it is what you absolutely expect; imprint on that. Imprint on being adored and gazed at and loved and known. Start there. That's what I want you to know, in your core—love. And when it's not there, walk away. Be done with non-love in all of its disguises.

This is what the mother and father first model. This love by gazing. We are built to see faces, to recognize them, to search them for signs of danger, to fall in love with them, to see how they see us. In part, we come to understand who we are by how we're seen.

At first, it's just gazing. But then it becomes crucial to be gazed at as you see yourself.

At this time of your life, in your cupcake dress but still being referred to as *he*, we were seeing you incorrectly. Hauser's line is self-blaming. "To keep becoming a woman is so much self-erasing work." You had an identity. You had a clear self. You were showing that self to us, asserting yourself into the world. By not seeing you, we were the ones doing the erasure. Not you.

You were becoming. We were erasing. You were becoming. We were erasing.

Becoming, erasing.

Becoming—and with a glance, a pronoun—erasing.

How long could this go on without something breaking? You from us? You from yourself?

We moved from "You're a boy who likes girl things" to trying "Okay, you're a girl *on the inside.*"

But you'd moved on past us. You were done with equivocations. You told us that we were wrong. "I'm a girl on the inside and on the outside." You wanted to be gazed at as you stood before us on the most obvious terms: a girl.

You were right. And this concept of being seen is crucial because of how we are wired.

I imagine what it must feel like to try to exist less and less. Why keep looking in a mirror that shows you only a distortion of yourself? To avoid the pain of being seen the wrong way, one might hope not to be seen at all. And start to disappear. This disappearing, I believe, is a mental act that has physical consequences. If someone disconnects from their body, they're vulnerable. Our bodies rely on connectivity. Our bodies rely on systems that operate on feedback.

There is pain in not being seen. Pain resides in the brain. We know that something is painful because our brain tells us this. (When pain is blocked from the brain, due to paralysis or an epidural, for example, we don't register the pain.) Nerve endings send messages to the brain. The longer one is in pain, the more messages are sent, creating pathways from the injury to your brain and back again. If you create too much connectivity, if the pathway becomes a heavy-duty superhighway, you'll keep feeling the pain even after the injury itself has healed. If your body pains you, if you find it hard to live within your body, then what happens?

I am saying two things might be happening at the same time: (1) The child who is seen incorrectly might be actively disconnecting from their sensory world and from the body they use to move through that world. (2) While disconnecting, the child might also be building up neural pathways of pain.

I didn't understand this at the time. But I also did understand it, deep down. I knew that I didn't want you to disconnect from us or from yourself. I didn't want those to seem like the two options. I didn't want you to be in pain.

Look, one day, you might be sitting in a classroom or on a balcony among friends, you might be at a cocktail party or overhearing strangers on a subway, and one person will say—to the class, to you, to a stranger—that "gender is a social construct."

They might even think they know what they mean.

That pink is for girls, that blue is for boys—those are social constructs. That women are the nurturers, that men are the doers, the solvers of problems—those are social constructs. Agreed.

But they might go so far as to say that gender is an idea, and that idea itself is a social construct, that gender is over. If this makes sense of their experience, then they're right. But if they try to apply this to everyone, they're wrong.

This is why.

I wake up in the morning, and I know that I'm a woman. I wake up and I am. I feel my womanness as a deep-down truth about who I am—while I'm wearing pink or blue, nurturing or doing or solving.

The self is a construct, yes. We have the story we tell of ourselves, in all of the various versions for all of the various audiences. We have the body as it exists in a moment, in a living room, at a kitchen sink, bustling among other bodies down a crowded street. And we have memories, and we imagine the future. (Both imagination and memory overlap in areas of the brain; remembering is an act of imagining.) Both remembering and imagining are collections of the self; we have the sense that memory and imagination are happening to the same person, us. This self.

The story takes shape around us. Character, in the best writing, can't be torn away from the plot. And yet who we are is different from the plot that we create, the plot that gets enacted upon us.

Why do newborns scream with such unrelenting suffering and rage and pain? Sometimes I think it's simply that they exist. Existential angst comes early.

Out there in every culture in its own way, gender gets constructed like scaffolding for us to engage with or not, challenge or accept. It can be dangerously confining or blissfully liberating. But the place where gender really matters is embedded within us, within the scaffolding in our brains, the busy intricacies of glands, the shapely twist of chromosomes, and then in the stories we construct of who we are, who we want to be, and how we want to be seen. There is scaffolding within scaffolding within scaffolding.

That part of our gender—that gloriously protected self-knowledge—is not a social construct. If that self isn't seen, if it isn't realized in the body, then that is an act of neglect.

Your teachers renamed you while you were still in pre-K. The boy's name we'd given you simply didn't work for them. They shortened it to a cute nickname, one without an indication of gender. Your father and I, your siblings, the larger family and friends, we took it on. We kept it.

The cashiers at various checkouts saw a little girl, whether you were in a cupcake dress or shorts and a t-shirt. "Does she want a lollipop?" they asked.

At first, your dad corrected them.

But then, one day, as he was pushing the full cart through the parking lot, he asked, "Do you want me to correct them when they think you're a girl? Do you want me to tell them you're a boy?"

"No," you said.

Of course you didn't. They saw *you*.

We were playing in the yard. It was shortly after Halloween. You were dressed up as a flight attendant. One of your babysitters was inspired to make an airplane out of cardboard boxes for you to get into and out of. This was what you were doing when you told me that God got two things wrong.

I was intrigued. What would a preschooler's critique of God be exactly? "What things?" I asked.

"Fire ants." This made sense. You'd been bitten recently and had just figured out how vicious fire ants can be and that their bites itch like mad — but even so you shouldn't scratch them.

"What else?"

This one was more complex. You told me, "God gave me a boy name, and I'm not a boy."

"God didn't name you," I said. "Your father and I did." I was not ready to say that we'd gotten it wrong, not yet. I asked you if you liked your nickname.

You did.

God didn't get anything about you wrong.

Nature loves diversity.

As for fire ants, if left alone for a century in a cattle field, they will slowly kill the grass by shading it with leaves and limbs which, in time, become fertile soil for trees. Eventually, a forest sprouts and grows and takes hold. What emerges is a lush habitat for birds and foxes, rabbits and squirrels, an entirely new rich ecosystem, brimming with life.

But what might be more relevant to this story is how fire ants rush to the surface of their nests when something goes wrong.

They protect their own.

There is also the science of memory and how we construct a self through memory. While you were trying to exist as you were in the present moment, asserting your sense of self, you were also building a story of self. Maybe because my girlhood resided solely in my memory now, I was keenly protective of girlhood—mine and yours. You were trying to exist in the present, to build a present moment around yourself, but what about building a past, your girlhood, and the memory of that girlhood?

Alex Haley once likened the death of someone late in life to a library being burned to the ground. I had the instinct to hoard memories. This was probably because I was a teen when my father's mother was suffering from Alzheimer's. She lived in our house for a while. It was sometimes my job to help her get dressed and to knock on the bathroom door to see if she needed help. My mother and I were the ones to bathe her. Unlike your great-grandmother, who wanted to die the way she'd been born, completely naked, this great-grandmother was painfully shy. It was a breach of privacy, an invasion, every time we had to help her. Eventually her care was too difficult. When she moved into a nursing home, my father visited her every day. The nursing home became an extension of our own home.

Her loss of memory wasn't a fire. It was a slow-moving flood, washing down one corridor of the library then the next, water rising up the stairwell, shoving books from shelves until they popped loose and floated, bindings spread like the wide undulating fins of dying fish. Eventually, Alzheimer's caused her to lose her sense of self. But first it broke down the formation of her short-term memories, which meant there could be no more layering of memory, and the narrative of who she was stopped being collected. The disease marched on, eroding larger and larger swathes of her memories, the memories that had constructed her self.

Although she forgot her present and recent past, she held onto her girlhood for a very long time. Her oldest memories were the most protected, especially the oldest memories that resided in her body. When language was gone, we could put on music and she would start clogging, as she had as a little girl in the mountains of West Virginia.

You didn't have to create a hidden self—a library of outward-facing stunt books like the ones in Jay Gatsby's library. I didn't want you to lock away the girl inside of you. Because I believe that that hidden girl will continue to grow up inside of you—a girl who becomes a woman. I imagined the trans person who transitions later in life being reunited with that self. They finally get to know the girl they were but never fully got to be. She existed, of course. She was there all along.

I wanted that girl to exist from the inside out, without boundaries. I believed that this was what you meant when you said, "I'm a girl on the inside and the outside." You were refusing these demarcations. I wanted you to build a full rich library of your girlhood—not the story of someone you had to pretend to be, but your *true* self. I wanted your brain to hold onto those memories: buying a dress for your cousin's wedding, sleeping in your grandmother's old-fashioned hair rollers, having sister time with Sophie where she talked you into playing spa day so you'd rub her feet, figuring out feminism one annoying middle school boy at a time. I wanted your brain to layer one memory on top of the next, to construct a story of you. I wanted to protect you so that you could have a girlhood. This was my goal, my promise.

It was becoming clearer and clearer that we weren't seeing you as you needed us to see.

And then something happened to change that.

IT WAS THE SUMMER of 2011. We'd been to New York City, hitting museums and FAO Schwartz, crossing over the Hudson on the tramway to Roosevelt Island. We met up with *this* set of cousins and *that* set of cousins. It was a free-for-all.

And then we stopped in to visit your grandparents before heading south again. I was tucking you in one night. The windows of the guest bedroom were open. White curtains lifted and trembled. We'd said our prayers. And then you told me this: "When you say I'm beautiful, say, '*She, she* is beautiful.'"

Beauty. *Your* beauty. We'd taught all of the kids that beauty isn't an external measurement. Beauty is a reflection of your soul. In this moment, talking about your beauty, I knew that you were talking about your divinity, your soul, your deepest sense of self. "When you say I'm beautiful, say, '*She, she* is beautiful.'"

This was something I knew not to mess with. How a child sees their beauty is sacred. It's the cathedral of self that resides within them. It's full of light and air and God.

"I will," I told you.

And in that moment, you became my daughter.

IN MY MEMORY OF all of this, the conversation was short and we switched pronouns the next day. But that was not what happened. I'd taken all those notes. And looking back at them, it was bedtime, yes, but you actually said, "You should pick one. You should say, '*She* is beautiful.'"

I said, "Who is *she*?"

And you said, "Me! I am!"

In this moment, you were giving me a test and supplying a cheat sheet on the right answer. *You should pick one*, you were saying. *Pick one. He or she. Make the call.*

And, by the way, you should pick she.

But the most interesting thing was that you linked your gender with your beauty. Your example was profound. It was deep and essential.

I slowed things down. I said, "It's a big deal to change from *he* to *she*. It's important to talk about and to keep talking about." This meant I wasn't ready to change, not just yet. "I love you," I said. "And you're really smart."

You were always so smart, but in this particular moment you weren't showing off your understanding of healthy childhood development. You were talking about your beauty. We see beauty through the lens of love. You were telling me how to *love* you.

"It was an ultimatum, in a way," I told your dad, explaining what had happened. "But I don't know what's on the other side of it."

Jeff was shaving in my parents' guest bathroom. And I was watching the kids in the backyard through the window. We had decisions to make.

"The school year's coming up," Jeff said, rinsing his razor off in the sink. "Won't it be easier to go in fresh? To start out as a girl rather than change in the middle of the year?"

"I think so, yes."

"We should do this, right?" He washed his face.

"I think we should do this," I said. "If we don't, I think it'll cause issues. I think..."

"I agree."

"I want to talk to my parents," I said. "They don't have any experience with this kind of thing but—"

"They have experience raising good human beings," Jeff said. "Get their take."

My mother had converted to Catholicism when she was thirteen. Converts are almost always staunch. My father was a corporate lawyer who also did pro bono civil rights cases. She was a fiery redhead now faded to a soft gray. My father, when young, looked like Alan Alda. He's now white-haired, tall, and spry.

I'd say that nothing in their lives had really prepared them for this conversation, not specifically. But that's not true. They'd helped raise the daughter of my gay uncle, Jack. They were always accepting of him. My father had gone through sensitivity trainings that included the gay and lesbian community, if not trans; it was corporate America in the eighties. My father told us one night at dinner that as the head of his department, he'd led a meeting by saying, "According to the training, one in ten people is gay. So that means that we already have gay and lesbian colleagues and that every single one of us has family members who aren't straight. We can start out acknowledging this fact." This got a chilly reception. The room was dead silent.

For the trans experience, they had little context, historically, scientifically, medically. Or legally, though in the years to come, my father would become well-versed in trans rights. Or religiously, though one day my mother would be able to school a diocese on faith-based love for trans students, as children of God.

But here, this summer afternoon in their kitchen with pimento cheese sandwiches on little plates in front of us, they were quiet. They listened.

When my mother interrupted, it was because she was nervous about getting this right. "Can you go over the part about how sexual orientation is different from being transgender one more time?"

I obliged.

This made sense to her because you made sense to her. "This is what I feel like when we're together," she said. "I'm with a little girl. It's plain and simple."

I then told them what happened—the story of how you wanted me to express your beauty. "Jeff and I are thinking of switching pronouns—to *she*," I said.

My mother is deeply anxious, a permanent feature of her makeup. So I was prepared for alarm. She speaks quickly, with urgency, no matter what she's saying. But she was calm. "I know one thing. You're the mother that your child needs right now. It is you. And you will do it right. I know you will."

My father is hyperintellectual and thoughtful. His father died when he was young, so he was raised by his mother and unmarried aunt, alongside two sisters. He'd spent his law career defending a massive corporation, yet he's the gentlest person I know, and so it was hard for me, as a child, to imagine that his job required such a sharply aggressive intellect. He has this gentleness too, like a good pediatrician. When I was a kid, he played four square with my friends and me after work, still in his suit. And though he'd make up complex overly litigious rules, he was a great player—funny, silly, generous. When we passed by the cows in the fields of the agricultural department at the local university, he'd sometimes moo at them, loudly. He'd been raised in poverty and was never interested in the trappings of wealth, but he spent money on travel and education, going to theaters, museums. "You have to listen to the child," he said. "You pay attention. That's what love is. That's good parenting."

This was all I needed to know.

This steadied me.

I wrote about my fears to a friend who I'd been put in touch with by a mutual acquaintance. Her son had transitioned to male pronouns. Much of my email was about wanting to open up the middle space for you. I preferred this in-between. I'd gotten used to it. I wrote that I was afraid of using female pronouns, that I feared "people will find out and feel manipulated, tricked. This feels dangerous to me."

As I continued in my email, I was aware that at such a young age, you had no idea that people are "threatened by this—our violent history and present dangers." But I didn't really know anything about "our violent history and present dangers." (I would come to. But I would also learn about trans beauty, trans intellectualism, trans art, and activism . . . and trans ordinariness too. Dentists and archivists and on and on. What I mean is— I knew almost nothing at this point.) With all of these gaps in my knowledge, I was pushing old fears, prioritizing other people's feelings of being tricked over . . . what?

Over your own right to exist, your right to live your life as you yourself. Your right to be seen, your reality.

———————

Was now the right time to make the change? It was summer. The new school year would offer a fresh start.

A week had passed since our conversation about pronouns and beauty. We were tending the row of tall weedy cosmos and other wildflowers in our flower garden. I reminded you about what you had said and asked, "Do you want to talk about it?"

You told me that you didn't need to talk about it.

"Why not?" I asked.

You said, "Because I'm me in my own land."

You'd moved on without me. You didn't need me. That was what you were saying. You had your own territory. You were determined. You'd created your own space, and in that space, you were already yourself. With or without me, you were going to be who you were in your own land, one you'd been creating, invisible to me. This is how, as writer Jan Morris put it almost a century earlier, the knowledge of gender recedes and becomes a cherished secret, a blur, tucked away in the back of the mind. This is how it loses its hard permanence in the shared land that misunderstands and becomes soluble and diffuse as it's transferred to the inner landscape that the child alone rules over.

I imagined a child cut off, shuttling the self between the land of being unseen, to the land of being who they are, a land of their own making, in which they can't be seen because they're alone. In both cases, they aren't truly seen.

Maybe the moment when you descended the stairs as a girl wasn't as huge for you as it was for your father and me. Was this the moment of two lands—ours and the one you'd already created for yourself—meeting?

Maybe you were never lost within yourself. You'd held onto your girlness resolutely. We were the ones who were lost, waking up in that moment, shaking off the dust of the foreign land where you already had taken up residence, creating a home of your own making.

But our eyes were clearing. And I was not going to accept that you had to create your own land because our land couldn't hold you. Our family was your land. Our house was your land. I wouldn't let you go.

———

James Baldwin said, "It comes as a great shock to discover the country which is your birthplace, and to which you owe your life and your identity, has not in its whole system of reality evolved any place for you." He was talking about a Black childhood. He was talking about a child of "five or six or seven" who, although they can't yet articulate it, comes to this understanding. It was the understanding that you'd already had and begun to imagine a way around. *I'm me in my own land.*

I'd never had this realization because I never had to. James Baldwin was Black and gay. I'm white and straight and cisgender and able-bodied and . . . this country has been mine. All of it. Yes, as a woman, there are many places I've been told I shouldn't be. And, yes, I have seen myself reflected back in unhealthy ways in film and television, magazines and books. And there has been a lack of female representation. There were teachers, artists, a lawyer here, a doctor there, an occasional politician. . . . There hasn't been true equality, but still there have been reflections. For the most part, I could live where I wanted to live. I didn't have to look for a place to exist.

And now I wasn't *a child* having a realization. I wasn't five or six or seven. I was a grown woman about to turn forty, about to realize that America's "system of reality" had not evolved, not fully, not enough to include you.

All of this talk of lands—lands that you created, lands that belong to you—these are all metaphors that can break down into realities. America would soon become a map of places where you were protected by law and not, territories where you could exist and where you'd be denied. It would become literal for your father and me. But this was a limited view. Your understanding began figuratively, began within you. I believe it exists within you still.

And, as much as it scared me then, I've also come to see it as a comfort. You have the power to create an inner landscape, a land of your own if you need it. Don't we all need a land our own sometimes, especially if the land is rustling and teeming with life, fecund marshlands and brimming rivers, hills and hollows and tall grassy fields, slick with sun?

We'd recently inherited a record collection, a mix of what was at my parents' house while I was growing up and in my grandmother's collection, heavy on Elvis. Your father was at one of his adult-league soccer matches. The other kids were doing homework—or at least pretending to. It was quiet, just you and me. The day was winding down, and I was looking for the first record I bought at a secondhand shop, a Marvin Gaye album. You dug through the crates with me until we found it. "I don't know if I'll remember how it goes," I said.

I put it on, and you said, "Do you remember? Do you?"

And I did. The words appeared just before Marvin sang them. Marvin sings about his pride and joy, but also that he's no baby boy. Of course he's not talking about the trans experience, but still, his words struck me. Why did I want to find this record now? Did I remember this part deep down? What did I need from it?

By the time your father came home from his game, muddy and sweaty and flushed, you were asleep.

"I found this old Marvin Gaye record," I told him as he kicked off his cleats in the breezelessway. But as I explained what happened, I started to cry.

"What is it?" he said. "What's wrong?"

The crying had caught me off guard. I wasn't sure what was wrong. I wasn't crying because you were different or because I was mourning a boy. (Some parents express this; I never felt it.) It was just because the moment had been sweet and you were mine. I couldn't quite explain this, though. I wasn't saying anything at all.

Your father, still sweaty and dirty, hugged me. The song had made me feel lucky and overwhelmed with gratitude and joy and love but also maybe fear. "I don't know what's coming," I finally said.

But this meant that I knew that *something* was coming, something I couldn't imagine or name.

And so he held me tighter and the moment changed—this was two people hugging each other in a quiet kitchen, yes, but this was also two people bracing themselves. They just didn't know what they were bracing for.

YEARS BEFORE YOU WERE born, your dad made a swing out of PVC pipe and strung it from a tree in our front yard. We had an old mattress that we would pull out of the garage so the kids could swing, let go, and get launched to a soft landing. I'd told my mother that we were one of those families that the neighbors must hate. "We have a mattress in the front yard? Who *are* we?"

My mother touched my arm. "It's so middle class to worry about what the neighbors think."

It was funny because my mother's father, who'd been a rumrunner during prohibition and eventually owned a bar, couldn't read or write; my grandmother, who had a sixth-grade education, kept track of the books. They were lucky to become middle class.

This story was important in understanding how I reacted when your father brought up what his friends would think. We were in the bedroom, getting dressed for a party to celebrate someone's promotion. I was still trying to figure out what to wear, digging through my closet. He was buttoning up his shirt. He said, "You know the guys I play soccer with. The stuff they say all the time. I mean, there's no way they'll understand this."

"It's so middle class to worry about what the neighbors think," I said to him over my shoulder.

(It was a joke that I will come to regret. We had underestimated the neighbors.)

He laughed a little but not much.

"What is it?" I asked him. "Really. Tell me."

These moments in our bedroom were important. This was the place we could try to see our way through—without the kids sensing anything.

He took a deep breath. He crossed his arms like a soccer coach. (They all seemed to have identical stances on the sidelines.) "I'm afraid that it's my weakness," he said, "made manifest."

I wanted to respond, but I knew to shut up and let him talk it out.

"It's like I'm not tough enough, like I haven't been brave or violent enough. No military service. I played soccer, not football. Did I ever tell you about the time I got the shit kicked out of me in a brawl in high school?"

"When you and your friends were jumped and you rolled under a bus so they would stop kicking you?"

"Yeah, and my father was, I don't know, good to me. Not one of those raging types."

"And you're a good father too," I said. "The kind who wakes up in the middle of the night if one of them is scared or sick."

"Yeah, that's just it. I cook most of the meals and do laundry and play with the kids in the yard. People will think it's my fault. I'm not that tough-guy guy so my kid. . . ." He sat on the edge of the bed and put his hands on his knees.

I let the room grow quiet. Finally, I said, "Do you feel better now?"

"What do you mean?"

"You said it out loud, and it had to sound a little far-fetched. Like, as you were saying it, did you still believe it?"

He shrugged.

"These are all the things I love about you. These are the things we agree on. These are things that make you a good father. That make you . . . good."

He was not convinced.

"I mean, do you really think you have this much power? As you were saying it, didn't it sound a little . . ."

". . . egocentric? And crazy? Like if only I'd bought more matchbox cars."

"You bought a lot of matchbox cars."

"And none of them tipped the scales to making our kid more boyish."

"Weird," I said, sarcastically. "You'd think matchbox cars would really have more impact."

"I know."

"Is Sophie's girliness because of me?" I asked. "Did you make Isaac and Tate more boyish because of your toughness? Are you an expression of your own father's strength and weakness or are you just who you are?"

"I think this has to do with our era—what we were taught," he said. "And the importance of nurture versus nature."

"Yes, and we've already been shocked by nature, right?" What had been so stunning in raising children, early on, was how our kids came prewired.

We'd both taken basic psychology classes. We'd both been introduced to a healthy dose of feminism. We were familiar with the concept of "gender as a social construct." We weren't hell-bent on deconstructing it, but we did push against it. "We offered trucks and balls to Sophie and dolls to Isaac and Tate—a mix of toys. But each was drawn to the toys they were drawn to."

"True," he said.

"They didn't care about our feelings about the patriarchy, our desire to end sexism," I reminded him. "Sophie outgrew dolls quickly and never liked Barbies." She was a rough and tough tree climber who could spend hours painting. She turned against the color pink and all that came with it. She despised velvety holiday dresses—of which we had an endless supply through hand-me-downs. In fact, she still hates velvet in all forms. I liked this rebellion in her. It was reminiscent of my own. "Isaac liked superheroes and dinosaurs. Tate wanted to play with balls—footballs, soccer balls, baseballs. We referred to his babysitters as coaches, remember?"

"People will think what they're going to think," he said. "And, I don't know, but I think she's going to crack us open. Our views of the world aren't just going to shift a little. We think we're progressive. We think we understand the issues facing vulnerable populations."

"We use words like *vulnerable populations.*"

"But I don't think we really know anything."

He was right. The knock on the door would change your father's life, his emotional trajectory, his way of moving through the world.

It would change all of us.

"It's not about me," he said. "It's about *her.*"

It was that quick. He progressed through the stages—whatever those might be—completely.

A few nights later, we watched a television special about transgender children.

The host said something like, "Unfortunately, she was born in a boy's body."

Your father immediately countered. "*Unfortunately*? Why not *surprisingly*? Why condemn it right off the bat?"

All of this said, you would challenge my feminism. Your love of pink will be undying. You will adore makeup, glittery high heels, all things fashion. One of your earliest word combinations was *'mokey eye*, from a Drew Barrymore ad about eye shadow. Your great-grandmother, the matriarch who once looked like Marilyn Monroe, who admired Liberace for his good taste, would have loved going shopping with you.

You adore Barbies. You hate "Messy Day" at school, when all the kids are encouraged to play in the mud.

When all the kids at recess played superheroes, you chose your superhero: Tinkerbell.

The first name you made up for yourself is Pursebella. You just loved purses that much.

Of course, this isn't because you're transgender. This is simply you. I'll eventually understand that there are a lot of trans girls who are rough and tough tree climbers like Sophie. There are trans girls who hate pink and glitter, who don't play with Barbies and love Messy Day. Gender identity is what each of us feels, deep down; gender expression is how we express that feeling or not.

And I will have to change my form of feminism—it can't solely be about being freed from all things girly, but being free to choose.

You collected fashion magazines and flyers and circulars that landed in the house. With a red magic marker, you colored in all of the lips of the models who you thought weren't given bright enough lip color.

"What are you doing?"

"They need some help." It was an act of great generosity.

I couldn't rely on my mouth to say the right pronoun—even as I tried to slow down and be more intentional. There is the linguistic act of changing pronouns. We don't realize how linked a pronoun is to a person and the built-up memories of that person. There is also the kinetics of saying a pronoun—what the mouth itself has learned to do automatically has to be undone and retrained.

I realized quickly that I had to go to the pronoun's source—you.

I started with the *you* in front of me. I practiced seeing the little girl. I found that if I looked for boy traits, I found boyishness. If I looked for girl traits, I found girlishness. I had to look for the girl to see the girl. I had to re-see you.

To do that, I would practice, dreamily, reimagining the past. I saw you in recent weeks and then months as a girl. I replayed the memories in my mind and re-saw you in them. (Eventually, we would use female pronouns all the way back to your birth, but not yet.)

When I was alone, I'd practice conversations *about* you. "She's doing great. She loves school. This is her latest drawing. . . ."

When your dad and I were together, we'd correct each other each time we slipped. After a quickly whispered *she*, the other would say the sentence again the right way.

During this phase, pronouns themselves started to detach and wander off. As I was getting your pronouns right, I often got other people's pronouns wrong. It was as if my brain, having loosened the attachments, decided that pronouns in general were now up for grabs. This didn't last long, but occasionally, still, if I'm too conscious of pronouns, I can feel this unhitching begin.

The thing that I remember most clearly is when, after you'd fallen asleep, I'd check on you. I'd look at the child there—the soft breaths, the fluffy curls, the lashes—and I would see my daughter, my little girl. "There *she* is," I'd whisper.

In Uganda, the Lango people refer to male-assigned people who live as women *jo apele* or *jo aboich*. The Lugbara people use the terms *okule* for trans women and *agule* for trans men. The Kenyans who speak Swahili call trans women *mashoga*. The Samoans use the term *fa'afafine*, a term that dates back to the beginning of the twentieth century, and the word *fa'ata-maloa* encompasses trans men and tomboys. In Tonga, the word for trans women is *fakaleiti*, but they often just use the term *leiti*, meaning lady. In Fiji, they say *vakasalewalewa*. In Tahiti, *rae rae*.

I kept getting tripped up by the stage of fear.

I worried that we might go through the process of changing to girl pronouns only to have you want to switch back. This is called *desisting*. I obsessed over it. "We would have to tell everyone that we were wrong. We'd have to take it all back," I said to your dad.

"And?" your father said.

"And . . ." I stalled out.

"We'd be raising another son. The kid we thought we had. A boy. I think we've got that down."

"But we'd . . ."

"Have to tell people that we were wrong?" your father said. "At that point, I don't think we'd care."

And we realized that by making it simple to change pronouns, we were modeling that it would be simple to change back. This fear was put to rest. It fell into the worrying-about-what-the-neighbors-think category.

Another fear wasn't as easy to get over. In fact, I still have it.

Your father was driving me to work. We were on this familiar stretch of road, the local high school up ahead on the slope of the hill. Scrolling through my phone, I'd come across more data on violence against trans people and was overwhelmed by it all. I started to cry. There were days like this when I felt newly vulnerable, aware of my limitations as a mother, aware that the world could be hateful.

"What's wrong?" your father asked.

I said, "I don't know how I can prepare this child for the world when the world's reaction to her is going to be so polarized and disjointed. Some places will see her as a sign of progressive hope, but in most places in the world, she's more likely to get murdered. How do I prepare her for all of that?"

Your father took a moment, and then he said, "We'll parent her like our other kids. The world is always dangerous and hateful and violent. We can't control that. We can only control the home we make for them. They have a place in the world where they know they're safe and loved. That's how we'll do it."

This is so like your father. He's a steadying force. You can rely on him. This was how it went and still goes in raising all of our children. At one moment, I can ground us; in the next, he does the work.

However, as this idea of home became a guiding principle, we were living in a progressive bubble—or so we thought. This bubble would not hold.

————————

There are red deer who live in the forest where an electric fence marking the Iron Curtain used to divide the Czech Republic from old West Germany. In 2014, a study that tracked three hundred deer with GPS collars revealed that over a quarter of a century since the fence came down, the deer on both sides still didn't cross the boundary line.

Somehow, generation after generation of deer have passed along their fears.

I've sensed for a very long time that you knew that the world was dangerous in a primal way. You were aware of invisible dangers. I've been raising all of you very intentionally, doling out precautions when I thought you were ready for them.

Of course there are fears I've passed down without knowing it. How are my fears informed by the spoken and unspoken distress of the generation who raised me, the generation who raised them, and further and further back? How much fear is written into our epigenetic coding? You come from poor, hungry, fevered, fearful, beaten-down, violent stock. How much of the time am I teaching you and the other kids, by my way of moving through the world, this vigilance like that of the red deer?

And now there are new fears. The rates of violence against transgender people are staggering. By the fall of 2019, murders within the transgender community will be so steep, especially murder rates among transgender women of color, that the American Medical Association will deem it an epidemic.

One day you might come across lists of these murders. The lists are long. In November 2012, I found myself at a memorial on Transgender Day of Remembrance. I went alone. The participants stood in a circle outside. The names of the victims of murder were printed on paper and handed out to the twenty or so people who'd shown up. We said the name, the age, and the cause of death of each person while in a large circle, candles lit. Look at any list of murders of trans people. You'll find them marked by extreme brutality. Rare is the single gunshot wound. And often the murderer isn't alone. It's often a group—a group of men. The bodies are left behind, abandoned, often in a public place—an alley in Burlington, Iowa, in a burned car in New Orleans, in a field in Dallas.

You are going to have to navigate your life—online, in real life, in public spaces, and private. You'll have to be more careful, more vigilant. You'll have to trust your instincts. At such a young age, you'll have a heightened ability to read people. You will keep reading them. You will decide if and when to tell someone that you're transgender, and that decision will always be, first and foremost, about your safety.

I'm not the only kind of parent who has had to explain that the world that takes shape around a child is different than the world that takes shape around other children. We live in a racist, xenophobic, misogynistic, homophobic, ableist culture; othering and dehumanization put certain people at higher risk. You have advantages—the color of your skin, that you blend in with other girls, that your family has enough money to live in safer communities.

These things and many others will make you less likely to be a victim of violence. Transness collides with race and class—and *passing*, that word with its long, complex history, that word that isn't just or fair or right because you aren't passing for a girl; you are a girl.

But let's say your family is a kind of herd. We will survive only if—like red deer in a forest once divided by an electric border—we keep our heads up, our ears pricked, our eyes darting through the trees, always aware there are dangers we can't see but that we sense nonetheless.

IN COLLEGE, I LOVED psychology classes. I especially loved the books on birth order, which felt basically like a slightly smarter form of astrology. My own family aligned with the birth-order books pretty closely. I was the youngest of four after a sizeable gap, so I was both a baby and an only child because the older kids were out of the house for much of my childhood. My siblings were my great abandoners; they left me, one by one. Luckily, I preferred to have my parents' full attention. You're also the youngest of our family with four kids, born after an even more sizeable gap. So, with birth order in mind, here's how your siblings were doing throughout all of this.

Sophie was fifteen and completely supportive but also, at first, a little confused. If she overheard me asking your dad a question like "Where is she?" Sophie might answer, "I'm right here."

"Not you. Your sister."

"Oh." This took a bit of processing. "My sister. Right."

When I explained your transition to one of my friends from college who was the only girl in the middle of six boys, she immediately thought of Sophie. "She's no longer the princess. She's going to have to deal with that."

It seemed crazy, but a few days later, Sophie pointed out that she'd lost her status. "I have this adorable little sister to contend with now?" But, of course, she was joking. Your relationship with her was never based in sibling rivalry. When she said the word *adorable*, it was shot through with maternal pride.

She also missed your name. Your dad and I had a few names that we'd picked out and put forward for discussion; the kids picked sides and argued it out. Sophie's favorite name had won. It was hard for her to give that up. But, of course, what was she giving up? A name, not what the name holds. Getting the name right, being called and answering a call, are crucial to that sense of self. Each time the name is right, the resonant reflection flashes back.

While you were stealing your sister's sole-princess role, you gave something back to your brother Tate. According to birth order research, he had an enormous amount to gain from your transition. Instead of being the middle son, at sea, bobbing between the primo spots of oldest and the baby, he now became your father's last shot at reliving his own glory days. What's more, Tate looks a lot like your father, and he's better at soccer than his old man. Tate is not only allowing your father to relive glory days but also creating new glory.

Tate was ten. As our only southerner, he had his own identity. Also, he wasn't anxious like the oldest two; instead, he had a deep well of calm to draw on. But he was fearful, which is different. He was the one who reminded me to be vigilant, to trust no one. That said, he accepted your transition easily. He knew you. He'd seen this coming. "Sounds right," he said, a boy of few words. Done.

Your oldest brother, Isaac, was thirteen and going through puberty. He said to me, frankly, "Look, she's allowed to be who she is. Absolutely. But I'm allowed to be a little uncomfortable about it."

This felt completely fair. I think, and I could be wrong, that it was simply his age. He was moving toward becoming a man. He was uncomfortable in his own body. "Okay," I said. "I can appreciate that."

As he expressed his discomfort, it seemed to evaporate in the same way your father's fear of his weakness made manifest disappeared once said aloud. This would happen over and over again, for each of us—this expression of fears, let loose in the air, often allowed for their dissolution.

Isaac was the one who told me not to be so afraid, to let go, to have more faith in you and the world. Unlike Tate, Isaac was anxious and restless in his day-to-day, but also fearless about the larger things in life.

Around this time, he started dating a girl in school. She was tall and blond and blue-eyed and very, very Christian. She took him to events hosted by an uber-Christian youth organization. For reasons that he still doesn't understand, they hosted an obstacle course that involved wrestling a full-grown shirtless man in a pit of oatmeal that had been dyed purple. This organization was *not* his thing, but he was crazy about the girl. And he spent a lot of time at her big, beautiful house with her family, who adored him.

I first met the girl's father when I came to pick Isaac up one day. Her father answered the door. He was a tall, broad man with his own blond head of hair. He was wearing a polo shirt and salmon-colored pants. He quickly told me how great it was to have Isaac around. "It's like our daughter is dating Ferris Bueller!"

As a woman of a certain generation, I'm a Ferris Bueller fan. It felt like something I should downplay. I said, "Yeah well, how far can you get on charm?"

He looked me dead in the eye and said, "You have no idea how far that kind of charm can get you."

—————

My parents were easy to tell because I'd been telling them all along. Even if I hadn't looped them in when you first told me to say "*She* is beautiful," they were prepared.

For example, just the previous winter there was what we've come to call the Christmas of the Matching Button-Downs. My parents were at our house for Christmas morning. My mother had bought gifts for you and your brothers, identically wrapped. They opened theirs first, among lots of other presents. They were striped button-down shirts.

When you came to your gift from your grandmother, I guess it didn't dawn on you that yours would also be a striped button-down. So when you tore into it and revealed a striped button-down that matched your brothers', you were at first confused.

And then you threw it and said, "I yate it!"

You weren't the kind of kid to have outbursts like this. And no matter how much a kid doesn't love and adore a button-down from their grandmother when they're still at the I-want-toys age, our kids had enough decorum to lie. On top of all that, our kids aren't allowed to say "hate." We reserve it for extreme circumstances.

So, at first, there was stunned silence.

And then we burst out laughing.

Eventually, "I yate it" became a family catchphrase. We still sometimes will say how much we "yate" something.

You didn't "yate" the button-down because it was a button-down. You "yated" it because it said you belonged with your brothers. It said, "*You're a boy.*"

All in all, my parents quickly changed pronouns. Years later, my mother would tell me, "We don't think of her except as a girl. We don't think of her as a trans girl." She knew this wouldn't work for us, as your parents. It has to matter to us, but it's wonderful that it doesn't matter to them. "This is what grandparents should do, just seeing her like all of our other granddaughters. This is our role."

Your dad told his mother. She was lively but a bit awkward, uncomfortable with ordinary emotion. Her father was a minister who also sold insurance. Her mother came from money, substantial money. One day, you'll look at the steamer trunk that we've hauled around everywhere we've lived. You'll read the name painted on it and you'll understand that this is one of those names that casts an American shadow. They didn't have access to that money but were monied, I guess you could say. Your grandmother was sent away to a boarding school at the devastating age of five. She didn't marry the man she first fell in love with. Instead, she married the man her parents wanted her to marry, your grandfather. In the seventies, they divorced. She was liberated by feminism, but she couldn't ever be liberated from the trauma of her childhood.

She was a nurse working in an optometrist's office during a famous eclipse. As part of her work, she taught people how to view an eclipse without damaging their vision. But when the time came, she stared at the sun with one eye and went blind in it. This story might make her sound flighty. She wasn't. She was rebellious and stubborn in ways I could never figure out, often to her detriment. Metaphorically, her blind eye gave her a place to store the things she didn't want to see.

But, as your father explained that you were now going to be seen wholly as a girl, she listened quietly. "Yes," she said. "Okay. I see."

If she had reservations about your move into girlhood, if she had any emotional reaction to the news at all, she never showed it. She changed pronouns, used the right name, and never mentioned it. And this was hard too, in its own way. She never asked how things were going for us, never asked what your father might need. It was as if the past never existed, the change never took place. It's a fascinating skill set.

Your father was nervous about telling his father. By this point, their relationship was strained. Your grandfather remarried before your father and I married. His wife stopped speaking to us decades ago. For reasons we don't understand, your grandfather edged further and further away during the years we started having kids. He's a progressive—a liberal Democrat and proud of it. For all of the acrimony and distance between your dad's mother and father, they responded almost identically. They said almost nothing about it when your father explained it and then never brought it up. He also didn't really know you. He has his own trauma—a father who abandoned him, a mother who died of a brain tumor while he was in college, a first wife who cheated on him and divorced him. He's a messy man who has made some cruel decisions that have made him sad. We assume that he's had a good life too, that his decisions have made his relationship with his second wife easier . . . stronger? It's hard to say.

Your aunts and uncles on both sides—including the Republicans—were terrific. Our friends were also all good, including our Catholic friends and the nuns I stay in touch with from my Catholic education and the monsignor who married your father and me and baptized all of you kids. The Catholic Church itself would prove much tougher, but that was years off too.

Your school was amazing. The teachers who asked us what to do were relieved. The nickname they came up with was now your go-to name. The head of school wrote a note to the families who'd known us from the year before. They wrote that the administration and the staff "are proud to be serving families that reflect the diversity of the human experience." They said they were grateful to you and to us for prompting them "to return to our mission statement for guidance and affirmation. . . . As a school we have always seen diversity as a valuable gift, a gift that enriches our community and the individuals in our community." They ended by saying that they happily embraced the role they were playing in your life.

It was beautiful, most of all because it was signed by the full faculty and staff—the bottom of the letter was ornate with signatures.

———————

There was someone who didn't need to be told of the change. While we were getting your gender wrong, there was someone who always got it right. Your cousin, Liam. When Liam was born, he seemed perfectly healthy. But, early on, he had trouble eating and digesting. He was slow to hit the typical milestones. As time went on, it became clear that his IQ would remain low, and he would need help with a lot of things that come easily to the rest of us. But one thing Liam has in abundance is joy and love. He loves his big extended family, his dogs, his school, and the New England Patriots.

He looked at you and he saw you. Really saw you. He always referred to you as she and her. Once he called you a cowgirl. My sister tried to explain to him that you were not a girl. He nodded and smiled, but he knew what he knew.

While our minds were cluttered, his was the clearest of all. He's never gotten your gender wrong—not once.

There were two things that people said again and again: *She chose you.* It wasn't something I'd ever say, because it's not the way I see the universe or the soul, but I love where it comes from and how it's said.

The other was: *She's lucky to have you.* This line hints at the brutal truths. We've come to understand what happens to gender-nonconforming kids whose parents don't support them. But we know the truth. We're the lucky ones. You're brilliant and hilarious. Your laugh is one of the sweetest sounds in the world; at this moment, it's rippling up the stairs and into this room where I write, a room that's gone from afternoon light to dark in what seems to have been seconds; time sometimes lifts from its confines and spills out.

We can't imagine our lives without you. How reedy and brittle and small those lives would be. You have expanded yourself and you have expanded each of us. You were ushering in a lush and vivid landscape, that land you created was becoming part of our living, breathing home. *This* home, *these* lives. You created so much of it, new and unexpected and doused with joy.

It wasn't that we didn't get some immediate pushback. We did. But it was mild, and we were pretty sure it would remain mild. And we handled it as it popped up.

Your dad and I had a good-old-boy doctor at the time. When we brought up your transition with him, he said that you could just go live in Charleston when you grow up—subtext being that, in Charleston, that dandy stuff is tolerated.

I was talking to a very intense woman at a party. She had a young son, who would later go on to come out; he was noticeably effeminate. "Are your kids here?" she asked.

I pointed you out. You were dressed as a girl. "Oh," she said. "I didn't know your son was theatrical!"

I felt the whole room shift around me, lift, and then reconfigure itself in . . . 1964? I stood there and listened to her explain the local scene for ballet lessons and a theater school for young performers. "Well, okay," I said. "And thank you. I see . . ." Was I supposed to say things that would open a door to a room where we could say the real words we needed to say? Or not? I guessed not. I guessed these were the only words available.

And there was our next-door neighbor. He was a lawyer and a former Republican who'd been converted to the Democratic Party by his wife. We were good friends. Every Halloween, the kids got on a ladder of his and threw our old pumpkins off of it, smashing them in the street. Then he ran over the pumpkins with his Jeep, a holdover from his bachelor days that sat slowly rusting in the driveway. He and his wife had two young sons. And one late afternoon, the husband and I were sitting in lawn chairs in the shade of our garage, watching our kids play. We agreed on some things and disagreed on others. But we were both straight shooters.

He said, "I just wouldn't have the girl toys around. I mean, if they don't exist . . ."

"So you're suggesting that I get rid of all my shoes and pocketbooks and lipsticks. That we chuck all of Sophie's childhood toys and books, her dollhouse, her barrettes and makeup, and all of her clothes and shoes. That we just masculinize our entire existence?"

"Maybe I'm just saying that you should . . ." And here he made a gesture like he was pushing something in his chest down to his stomach.

"You're suggesting repression?"

"No, no. That sounds bad, like something that would just rear up later. Just . . . discourage. That's what I'm saying."

"Sorry," I said. "I was raised Catholic. Can you be more specific? Are you talking about guilt or shame?"

It's hard to explain that this was banter—a little heated but not too much. It existed under that guise of we're just batting this around; we're just going back and forth.

"No, no," he said. "Just don't *encourage* it."

"So, what you're saying is just slowly erode the child's self-confidence in a way that emerges later as . . . self-loathing?" I was doing this mock confusion face—squinting, head tilted, one finger raised. "Tell me when I'm getting close."

He shook his head. "I'm just saying. . . . I wouldn't let my sons play with girly toys."

"Here's the thing. If I were to take parenting advice from three people and those three people were you and Dick Cheney and Archie Bunker, my order would go—bottom to top—Dick Cheney at the bottom, then you, then Archie Bunker at the top. You'd rank *below* Archie Bunker."

And he laughed and nodded. "Got it. Got it."

And he did get it. He would prove invaluable to us later, on the day of the knock at the door.

11

BEFORE THE KNOCK AT the door, I found the number of an organization in town that supported the transgender community. I left a message, asking for the meeting times for the parent support group.

The next day, I got a call back. It was Marguerite; she ran the organization. "I'm so sorry. There is no parent support group for parents of transgender kids."

"Oh," I said. "Then what do you tell the parents who call in?"

"You're the first parent to call in," she said. (In a few years, there will be a vibrant support group for transgender parents in the area with weekly meetups.) "You can come to the adult support group for trans people," she said, "if you think it would help."

I wasn't sure, but I knew that I needed community.

I remember the room where we met, vividly. I could tell you where every person sat, who came on time and who came late. But I can't remember anything outside of that room—not the building, not which part of town we were in.

Everyone there was trans or gender nonbinary. Marguerite, tall and thin, was facilitating. She was warm and patient. The other folks introduced themselves and gave updates on their lives. While most offered vignettes, one trans woman who worked for the state had a lot to report. She'd been trying to transition at her office. A young gender-nonconforming yoga instructor knitted quietly.

A seemingly cisgender man, dressed in a suit, came late and talked about his gambling addiction as if trapped in the wrong support group. He explained the problems it was causing with his wife.

But when Marguerite asked a few questions, he came clean. He had no gambling problem. It was a joke. It was supposed to be funny.

Everyone in the room knew this person, and I assumed he often spoke in metaphors, in jokes. But he kept coming back to the group. Some of the histories here were long.

The moderator then explained how I'd come to the group. I told my story. It was a fairly short story at that time. I was new to all of this.

At the end of it, everyone was very generous. They told me that I was a good mother. They said how they wished they'd been raised in a household like ours.

Except for one woman. Earlier, when it was her turn, she'd introduced herself as an engineer from my home state, far away from this hot southern town. Sitting directly across from me, she listened to my introduction with her arms crossed. She stared at me, unmoved and unfazed. As everyone else's encouragement died down, she said, "They're going to blame you. They always blame the mother."

Marguerite gave her a little reminder. "We're here to listen and support." I got the impression that this woman was known for her frank honesty. This didn't seem like her first reminder.

She stood her ground. "I'm only telling the truth."

I thanked her for the comment. "I appreciate it."

On the way home, I realized I shouldn't have gone. Kind as it was to invite me, I didn't belong. I'd disrupted something sacred. I felt more alone than before.

As I replayed the moments from the meeting, one voice kept coming back again and again—the woman who said, "They're going to blame you. They always blame the mother." I kept returning to it not because it scared me, though it did, but because it was true.

I knew, deep down, that she was right.

The word *transgender* can be found in a medical text in 1965, but its first use by a transgender person dates back to 1969. That's when it matters. Virginia Prince, a controversial American transgender activist, wrote, "I, at least, know the difference between sex and gender. . . . If a word is necessary, I should be termed 'transgenderal.'"

I like it too. It feels like a combination of *transgender* and *ethereal*.

But 1969? That's a very young word in the history of the English language. As I write this, it's fifty years ago.

In fact, on June 28, 1969, your grandmother was six months pregnant with me. It was the night the Stonewall Riots began. Your grandfather probably read about it in his Sunday *New York Times*. I imagine him now on the sofa, reading the article. Trans people won't be mentioned; acknowledging their pivotal role will take decades. The Stonewall Inn was a gay bar, owned by a Genovese crime family. The bar was raided from time to time by cops in a perfunctory way, and the bar owners were usually tipped off first. But on this night, they weren't tipped off. It was hot. Judy Garland had just died. The patrons were mourning and in no mood. The cops barged in, roughed people up, started making arrests. (It was standard for the female cops to usher those they thought were cross-dressing into the bathroom to check their genitalia.) As the story goes, a woman known as a butch lesbian, Stormé DeLarverie, resisted arrest, igniting the events that escalated into a full-blown riot. Marsha P. Johnson, who became a beloved activist for trans rights and only received true recognition after her death, showed up to fight the good fight. The fire department and riot squad were called. The crowd dispersed but not for long. The riots went on for five days.

In 1973, at the Christopher Street Liberation Day Rally, a commemoration of the Stonewall Riots, there were speeches and bands and Sylvia Rivera. She stormed the stage and grabbed the mic. Her speech was caught on tape by a Belgian film crew who was following around Bette Midler. Sylvia was a Latina transgender woman who'd survived on the streets since she was ten years old. Her speech is only four minutes long, and while she speaks, she's shouted at, cursed at, told to shut up—and worse—by a crowd that is pre-dominantly gay and lesbian and white. (There are hierarchies everywhere.)

But she doesn't shut up. She tells them her truth. She speaks for her broth-ers and sisters. All these years later, I feel like she's shouting for you and also at me. It's a cri de coeur and a lecture on race and power and liberation.

She's calling out the "white, middle-class, white club." She is calling me out through the static of time, the reverb of the mic, and the crowd noise. She starts a chant, rousing the crowd. She spells out G-A-Y P-O-W-E-R— "Give me a G!" she begins. By the time she arrives at the final letter, her voice is choked with tears. She barely has a voice left. Her body is weak. She liter-ally drops the mic.

I imagine how you will feel when you watch this video clip—her heavy New York accent, her broken grammar, how she's so thin and fragile and yet shot through with strength. She and Marsha are aunties, in a way. Their power is in you.

You can find traces of transgender people in the earliest scraps of recorded human history, but as recently as 2018, the *Oxford American Dictionary* added the word *trans**—an umbrella term that popped up to cover a broad spectrum of gender identities.

Transgender people have been here forever, and at the same time, this movement is so new it's still creating a language.

Also, you should know, before the knock at the door, I found out I was pregnant—at age forty. I was surprised by the home pregnancy test when it turned positive. Shaken. I'd taken it not really expecting to be pregnant; I had a reputation for taking pregnancy tests on a whim. My cycles weren't typical, so I'd often wonder, and I preferred to know things for sure. And I had a fear of pregnancy; I knew too much. I understood the toll on my body.

Jeff was at the store. He'd taken you with him. Sophie and Tate were with friends. Isaac was somewhere in the house.

I paced around the bathroom for a few minutes, trying to reason with the test. It made no sense. It couldn't be right.

I walked out of the bathroom and found Isaac sitting on our slouchy IKEA fold-out couch. I said, "Hey, friend. A minute of your time?"

"Sure." He could see I was a little wide-eyed.

"This test. Does it look like a plus sign to you?" This was bad parenting, by the way. I do not recommend it.

"It does, in fact," he said, slowly and very formally. "It looks very much exactly like a plus sign."

"I thought it did."

"And it does," he said.

Here I started crying. He made a top-of-the-morning-to-you gesture as if wearing a top hat and disappeared. Months later, he told me that he didn't care to be the person who read the pregnancy tests and, in the future, to do that without him.

Two of the kids were born C-section. I'd had my first by cesarean at age twenty-five, my fourth at thirty-seven; the differences in my body's ability to bounce back were notable. At age forty, was I going to go through it all again? Would there be any bounce left?

I waited for your dad to come home. He was just out grocery shopping, but I pulled him away from unloading the bags into the mother-in-law suite.

"What's up? What's wrong?"

"I'm pregnant?"

"Are you serious?"

"I'm very, very serious. I mean, I'll have to take more pregnancy tests—just to be really sure. But these things are pretty accurate."

He was thrilled. He couldn't hide it. He picked me up off my feet. "I'm so sorry. This is crazy. But I'm really happy." He put me back down. "A baby. Babies are good!"

"Babies do tend to be good."

"They're very adorable. We have an excellent track record. Have you *seen* our babies? I mean, they're amazing babies."

Having been raised in a mostly Irish Catholic mindset that promoted the joys of a big, loud, messy house full of heartbeats and stories, this kind of joy worked for me.

Our imaginations quickly took hold. Our concept of family popped open to include a new baby. We decided to be cavalier. We'd done it before. What was one more?

We sat the kids down in the living room and told them, but Sophie and Tate already knew. Isaac had spilled it, as was his right. I hadn't told him not to. You were sitting there too, curled up on Sophie's lap. I could see that you were slowly starting to understand.

"A baby?" you said. "From you?"

"Yes. A baby from me."

Sophie was still stunned. This was derailing her plans. "I'll have to go to college closer to you all."

"No," I said. "You can go anywhere. Don't limit your options."

"Oh, I'm supposed to let *you two* raise a baby without me?" She was appalled.

Tate was fine with the news. He shrugged. "I'm already used to it. It's not a big deal."

"Or we could end up with two," Isaac said. "The twinnies?" You have twin cousins—my brother and sister-in-law decided to have a fourth child and had a fourth and a fifth.

Tate was unshaken. "Okay. Or two." He tended to roll with things.

The idea of twins hadn't dawned on me. I was a little rattled by it.

But then you smiled. You really got it—a new baby in the house. You beamed at all of us and said, "He's gonna be a girl!"

At this point, your father and I got bullish—like it was our job to upside the hell out of everything. We became haughty—the best offense being a good defense. We were going to have five kids, and we were going to have this big loud house, and we hadn't given away *all* of the baby stuff, so we'd just pull those things out of the attic. . . .

And, at the same time, we were going to be the best parents of a transgender child in modern history, loud and proud. We were critical of the hypocrisy all around us. Parents told their children that true beauty resides within. Mr. Rogers put it this way: "We need to help our children become more and more aware that what is essential in life is invisible to the eye." Our sense of self, our souls (if you will), our consciousness. Love. God and faith. Our true beauty. I'd been raised in the tradition of Saint Francis de Sales, who famously advised, "Be who you are and be that well." So, why didn't people *live* that?

We would betray all of this after the knock on the door. When that time came, I wouldn't want to hand over any part of the self—not mine, not yours, not the self of our family, not the true self that St. Francis de Sales suggested. For all of my lofty ideas about authenticity, I would become a coward so quickly.

This story doesn't define you. It's just a small piece of who you are. I want to say that it doesn't define me either, but it always will. This is something I have to reckon with: As soon as I felt that we were in danger, I wanted to create a fake version of a family—veneers for us to hide behind, sturdy, hardened, and polished like candy apples but made of depleted uranium pressed between sheets of steel armor plating.

I wanted us to be a family of tanks.

Part II

THE KNOCK

YOUR SISTER WAS THE one to answer the knock at the door. Sophie was probably fierce even in the simple act of seeing who was knocking at the door. With long glossy hair, pulled back, and a way of talking that's a challenge, something to rise to and meet or shy away from, I can imagine that the conversation was chilly.

She found me in the mother-in-law suite, seated at my desk. "There's a man at the door," Sophie said.

"What kind of man?" I asked, because her tone was off.

"I don't know. He wants to see you."

I headed to the front door. I was wearing a flowered skirt, and I'd put on a polka-dotted sweater earlier in the day. Clashing wasn't an issue when I was alone at my writing desk. I didn't think about what I looked like.

He was middle-aged, white, with brown hair. Not very tall, not very heavy. He had a folder, so I assumed he was selling something—lawn services or water purification or redemption. "I'm from the Department of Children and Families. A call was made. Do you know why someone would make a call about your family?"

It took me a few seconds to process what he was saying, but soon my chest flared. I said, "Yes, I think that someone might have called because of our daughter. We started using female pronouns and a new name recently. We've been letting people know. Maybe that's why someone called?"

That was exactly right. "Your child's name is _____?" He said a name that was not a name we'd ever called you. It was a long, elaborate name—one I'd never heard before and I've never heard used since.

"What?" I asked. "No, that's not her name." I gave the name we actually call you.

"Oh," he said. "Okay." And he made a note of it.

He asked to come in. We sat on our long yellow sofa from the 1940s, one that belonged to my Aunt Ruth, who'd kept it pristine; she'd had no children. Her own childhood had been brutal. There were stories passed down to me that she'd been raped by her stepfather. Her mother knew this and didn't leave him. (There are some homes where children need protection.)

We sat on that sofa.

He asked me questions and I answered them. I explained things, as best I could, including the research that I'd done. I walked him through the consultation we'd paid for with the gender specialist. I told him that your behavior was "consistent, persistent, and acute"—a phrase the expert used.

I talked about your school, telling him about the beautiful letter signed by the entire faculty and staff.

At a certain point, I started to cry. "I'm crying because I'm scared. There's someone out there who would do this to us. If they're capable of this, what else are they capable of?" We had an enemy. "Can you tell me who made the complaint?"

"It's anonymous," he said, explaining that the calls had to be anonymous; sometimes they were made by the children themselves.

"I understand," I said. "I appreciate the policy." But now I realized that my clashing flowered skirt and polka-dot sweater weren't merely a reflection of bad fashion. They made me look unstable. What was going on here? Was I being accused of something? "Tell me the procedure. How does it go?"

"When we receive a call, we have twenty-four hours in which to make a visit to the home. We have to interview every family member in that home, coming back every day until each one has been interviewed." He looked at his notes. "Who lives with you?"

"My husband and our son Tate are at a soccer event, two hours away. Isaac is at a friend's house. Our youngest is at the movies with the babysitter. Only Sophie and I are here."

"She's the one who answered the door?"

"Yes."

"I'll have to come back every day until I've interviewed everyone. But since Sophie's home, I'll ask her questions now," he said.

"I'll go get her."

"I'll have to talk to her alone," he said.

"Of course," I said, standing up.

While I talked to the investigator in the living room, Sophie realized that the man she'd mistaken for a Mormon going door-to-door was not a Mormon at all. She'd lingered in the dining room, eavesdropping. She had a friend over, a classmate from school; I knew her mother from work circles.

I explained to Sophie what she already understood because she'd been listening in. "He needs to talk to you now."

Sophie went to the living room for her interview. I was left in the kitchen with her friend. Did I offer her something to drink, cookies?

After Sophie's interview, after walking the investigator to the door, I told both girls not to tell anyone what had happened. "Except for your mother," I told Sophie's friend. I trusted her mother, and I don't believe in telling kids to keep secrets from their own parents. "Tell no one at school. Okay?"

Sophie's friend was on our side. The man who'd knocked at the door was a threat. She promised she'd tell no one. "Don't worry," she said. Was she more prepared for this kind of fear in a way we weren't? She was Black; had her mother taught her about a different set of risks when a white man from the government shows up at your door? Would her mother have been more scared right from the start?

Looking back, Sophie also remembers the yellow sofa first and foremost—how awkwardly long it was, how she sat as far away from the man as possible. She was already defensive.

The caseworker asked about her hobbies.

"I like art."

"Do you have a favorite subject at school?"

"Yes. Art."

"How does discipline work in your home? When you get in trouble, what happens?"

"We talk about it."

He asked questions.

She answered them, without elaboration.

She remembers his body, its size and shape. He wasn't too tall, not too broad. She had never been in a fight in her life. But she was thinking, "I can take this guy if I have to. I can take him."

We called him a caseworker maybe because that was how he introduced himself. But on the actual report, he would have a different title: *investigator*. I wouldn't see this final report for a long while. And I didn't yet really understand that we were being investigated. I would very soon.

I called Jeff. "You need to come home."

He remembers the call, vividly. It was a beautiful day, hot and clear. He was standing between two soccer fields, pacing the gulley between the white lines. Both fields had games in full swing. Parents were shouting at the children. The refs' whistles pierced the air. It was hard to hear me. He remembered pushing the phone's speaker to his ear. He was worried there'd been some kind of accident. In some ways, there had been. "Is the baby okay? Are you?" I'd had a miscarriage between Isaac and Tate; these were the early months, when everything felt precarious.

"Everything's okay. It's just . . ." And I tried to explain the knock at the door, the investigator, the interviews . . .

Jeff had questions that I couldn't answer. Then he said, "I'm the coach. There are back-to-back games. I can hand the team off to . . ." He was trying to think through the parents, but then he remembered. "I drove a carful of kids. Is there anything we can do now?"

"I don't think so," I said. I was strangely in shock. Though I was afraid of this unidentifiable enemy out there, I didn't actually think through any of the things that might happen as a result of the knock at the door. "Just keep doing what you're doing. I'll figure this out."

He wouldn't be home for hours.

I tracked Isaac at a friend's house and asked if they could drop him off early. They could.

I called the babysitter, who was in a movie theater with you.

"Hello?" she whispered.

"I need you to come back home."

"In the middle of the show?"

"Yes. Thanks. Yes, sorry."

I wanted to hold you.

I then did what I so often did when I had questions about how the world operates. I called my father. He retired as early as possible from corporate life—got out and never looked back. He helped out raising his grandkids, carpooling, and babysitting alongside your grandmother. Known as the baby whisperer, he can quiet any crying baby. As I mentioned, he has the air of a pediatrician—unless you're looking for legal advice; then he's a shark.

His first question was simple. "What has someone accused you of?" He wanted to know if there was an actual charge.

"I don't know."

"It's your right to know," he told me. "Find out what has been said against you. The person can remain anonymous, but the charge can't." His voice was calm, stoic, as it often is, but he'd switched into his other mode. I could sense it. I was talking to a lawyer now.

I asked him if he was worried.

"No, not really. But find out the charge."

I called up the investigator. He'd left his number in case I had questions. I asked for the accusation, for as much exact wording as he was allowed to offer.

He read to me from the call notes. Was this when I decided it must be a woman who called? Did he slip in a little female pronoun accidentally? Pronouns are tricky, you know. He said that the caller was concerned that we were dressing our son in girl clothes, that we were *forcing our child to be a homosexual*.

The coming months would be marked by paranoia—who made that call and why? This bit of wording gave us clues. This was a person who, most likely, didn't know what gender identity is; this was someone who'd never heard the term *transgender*, didn't know it as a concept, and couldn't separate gender from sexual orientation. This was someone who still used the word *homosexual* instead of simply *gay*. I assumed a generational gap. I thought: a woman called this in, an older woman.

I started to imagine running into someone at a grocery store, having just a casual conversation—and then they would ask how you were doing, but they would use the name the investigator used, and I would know, in a stark moment, a smile still fastened to my face, that they were the one who called.

The man who knocked at the door was coming back the next day, a Sunday. We didn't know when. But we were trying to remain steady, calm, *ordinary*.

After dropping off her friend, Sophie went to soccer practice. Your dad was making his way through the games, anxious to get on the road.

The sitter brought you back from the movies. She was a student at the well-known historically Black university in town where she was preparing to get her master's in education. I filled her in, briefly.

"If you need me," she said, "let me know how I can help."

"Thank you," I told her.

We had a few sitters. With four kids, it helped to have a team. We would need them. We would need a lot of people—and very soon.

What followed was a series of coincidences—or divine interventions, depending on your leanings. (You lean divine interventions.)

I went out, running an errand. I don't know where. I only remember pulling into the driveway after.

At the same moment, our neighbor, the lawyer, was also pulling into his driveway. We often would wave and chat. My first instinct was to wave and move on. I was feeling anxious, a hive in my chest had begun to buzz. But I didn't just move on.

I waved and walked over. He asked how I was doing.

And I told him, "Well, this strange thing happened. . . ." I think I was trying to lighten it. He was the steady kind of person who might laugh something like this off, right? I was looking for someone to put it into context, to frame it for me.

He got very still. He listened intently. By the time I wrapped it up, he had switched modes, like my father had. "Okay," he said. "I've got friends who work in this area of law." His mind was spinning through contacts. He was landing on a few. "I'm going to make some calls. I'll let you know what I find out."

Now panic set in. *This area of law*. What area? What was happening?

I went into my office and sat at my desk. I thought I should research, should do something. What? What should I do?

There was an email from my friend who was raising a trans son—just a quick email, checking in.

I wrote back. *Funny that you're writing me today of all days.* . . . Again, I explained.

My phone rang within minutes.

"This happens," she said. "I've heard stories. I'm going to put a call through to someone who advocates for transgender kids on the national level. She'll tell you what to do."

The escalation was terrifying.

Meanwhile, my neighbor showed up. Your father was driving back from the games, dropping players off at their houses around town.

I remember where my neighbor was sitting, where I was sitting, how he started talking about his lawyer friend. He was giving background information. None of it was pertinent. He was stalling.

"Please," I said, "just say it. Tell me."

What he had to say pained him. The bravado about not letting his own sons play with girly toys, all of that was gone. He was sitting with his elbows on his knees. He straightened and explained that we could lose custody. That if things progressed, if you were taken from our home under suspicion of abuse that, in that red state, with its appointments of far-right judges, we could lose the case. If we lost custody, it could take a long time to get you back.

He gave me his friend's phone number. "Call him."

We could lose custody.

We could lose you.

BEFORE I COULD CALL the lawyer, the woman who ran a national organization that supported families with transgender kids called me. She told me that she'd gotten word from our mutual friend, but she wanted to hear what was happening directly from me. I gave her some background on you and then about the current situation.

Her first question was this, "He comes back tomorrow?"

"Yes."

"I'm going to ask you a list of questions. Are you ready?"

"Yes."

"Are you white?"

"Yes."

"Are you married?"

"Yes."

"Are you both straight?"

"Yes."

"Your husband is also the father of the child?"

"Yes."

"Do you have money—and by that I mean, if this becomes a legal situation, can you hire lawyers?"

"Yes."

These were the questions she asked, reading them off from a list, I assumed. These were the questions she needed answers to in order to assess our risk. This is the checklist of privilege. This was what would help determine whether or not we would lose our child. I was haunted by each question. I was able to say yes to all of them, but each cast a shadow. What happens to the person who doesn't get to say yes? What happens if you're Black or brown or poor or dealing with custody issues or not married or gay, lesbian, transgender, or queer yourself?

I knew the answer without asking. You were more likely to lose your child. The list existed because parents had lost their children.

The woman was straightforward. She didn't have time to be prissy about what one should and should not point out about our ugly bigoted culture.

And, actually, we didn't skate through the checklist. At the end of all the questions, she said, "You have two strikes against you. First, your daughter was assigned male and identifies as female. If it were the opposite, people would be calmer about it all."

"Because girls can be tomboys?"

"In our male-dominated culture, who wouldn't want to be a boy?" she said, flatly.

But to want to be a girl, there must be something wrong with you or your parents, some perversion along the way? "What's the second strike?"

"Her age. She's young. If she were over nine years old, people accept that she's making the call herself. They don't understand the formation of gender identity. They think that kids can't be transgender, much less at a young age."

At a certain point, I stopped and asked if this happened to families like ours regularly.

"Yes," she said. "It's not unusual. The calls are sometimes made by someone in the school, like the school nurse who's privy to what's sometimes confidential. It's sometimes made by neighbors or from the church congregation. Sometimes it's within a family—a grandparent calling in their own son or daughter or an aunt, an uncle, a stepbrother, an in-law." She said that in a group of parents with transgender kids, a workshop or a group session, there were always people there who'd gone through it. "Sometimes it can almost feel like a rite of passage for these families."

Did she use this phrase here? Am I blurring this with another conversation? Someone said this to me: *rite of passage*.

Then she told us what we were supposed to do before the caseworker returned. "You have to create a safe folder. Get letters from as many people as you can to vouch for your parenting. Get a letter from your pediatrician, any social workers or nurses or teachers, family and friends."

"I can do that."

"Overnight?"

"I think so."

"Get photographs of your daughter living her joyful life in the clothing of her choice."

"Okay."

"Print out articles that explain transgender children. I'll send you links."

"Thanks."

"And self-portraits. Collect any drawings that she's done of herself."

Your self-portraits and drawings of princesses and flight attendants always had huge eyelashes and triangles for high heels. "Got it. Thank you."

"One more thing."

"Yes?"

"If you have the means to move to a progressive community out of the South, especially to a state with good antidiscrimination laws, do it."

I would see this woman years later at a conference for transgender health, far away from the South. I would tell her who I was and how she helped us. She would remember our story, this call. I would hug her in a huge hall of booths and tables and buckets of free pens and stress balls. I'd cry and she'd cry, two strangers holding onto each other.

Sometimes strangers can save you.

When all of this happened, my body was working hard to make another body. I'd been fighting exhaustion and nausea. I could only eat certain foods at certain times, depending on what tasted right. I had to ignore that now. I had to press on.

And then the call with the lawyer, the one our neighbor had recommended.

As he gave me instructions, as he explained how things worked in this southern town, as he explained what I had to do, I sometimes felt like an animal, my shoulders hunched protectively over my heart. I felt small and trapped. I had the instinct to claw my way out—of what? While he talked, I would lift my head and look around. I was just a woman—a mother, a mother pregnant with her fifth child—standing in a room, talking on a phone. A ceiling fan slowly spun overhead. But I was no longer the same woman I had been when I woke up that morning. The world altered around me, took a new shape, a new constellation of hatred. I was trying to orient myself. Everywhere I looked, the house was the same, but every molecule was different.

These are the things that he told me.

"If the investigator shows up tomorrow with a police officer, that means they're taking your child with them, in the cop car, immediately. This is their right. But call me right away."

He said, "You and your husband should choose someone you know who'll take your child in. Have the name and address written down on a piece of paper, ready to hand to the cop."

He said, "Sometimes they'll let the child stay in the home, but only if one of you takes the blame and leaves." This was presented as a more positive scenario. "You two should make this decision tonight so you know exactly who'll be the bad guy." Whoever left would have to live somewhere else for a long while. We'd have to prepare for that, too. "Think long-term."

He said, "If you go to court, it's hard to say if you'll win or not. I know how you'll be seen—lefties, hippies, weirdos. . . ." He'd gotten some information from our lawyer neighbor, and now I could see it distort—balloon animals twisted into a new strange shape. He was describing strangers.

"But we're not like that at all. We're registered Democrat but actually we're—" I wanted to say things about being Catholic, about Jeff's grandfather being a minister, about our Republican friends and family. . . .

"Doesn't matter. I'm not talking about who you are. I'm talking about who they'll make you out to be in order to blame you and keep your child from you."

While he talked, quickly, urgently, I drew up a picture of what he looked like in my mind—a lean, wiry man who talked all day long while rattling peanuts in his fist and popping them in his mouth. He'd seen things go badly. His job was to expect the worst. He was trying to get me to brace for the worst.

And he knew I was naive and stupid, that we'd been living in a bubble of our own design, and that we were going to have to become tough, very quickly. The progressive bubble of southern liberalism had popped, but it had never really existed to begin with. We needed to be ready to fight. He said things to me—about you, about us—that were hideous. I won't repeat them. As he was explaining the ways we'd be described by lawyers, he was, in a way, running me through a rough approximation of an ugly childhood in an ugly place so I could be a grown-up in that ugly place. I hated him, and I was full of gratitude. I didn't want him to ease up.

"Thank you," I kept saying. "Got it. Thank you."

Then the call was over. "Let me know how it goes." And he hung up.

14

I'VE PUT OFF WRITING this next part for years. I thought I didn't want to relive the fear. We had one night to get everything together, to prove we were parents worthy of raising our own child. But I realize now that I wasn't putting off the memory of fear. I was putting off the memory of love.

What happened that night was something that the person who reported us could never have imagined. It was an outpouring of love. It was a dam breaking, and we hadn't known there had been a dam at all.

That's the thing about this journey. I never know when I'm going to run into hatred. But I also never know when I'm going to run into love. And we have run into so much love.

As much as I believe that there is usually only an invisible skein, fine as muslin, that keeps humans from being brutal to other humans, I believe that most of the time we are actually hiding from each other our overwhelming sense of love. Love scares us. You can see it sometimes in these strange ways we hide our love—for fear of being overtaken by it. My grandfather had nicknames for all four of his sons. The nicknames were rough and a little mean, but when he talked about his boys, when he used those nicknames instead of their actual names, he'd sometimes go misty-eyed. If he were to say, "Those damn shitheads . . . ," you could guarantee he was feeling nostalgic.

Sometimes I think that those parents who don't let their children transition are afraid of how horrifically the world will treat their child if they came out and that they couldn't bear it. They love their child so much they can't imagine seeing them in that pain, and so they keep them in the pain that they think they know instead of the pain that they can't foresee. If they keep their children the way they are—which is an illusion—they can hope that their hearts won't be ripped from their chests. They won't be overtaken by the love held back by unseen dams. (They're wrong.)

I think that people love each other so much more than they let on.

And, my sweet, people love you. And on this night we saw their love for our family.

This is why, when things are bleak, I tell you that there will be heroes. This is why I sometimes whisper to you, in a quiet moment when we're alone, that you are powerful beyond measure.

Sometimes people love you and are helpless. There's nothing they can do to help. But every once in a while, you're in a situation where they can do something and then you see how quickly they rally, how quickly they spin into action, how quickly something breaks and there's love.

There was a decision to make: Which one of us would go if one of us were forced to take the blame? Would your father leave or would I?

"They'll blame me," I said. "They always blame the mother."

That woman in the support group was in her sixties. Had her own mother been loving? Had her own mother in the 1950s and 1960s tried to protect her a little? Had her mother allowed her to make her own land, the way you had once upon a time? Did she tell her mother the truth of her being? Had she created a library of her girlhood, one hidden behind the outward-facing books or locked away in the Special Collections, the archives? Had she been reunited with her girlhood self once she transitioned? Why did she think of mothers and blame? Had she been able to be a mother herself? She knew blame. And I assumed that she knew it well.

It made sense that I would take the blame. I was the one who'd done the research, read the articles, called the consultant, joined the support group.

If this was the only offer, I would take the blame and I would cave. I would talk about how I was wrong, that my husband, who'd fought me all along, was right. I'd say that I should have listened to my husband. I would ask for forgiveness. I would beg for it. I would agree to follow the suggestions of the court. I would follow my husband's plan. We would reverse course. We would put you in boy clothes. We would go back to male pronouns and your full boyish name.

We're not healthy when it comes to motherhood, as a culture. We denigrate it then sanctify it. Mothers are martyrs and saints. We're to be trotted out, given our little accolades, and then told to recede. We're cutesified, commodified, erased. There are pedestals and pits of damnation. We rarely talk about the realism of it all. It's something governments—made up largely of men—want to control. So, this would make them happy, right? This would restore order to the world. The girl would become a boy again, as it should be. The confused wife would be put right. All would be fine. We would reassure them. Your father would accept my apology and tell the court that he'd take it from here.

We would do all of this for as long as we had to, and then we would move. We would leave as soon as possible. We would be gone.

That was one plan.

Jeff remembers the ultimatum—one of us would have to go—but he doesn't remember that we decided on me. It was practical, he gets that. "I know why I blocked that part out. It should have been me. Men sacrifice themselves. How could I have let you be the one to take the fall, to leave?"

"It made the most sense, though," I said. "It's all there, on the page."

"It doesn't matter that it makes sense," he said. "I should have been the one."

"It's over," I said. "It doesn't matter."

What's been surprising for both of us, as I've plowed back through all of this, is how much it all still matters.

———————

Maybe, if someone were to erase all of the specifics, rub away the details, pull the stakes up from the damp, dark narrative soil of all of this, what I'm saying is universal. Maybe elemental.

Maybe this is only an agitation of meaning—or *toward* meaning.

It's a defense of motherhood and fatherhood, in general, and in specific. It's a defense of your being. (You might not need this defense at all.) But most of all, it's a love story, if you read this the right way.

Maybe that's true of every story.

———————

That afternoon and evening and into the night, Jeff, Sophie, and I made calls. We had three phones—two cells and an old landline. And we worked them. Your brothers were set to other tasks, mostly cleaning the house, getting it ready. For what? An inspection? We had no idea.

We chose someone to take you in, should the police show up at the door the next morning. We picked a family who had two sons—one was their bi-ological child, one was adopted from Africa. They'd also been foster parents. They have a midwestern gentleness and a midwestern toughness. It's hard to reimagine this call.

They remember it coming in the middle of a small dinner party they were hosting. The wife answered the phone. She agreed, immediately. She called her husband over. I talked to him too.

"Of course," they kept saying. "Of course."

I told them, "It won't be long-term. My parents will fly in immediately to take over." My parents were with us throughout all of this.

They agreed. No questions asked. Yes.

They went back to their dinner party, pretending everything was fine, but with this gnawing sense that it couldn't be real—the call, the dinner party. Neither felt real now.

We listed everyone else we thought would be helpful in an investigation. Our friends, it turns out, had jobs that were applicable. We reached out to one of the nurse practitioners who attended your birth, a city commis-sioner, a social worker, a well-known psychologist, a minister and his wife, a religious studies professor. There was my Catholic mother, my legal-minded father, friends who'd known us for ages, a few of the babysitters who'd known you since birth. We got a note from your pediatrician, a letter from the founders of your school.

Call after call, all three phones working at once, we explained what had happened. Your father called the psychologist, who was sitting in the stands of a college football game. He moved under the bleachers to hear what your father was saying. His letter would come later that night. One by one, people heading off to exercise, fixing dinner, getting ready to go out on a Saturday night stopped what they were doing and set to work.

The letters came quickly. They piled up.

Some began formally: *Please accept this letter of support . . . This note is to verify . . . As the biosketch appended to the end of this letter shows . . . The pur-pose of this letter is to provide . . . Dear Sir or Madam . . .*

But they quickly cut to the heart of the matter:

These are not merely wonderful but superb, loving parents . . . I can think of no better place for any child to be than in their home.

[This] family is one of the strongest, most loving families that we know . . .

Perhaps more than any other couple of my acquaintance, [they] place their children at the center of their lives.

Their goal and desire has been to protect [their child's] self-esteem and dignity. They are honest people who live their lives openly, with integrity and authenticity, and to deny their child the chance to do the same would be something they could not abide.

They talked about their own observations of your journey—your *desire to dress as a girl and to be referred to as a girl at school.* They stated how we let you *take the lead* and how our decisions were *supported by research.* Some noted that we were *equally prepared to support [you] in the event [you decide] at a later date to be referred to as a boy.*

One letter is very different from the rest. It's a letter from the sitter who'd been with us for a year and a half. We called her the G. She starts out describing a typical day with you. Your favorite games: *pretending to be flight attendants, Barbies, cleaning ladies, dressing up in skirts and high heels.* How you would always ask to see her purse, to hold it, and to play with the makeup inside. You two watched movies together, and you *would talk about the clothes of each character, being more concerned about shoes than plotlines.* You would also always ask to play "babysitters," which involved you pretending to be the G and the G pretending to be her sister/roommate Becky or Chloe. (You also requested that she do this in a British accent.) The G explained how you would put both legs in one trouser leg of your pants to make it a skirt but added that you *would turn your boy's underwear around so it looked like girl's underwear.* Like all kids, you loved going to toy stores. There was a Toys "R" Us right down the street, and you and the G would go there sometimes, *spending the majority of the time in the Barbie aisle.* You *loved playing Cheerleaders*; you would call yourself Abby and dance around the room while the G was *trying to keep up with the routine.* You *loved to gossip and have [your] hair brushed and styled.* You two *went to birthday parties together and [you] would ask for the girl's goodie bag at the end of the party instead of the boy's.* Action figures and rubber dinosaurs *were never as interesting to [you] as princess silly bands or scented lip gloss.* You would ask to go shopping at Old Navy and would drag the G *to the little girl's section, pointing out tutus and dresses* that you wanted. You really liked shoes and *ended up picking out a pair of purple sneakers to match the gray pair* the G had.

Don't you miss the G? I do. The G is now married with two kids of her own—a boy and a brand-new baby girl. She is an actual flight attendant.

And two of the letters aren't addressed *To Whom It May Concern* or *Dear sir or madam*. They were addressed to your father and me. They're from my mom and dad.

My mother talked of God and love:

You are a wonderful and loving couple who are the parents of four terrific children and one on the way. I have been in awe of you and your devotion to your children. You realize that what God has given to you is special and no one child is like another. . . . As parents, you did what you have always done; you sought the advice of experts. And, of course, you followed your heart. Just as you do, your father and I love [this child] just the way she is and would not want to change her in any way. She is going to grow into a marvelous person, and it will be because of your love, understanding, and smart parenting that her life will be so very rich and happy.

My father wrote:

I have witnessed over the past couple of years her strong bias toward traditionally feminine toys, play, dress . . . and have frequently heard her express her definite preferences to be called by a series of typically female names and ask that we refer to her as a girl. (Note: I have used feminine pronouns referring to her because she has asked me to do so.) He ends with this: The common denominator is always the love you have for each child and each other. I feel privileged to have been included along the way.

With all of my love and support,
Dad

Of all the lines in all the letters, it's my father's parenthetical note that makes me choke up while rereading it. There is something about this man, in his older years, having the humility to simply listen to a child. To you. He takes us out of the frame and focuses on you. You two have your own relationship.

I remember this one time, when you were three years old, my dad walked into the kitchen. He'd been playing some game with you in the playroom. My dad is an excellent game player. But he walked in with his hands in his pockets, looking a little rattled.

"What's up?" I asked. "You two having fun?"

He told me that you two were talking through some aspect of the game, and then you said, "Are you mocking me, Pop-Pop?"

You know this story by now. We love this story. You were so little that you couldn't even pronounce *mocking*. It came out *motting*.

But the best part of the story was that you were right. "And I was mocking," your grandfather said. "I was completely called out. I had to come clean and apologize."

The point is that you were always reading people. Always. And you had such dignity. At three years old, you refused mockery.

We talked to another lawyer friend. As I told the story, he stopped me cold. "Wait, the school wrote a letter? The teachers gave the nickname? It's almost as if you were following their lead on this. They're the experts on child development, not you." He was suggesting that we off-load blame onto the school. I was stunned by how quickly narratives could take on new shapes.

I was connected with a lawyer who worked for trans rights on the national level. He used the word *transphobia*. I remember the moment so clearly. I'd been on the phone, pacing in one corner of the mother-in-law suite. I stopped cold. I was saying, "Yes, uh-huh, yes . . ." But I was thinking, *Transphobia, that's what I have.* I knew I had it. I knew it ran deep. I'd never had a word for it, but I recognized it like finding a mirror in a wall of your house for the first time. The shock of your own face staring back from what you'd thought was a simple wall.

After the call, I told your father what the lawyer had said. I slipped in the word *transphobia*. Your father said, "Transphobia. I have that."

It seems insane that we could be transphobic while fighting for your right to be transgender. But we were. We'd been hiding it from ourselves but now we had a word for it—and it was such a simple word, one that's become so common it's hard to imagine that we didn't know it. Our transphobia was fueled by our ignorance and culture—and all of the various cultures within our larger disturbed American culture, like sports culture and joke culture alongside sexism and homophobia, machismo, far-right politics and far-left politics and feminism (which should be pro–trans women but hasn't always been, historically speaking)—mixed with religion and media with its

portrayals of trans people through the history of television and film. Here's
a small glimpse of what I mean. In November 1998, I was twenty-eight years
old when the enormous hit show *Friends* introduced a trans character.
Kathleen Turner, a cisgender actress, played the role of a trans woman—
except that the word *transgender* never even comes up. Chandler's *father*
was simply referred to as a gay man. The word trans didn't even seem to exist as a concept—or not one that American audiences would understand.
Again, I was twenty-eight; you'd be born less than ten years later. The episode floated back to me during all of this. I'd thought it was funny. (This is
the tiniest of tiny examples, of course. I'll get to the bigger ones.)

It would be years before I would learn that there are so many terms,
throughout cultures and history, used to describe transgender experiences
and trans people. Tacitus wrote about the *galli* priests of the Germanic Na-
hanarvali tribe wearing women's clothes in Rome. In Sumer, transgender
and androgynous priests are called *gala*. During the Akkadian period, they
were called *kurgarru* and *assinnu* and were part of rituals devoted to Ishtar,
who could transform them from masculine to feminine. There's evidence of
a third gender in various texts in India dating back three thousand years,
which are related to *hijras*, trans-feminine women. Despite the British col-
onists' attempts to erase them, *hijras* still exist. In Indonesia, third-gender
people are called *waria*. In the Philippines, *bakla*. In Thailand, *kathoey*. The
Native American Dine (Navajo) tribe uses the word *nadleehi*. Though the
nadleehi's gender identity can shift over time and even day to day, they tend
to be "a male-bodied person with a feminine nature." Nadleehi are often recognized at a young age, and sometimes they take on ceremonial roles that
can only be held by someone who is nonbinary. For the Bugis of Sulawesi,
there are five genders—the typical male and female, trans women, trans
men, and those who exist between genders. And these are but a few examples. In addition to my own transphobia and ignorance of the transgender
experience, I was also worrying about the internalization of transphobia.
If we are transphobic, deep down, are you? I know how it can happen. As
a woman, I'm capable of sexism while in a group of women talking about
sexism; the sexism I've encountered on a personal level has come from both
men and women, including women who are hardworking feminists. Inter-
nalizing the fear and hatred from others is so incredibly sly; it slips in without you knowing it. But then, once it arrives, it can take up a lot of space,

start stomping around, making proclamations, doling out injuries from within. But naming it makes a difference, like banding a strange invasive species so you can track it.

Someone else, I can't remember who, suggested that you should have a therapist. You were healthy; in fact, since the transition, you were thriving. We'd been the ones talking to experts. But, okay. A friend who was a licensed social worker made a call to someone who specialized in play therapy. She scheduled an emergency appointment for us the coming week.

Sophie collected your drawings of princesses and flight attendants. She had you draw a self-portrait before you went to bed.

I read the articles that had been suggested and printed them out.

The Safe Folder was a plastic three-ring binder. We hole-punched and arranged the proof of our good parenting. It took on a physical weight. This isn't what love should look like—a three-ring binder. But it was, in fact, what love looked like.

———————

Your father and Sophie and I worked late into the night, maybe into the early morning. After everyone went to sleep, I swept the house. I took down a painting of a nursing mother. It had been so benign before, but now it seemed dangerous. I took down anything that seemed political in any way. I cleaned the house all over again. I am not tidy by any measure, but I started cleaning inside of the cabinets, refolding towels, lining up coffee mugs—the way I'd only done when staging a house for sale.

I refolded all of the clothes in your small chest of drawers. I assumed they'd look here, to see what we were "forcing you" to be. I wanted the investigator to notice that you had boy clothes and girl clothes. At that point, you actually had far more boy clothes, in fact. All of this was still new.

What was I expecting? A raid?

I was expecting a raid.

I was thinking about how you had a diagnosis from your pediatrician, a diagnosis with standards of care from the American Academy of Pediatrics. How could they take you from us? Would someone see a child in a wheelchair and say that the parents were forcing that child to be disabled? I would find out years later that the answer to this question is yes. Babies with rare genetic disorders that are hard to diagnose, infants who fail to thrive for reasons not yet understood, children who bruise easily due to leukemia—people make those calls. When doctors can't figure out the diagnosis or their treatment plans fail, they turn on the parents. As Dr. Atul Gawande puts it, "Nothing is more threatening to who you think you are than a patient with a problem you cannot solve."

Your father heard me rattling around. He told me that I had to stop. In a hallway dimly lit by a nightlight at our ankles, he held me. "You have to get some sleep. You have to rest."

"Okay," I said, "I will. One more thing though. Just give me a minute."

I went into your brothers' shared room. I looked in on them, each in his bunk bed. They were peaceful. I checked on Sophie. She'd fallen into a restless sleep. And then I walked into your room. I sat on the edge of your bed, and I watched you dream. I put a hand lightly on your ribs, feeling the small expansion with each breath. I'd done this with all of my kids when they were babies, checking to see that they were breathing, gazing at the beauty of a face so carelessly and blissfully asleep.

But you had this habit that none of the other kids did. You laughed in your sleep. You were put on this earth with that gift of joy—it was so much a part of you that it was embedded deep down in your unconscious mind.

That was what I was trying to protect. Your joy.

WE WERE UP EARLY. Letters were still coming in. The safe folder was still growing. (It would continue to grow.) The kids were awake. We talked to the boys about what might happen and what kinds of questions might be asked. We didn't really know. We were guessing.

And then there was you. We decided not to fully explain it to you. How could we have? We didn't want to scare you. We couldn't imagine the other scenario—that a police officer would show up. In retrospect, maybe we should have. But we couldn't. Even now, I don't know how to explain that to a child. Instead, I said that one of my coworkers was working on a project about kids and wanted to ask you some questions. I didn't know how else to frame it.

It was midmorning when the caseworker showed up again. He was alone. No cop car. No police officer.

We welcomed him in. He met your father. They shook hands. We offered tea and coffee and lemonade. He declined, as we knew he would.

We handed him the Safe Folder. "We thought this might help give some context...."

Did he look at it? Did he glance through it? Did he even touch it?

I can't remember now.

He talked to your father, alone.

The one question your father remembers is something like this: "Have you ever been concerned about your child?"

Your father looked him in the eye and said, "Not until yesterday. Not until this."

The caseworker didn't understand. But this is what your father and I already understood: If a child has a problem that's only a problem when they go into the outside world, then that child doesn't have a problem. The outside world has the problem. Your father explained that he hadn't been worried until this threat to his family. We were fine before this. His child was fine.

Then the caseworker wanted to talk to you.

I told him how we'd prepared you for the conversation and then said, "Can I be there? I think it might be easier." The idea that you would tromp in and chat with a stranger alone seemed unlikely. You were shy around strangers.

So, we sat in chairs set up in the living room.

He asked you about school and things you liked to do.

You gave little peeps of answers.

He shrugged and looked at me. He didn't know what to ask, so I jumped in. "Tell him what toys you like to play with."

You mentioned some of your favorite things, your toy vacuum being a highlight among them.

I said, "Tell him what kind of job you want to have when you grow up."

You perked up and got a little animated talking about wanting to be a flight attendant.

And he shrugged again. "Okay," he said, "that's good."

He asked to see our oldest son.

Isaac was ready. He was a confident, funny boy with a wry smile and the demeanor of a guy in his late twenties. The kind of kid to prop his foot on his knee and say, "So, what you got for me?"

The rest of us pretended to be busy in the kitchen. But I edged as close as I could to listen in.

I heard him ask Isaac about what happened when he did something wrong, how punishment worked in our house.

Isaac drew in a deep breath. He said, in a very serious voice, "Well, it's not easy. I'm glad you asked about that. Because I don't like it. Sometimes, when I get in trouble around here, my parents take away screen time. No video games, no TV. It can go on for like a couple days, honestly."

It's hard to say, even to this day, if he was aware that this was comedic or if he was actually glad someone was finally on his side—or, most likely, a mix of both.

Tate was next. He was nervous. He can be a little shy, like you. He's not a chatty person. He answered succinctly and very earnestly. I didn't hear the question, but the last thing he said was this, "She's my sister and I love her."

Your dad and I walked back in. We asked if there was anything else he needed.

He was packing up his notes. "No, that's it," he said.

And then he told us that he planned to write up the report and that would be the end of it. "What's frustrating about this is that there are kids out there who need me, who really need me. And someone calls in a family like yours?"

I didn't feel relief. I should have. But my whole body was still locked. I could only say things that someone might say, do things that someone might do. I was supposed to go on a trip the next day for work. I hadn't canceled yet because offices hadn't been open, but I'd been preparing to. I asked if I should stay in town.

"No, go on your trip."

"Are you sure? I can cancel."

"It's okay," he said. "Go."

"When will we find out, officially, that it's over?" your father asked.

He gave a date a couple of weeks away. "They'll send paperwork or you can go pick it up."

For me, it wouldn't feel over until it was official. (It would never really feel over.)

We had his number to call; we had the department's number.

And, like that, he left.

16

HOW TO EXPLAIN THAT someone—maybe someone who's had many pregnancies—can know when they're no longer pregnant?

I went to the conference. My parents met me there. They were a comfort. They had a big family of their own. I was their youngest, their baby. They wanted to see me, to hug me. I understand the instinct. There've been many times when I've worried about one of my kids from afar, wanting to be there, wanting to be close. My parents were relieved but still worried.

I confided in my mother how I was feeling physically.

I wasn't nauseous anymore. It was that time when morning sickness should subside. In my previous pregnancies, my nausea started late, just late enough that I was hopeful that this time I wouldn't feel sick. But then it would kick in, and it always lasted longer than the books suggested. I'd had one miscarriage before. My pregnancies are actually statistically in line with rates of miscarriages per pregnancy. I had two healthy pregnancies then a miscarriage. Then two more healthy pregnancies and again what seemed to me to be the beginning of a loss.

With a person's first pregnancy, the changes to fullness, to showing, take a while. But once the body knows pregnancy, it bounces into its rounded shape. It pops into expansion. My body had popped. But when I looked at my body on this trip, it seemed slightly deflated. I was less round and full. I called the obstetrician and set up an appointment. When I got home, we quickly learned that there was no longer a heartbeat. My doctor suggested waiting to miscarry naturally.

My mother told me that, in the lead-up to seeing me, she'd been wondering how to help. She knew what I'd just been through; she'd been through it with me, albeit from afar. She decided it would be best to focus on the future, the baby. She bought a newborn outfit and packed it in her suitcase.

But then I told her what I was worried about, an impending loss, so she never gave me the outfit. She took it home with her. Once there, she learned of the miscarriage. She didn't want to keep the outfit for another baby. I understand this. She went to a home for families in crisis, a charity that was right around the corner from her church. They didn't usually take clothing. But she knocked on the door. She explained about the loss. The outfit was brand new, the tags still on it. "The woman told me that she would find a use for it and thanked me for it," my mother told me years later. "She may have just felt sorry for me, but I was relieved. It felt so important that it be used by someone who needed it."

I think of those two women standing on the porch—my mother and the stranger, negotiating my mother's sadness. The mutations of grief are sometimes small and quiet but necessary.

Recently, my mother was thinking back on it all. "I always wonder how much the heart can take," she said, "and then I see how much the heart can take."

I do not believe the loss was due to the knock at the door, to the person who made that call—and the stress that followed. But this was when I wanted to know who it was, this was what I wanted to explain to the caller. I wanted to show her what we'd been through. I wanted to show her the chaos and fear that she had caused.

The loss hit us all in different ways. Already reeling, we were hit with something so personal. A pregnancy is something that creates a new future. It reshapes the imagination. Our idea of our family, which had finally seemed locked into place, had suddenly sprung open. And now that future was slamming shut. That idea of who we would become was gone.

Still, your father and I had been somewhat prepared. We've had so many friends suffer miscarriages, and because we'd been through it ourselves, we'd put up our defenses. We'd already braced for this.

We told your brothers, your sister, and you.

It hit Sophie the hardest. She'd started to rearrange her life for the new baby. She wants a big family of her own one day. Again, she wasn't the kind of teen you'd think would be so invested. She had very clear ideas about her work, her career. She was putting time into her art. She was competitive and ambitious. And she really hated how mothers were condescended to, as if mistaken for babies themselves, or at least toddlers. But she was also raised by me, and I'd managed to have a good career in a competitive field while raising kids. And her father was not just supportive. He was a champion of my work, and he dug in with the family. Her life was proof that a mother could have a career.

Your dad went to a family wedding. There was no way for him not to go. I told him to go. We were waiting for the miscarriage. My body would know what to do. I would be fine. He took you and the boys. His back seized up on the flight. He hobbled around, trying to smile, telling no one what had happened. He didn't want to dampen the celebration or divert attention. But he kept calling me to check in.

This loss was very hard on him. We embraced this child, had already imagined their sweetness. And he'd started to reimagine the house, the kids' rooms, how our daily lives would change completely. Your dad was at the wedding, a quiet beautiful thoughtful wedding, pretending that all was well.

He was also furious that some stranger had felt this was their right, had been so reckless and yet also probably self-righteous. He was angry about the lack of acceptance, the bigotry that primed it.

But he was surprised that I wasn't angry. I was surprised too. I'm not someone who's cut off from my emotions. But anger felt like a lever that I couldn't pull. That I wouldn't let myself pull. It would do me no good. I was in survival mode, and anger would deplete my resources and put us at greater risk. I had to be the perfect mother. There was no margin of error, no room for creativity, no room for anger.

Also, deep down, I already knew this was a warning shot. I knew that we'd actually gotten off light. We needed to leave, and this was enough to make us go. It could have been worse.

Sophie didn't go to the wedding. She couldn't leave me. She had to stay. And it made sense. I might need help. Miscarriages can sometimes be dangerous.

The two of us were watching a movie when the cramping and contractions started. I didn't need her help. It was a little scary but never dangerous. The movie—I don't remember which one—was a comedy; we needed something lighthearted.

Sophie is terrified of miscarriages now. She felt this loss and wasn't sure what to do with the grief. It blindsided her and yet she had to just keep going. There was school. She was a straight-A student, and she wouldn't compromise. Her days became harder to navigate.

She made more art. The work became larger and more elaborate. It was all protective, armor-like pieces. The metaphors were clear. In some ways, maybe this was when she really became an artist—learning not only to express suffering but also to drill fear and grief into the work so the work can hold it for you; to let the work consume you, to let it insulate you.

And, to be honest, I hadn't really understood how shaken she was. We were all just trying to get our feet under us. And over the next few months, I would focus much of my attention on getting out of the South and where we might land, and what that new life might look like. And Sophie was becoming . . . she was learning how to exist in a world that had exposed itself suddenly as untrustworthy. Like so many artists before her, she created a practice that she could control, a world of her own; she created bodies that she could protect; she began to trust art.

17

THE KNOCK AT THE door wasn't terrifying in the usual sense. There's a difference between being terrified and feeling terrorized. Both refer back, in their roots, to terror. I felt terrorized during this period of time. But I have actually been more terrified as a mother. This was when your big brother Tate was in high school, hitting his stride during his senior year soccer season, and he got a fever. It spiked, and in the middle of the night, he called me into his room. The pain in his foot was so severe he couldn't walk. By the following afternoon, he was in the hospital. An infection in his bloodstream. The pain in his foot and now also in his hip was from the infection trying to burrow into bone. I knew that people died of this. When I asked the ER doctor, in private, what the rates of survival were, she said, "I couldn't tell you" and walked away.

The team of doctors were vigilant but kept it lighthearted in the room—until one day when each of them changed, one by one. Tate wasn't responding to the antibiotics; the cultures kept coming back positive. They stood over his hospital bed, arms crossed, scanning his body, trying to figure out what they'd missed. Had they not gotten at the infection's origin? Had it slipped into a place where there are few nerve endings, a spot where he wouldn't feel the pain? "Like in his heart valves," one doctor said. I already knew that staph, when carried in the bloodstream, can travel and take root wherever it wants—including the heart and, worse, the brain. Tate underwent surgery to protect the bones of his hip and foot.

And then one night, his vitals dropped suddenly. The medical staff swarmed. This was terrifying. It was fear at its most primal and uprooting. Your father was taking care of things at home. I called him at one o'clock in the morning from the hospital room and told him he had to come in now. I couldn't reassure him. I couldn't say, "It's probably nothing." I just said, "Come now. Get here."

He drove for a half hour to the hospital, not knowing if his son was dying.

You know how this story goes. Tate's vitals stabilized. One day, he looked brighter. His eyes could see us clearly. Something had changed.

I think of the care Tate was shown by the people in that hospital as a form of love. Love can be wild and terrified. It can also be precise and measured. It can be found in the lawyer who won't let up, who will tell you every horrific thing you need to know to brace yourself for what might come. Love can be found in the expert who calls you immediately, firing off a series of questions to quantify your risk. Love can be found in the straight-shooter at a support group—*They'll blame you. They always blame the mother.* Love can take the form of a flood of letters.

I've been terrified of illness, of disease, since my first pregnancy. I have been aware of the coldheartedness of statistics. I have a near-perfect memory of every horrible accident I've ever heard of—sledding, choking on hard candy, a dog that turns on a baby. We once saw a car at a gas station slowly roll backward downhill toward three lanes of traffic in a blind curve. The driver, who'd been strolling away, realized and ran after it, in vain. Before flying into the oncoming cars, it disappeared into a ditch. It was a wild thing to watch—no one was hurt. But as we were pulling out, passing people gathering to take photos, we saw car seats belted into the back. And even though no children had been in the car, the idea that they could have been made the whole episode suddenly terrifying.

Having children is saying yes to the unknown; it's accepting unquantifiable risk. It is an act of irrepressible optimism.

After the knock at the door, when the threat was gone, it didn't feel like it was gone. The moment when your brother suddenly seemed healthy, his eyes brightening, was the shift we'd been hoping for. The caseworker putting our case to rest should have worked that way too. But it didn't. Something had cracked. And even though it was over, it couldn't be fixed. Unlike an infection, it couldn't be treated. And so it wasn't over. This is why what could have been terrifying was more terrorizing. It created a present-tense anxiety, an ongoing urgency. I couldn't put it behind me because it refused to move to the past. It remained, reverberating in every room of our house—now tidy, forever waiting for another knock.

I went to the department the day that the complaint was to be officially completed. I picked it up. It's now part of the Safe Folder.

I called the caseworker with another question. I left a message, and he called me back. He was kind. That's the honest truth. I wanted an assurance. "Now that we've gone through the process and you've done a visit of our home, what happens if someone else does this to us? Or the same person does it, anonymously, again? You'll have us on file, right? We won't go through it again?"

"No," he said. "Sorry. That's not how it works. We have to investigate every call."

"Okay," I said. "I understand."

"But your case is going to go to the state level. We're going to discuss it because we need to educate our operators on how to respond to this kind of caller, calling in this kind of case." He meant transgender kids exist and those calls shouldn't make it all the way through the system. "We're going to review it."

Although that was hopeful, it didn't really help us. With no reassurance, we were still a target.

––––––––––

Because the call was anonymous, there was no way to connect with the caller, to give some background, to do some education. This was what my mother says to me now about all of this. "You couldn't ever face your accuser. You couldn't explain anything or make peace. So you couldn't stay. It was impossible."

And, for us, it was possible to leave.

Migratory birds developed an adaptation—their pituitary glands secrete a hormone when the days grow shorter. The hormone gives them a kind of wanderlust, which kicks off their migration. For us, fear kicked off our migration, a heady mix of adrenalin and cortisol.

We needed to head toward home. It was logical but also irrational.

A German scientist named Hans Wallraff transported homing pigeons far from any place they'd ever been before, in airtight cylinders with bottled air. Light and noise were used to disorient the birds. The cylinders were insulated in magnetic coils. The birds were unable to orient themselves using the sun or air, their sense of smell, or magnetic fields. They were then dizzied and released in areas that were completely foreign to them.

This is how I felt. Disoriented, dizzy, trapped without the normal bearings. And then released back into the world I'd known, yes, but one that had completely changed on me.

The pigeons found their way home.

There are many ideas on how birds migrate—theories about their internal olfactory maps; that they sense their position because of a sensitivity to the magnetic pull of the earth's poles; that they orient themselves by observing the sun's path across the sky (not the sun in isolation but in movement) or the rotation of constellations in the night sky.

Sometimes it was the voice of my mother and father. Steady and calm. I was a grown woman, but they were orienting.

Once upon a time, they'd gazed at me and I'd gazed back. We had family back up North. We were going to need all of that unconditional love, all of that gazing. All of us.

⸻

You weren't taken from us. You know this. But I can pinpoint the fear lodged inside of me. It sits at the base of my breastbone, now just the size of a finger poking into my chest.

We started our plans to leave the South because we had the means and the collective will. We're lucky, privileged. We told family that we would be moving back. And we had people waiting for us. (This is a privilege that wasn't on the list of questions read to me over the phone by the woman prepared to help families like ours, but it should be. It would prove invaluable.)

We searched maps and started clocking antidiscrimination laws. Most of all, we looked for places that had already been homesteaded, where there have been plenty of pioneers—lesbian, gay, bisexual, transgender, and queer people—who had come before us. We were following their migratory patterns, the ones established throughout American history. They have left and continue to leave rural areas, claustrophobic hometowns, Bible Belts and Corn Belts and Rust Belts, the Mormon Corridor, in hopes of freer or at least more anonymous lives in cities and progressive pockets of America.

That they moved to cities and progressive communities isn't unique to the LGBTQ+ community. During the Great Migration, which spanned much of the twentieth century, six million African Americans left the South for cities in the Northeast, Midwest, and West. As Pulitzer Prize–winning writer Isabel Wilkerson puts it, "They did what human beings looking for freedom, throughout history, have often done. They left."

Imagine how these places met the LGBTQ+ people who arrived. Our cities gave them a home, and those cities—they are mostly cities—grew richer and richer for all the community gave back. People, some of whom were just kids, were still forced to live on the edges, but they often made those edges their territory. They found books and art and theater and dance and science and creating and making. We are the collective beneficiaries of suffering that was turned into an expression that expands who we are, each and all of us, and expands what our humanity can accomplish. Maybe they were trying to save themselves, but with their creations and innovations, they help save all of us.

We've begun to learn the culture, the history of pride. We've begun to learn a new kind of gratitude. We've begun our education on heroes.

Sylvia Rivera and Marsha P. Johnson, Saint Joan of Arc, Diana Goetsch, Oliver Baez Bendorf, Jennifer Finney Boylan, Nick Krieger, S. Bear Bergman, Janet Mock, Laverne Cox, Lili Elbe, Dr. James Barry, Chaz Bono, Billy Tipton, Lucy Hicks Anderson, Gavin Grimm, Jen Richards, Sarah McBride, Danica Roem, Nicole Maines, Aimee Stephens. . . . Let the names become a litany. . . .

I stopped letting the kids play in the front yard. We now pulled our cars all the way into the garage to enter and exit the house. I kept the house spotless for the first time in my life. Just this year, I met up with a friend raising a transgender daughter around your age. He'd also experienced someone reporting a complaint, *the rite of passage*. "Sometimes it's late and I want to leave the dishes in the sink and go to bed," he confided. "But I can't. I think, what if tomorrow morning they show up at the door again. I have to do the dishes. I always do them." It had been at least eight years since their case was closed.

I lived in fear of another knock at the door. Didn't that person still have access to us? Couldn't they see us? They knew you weren't taken away. They knew their plan didn't work. How would that make them feel? Would they try again? Would they do something else?

I scolded the children if they were roughhousing. I was terrified of bruises. What if someone—what if the person who reported us—saw a bruise on one of you? And you bruise easily, a trait from my father's side of the family. I told your pediatrician that I was worried about the bruising, the occasional nosebleed. He did a test that proved that your platelets, though within normal range, are slow to clot. I put that in the Safe Folder. I wore my most conservative clothes. I was suddenly picky about what you kids looked like when leaving the house.

All my life I'd seen what I called "snatchy mothers" in grocery stores and malls and restaurants. I hadn't understood why they were so hard on their kids. *Don't touch that! Come to me when I call you! Get over here!*

My thoughts immediately shifted. As I'd walked around—white, middle class, respected as a good mother just because of what I looked like, sometimes even lightly sainted for being a mother, especially one with a lot of white middle-class children—others were treated with outright suspicion. I suddenly saw Black mothers, Latina mothers (fathers, too), the parents who don't fit gender roles, who don't look the way we expect, who don't roll out of minivans with kids in their stained athletic uniforms straight from team practice—in a new way. Trayvon Martin was still alive in a town in the South. He hadn't yet been shot and killed for just being a Black boy who'd run to the store to buy Skittles. But Emmett Till, at fourteen years old, had already been lynched for supposedly whistling at a white woman in her family's grocery store back in 1955. Slavery and racism are the American experience. And, still, we don't tell the truth about the terrorism that Black people have endured in this country, the violence and murder, Jim Crow, the New Jim Crow, institutionalized racism. Our collective white guilt and shame and supremacy actively alters and skews and marginalizes and erases as much of the truth as it can, devours it. It is a maw that eats and eats and eats.

These mothers aren't snatchy moms; they're protective moms. They know the world they navigate. They live in a world that treats their motherhood and their children with the threat of murder, violence, and imprisonment, the threat of having the manager called over, the threat of that escalating, or the threat of being watched from the moment they walked into the store. They have to keep their children close. Their children can't just reach out and touch things on the shelves; their lives are being lived in a heightened state of suspicion, scrutiny, and presumed guilt, with the possibility of danger in the most ordinary moments.

I'd had to create a Safe Folder to prove to someone who knocked politely at my door that I was a good mother. I'd never had to prove it before. I became obsessed with the identity of one person who'd threatened us. In that moment, it was one person. But, to me, that person represented America's homophobic and transphobic hate-fueled culture.

This is how we terrorize mothers. We threaten to take their children.

What's happened since this realization? That form of terror became American policy at our borders. The Trump administration proudly explained that taking children from parents who were immigrants, who were seeking asylum, was tactical, a deterrent. There was no practical reason to separate a father from his children or a mother from her infant, except to terrorize them. We've done this to Black communities with calculated precision. The mass incarceration of Black men and women in this country is another way to separate parents and children, to rupture families. Native American children were taken from their parents and forced into violent schools bent on assimilation. Immigrants in tenement housing were targeted and harassed, one group after another. At the auction blocks, slave owners and slave traders divided families, ripping children from their mothers' arms, selling off Black men and women and children into slavery and continuing to sell them throughout slavery without regard for their families, for their humanity.

It is a specific form of terrorism, an enduring one.

I WAS VERY AWARE of how fear could be translated in the child's mind to shame. I wouldn't tell you this story for four years, not even the simplest version. It's not a story we told. None of us really wanted to talk about it much. Within the family, we talked about how the move North would be better for you, that things were better there for all transgender people—in terms of the law and the open, progressive community we chose—but I also mentioned the other things too, that the public schools would be better for all the kids up here, that we would be closer to family again.

I kept my eye on our fear. I feared our fear. But I was even more worried about shame.

Fear is the danger from the outside in.

Shame is the danger from within.

You can get away from something you fear. You can't get away from shame if it starts to take up space inside of you.

I took you to the therapist who specialized in play therapy. Her office was cluttered with little toys. You played. She watched. She asked you questions. You answered.

She told me that you were healthy and fine. She wrote a letter on our behalf. I put it in the Safe Folder. You liked her. We kept going. You played. She watched. She asked you questions. You answered.

She made one suggestion. She told me to keep offering boyhood as an option.

"How?"

"Just let her know that she can always switch back if she wants to."

"How often do I bring it up?"

She wasn't sure. "Every couple of months?"

She was making this up. But we were all making this up.

"Okay," I said.

And so, I offered boyhood.

Each time I offered boyhood, you rejected it. It was simple and easy for you. But for our culture, it was radical.

What I was just beginning to understand in a blurry intuitive way, a series of sketches, watercolors without edges, is that you are dangerous.

Of course, you're just being. You're not doing *anything*. But from my viewpoint, I see how it can appear, which is something like this: By rejecting boyhood and therefore manhood, you have rejected the patriarchy. It's like someone who's been offered an endless feast of power, an all-you-can-eat buffet of privilege, and you've said, blithely, "No thanks." Some may see it as turning your nose up at the great gift of power. By claiming girlhood, you've upended what our culture values most: men, manliness, prowess, strength, dominance. How dare you?

James Baldwin put it this way, in the context of race, but it resonates: "What one does realize is that when you try to stand up and look the world in the face like you had a right to be here, you have attacked the entire power structure of the western world."

Just that—looking the world in the face like you have a right to be here.

By being.

This is why I want you to watch Sylvia Rivera's four-minute speech after she storms the stage at the Christopher Street Liberation rally in New York City in 1973. I want you to see her raw courage. As she yells at that crowd, as she tells her truth, having rejected boyhood and manhood, she seems to have no power—but watch her, listen. She said no to power, and in so doing, she claimed ultimate power. She is power. And the power she has resides in you.

In your refusal to take up boyhood, to choose instead—of all things— girlhood, you are powerful. Your no-thank-you is loud even if you say it in a soft voice.

And because of this rejection of boyhood, your body is a force. You are to be reckoned with. What I can't fully comprehend is how your being and your relationship with your body are so radical that people are terrified of them. Culturally, people want men to be men and women to be women. They seek this simplicity. They want the roles to be divvied up and clear.

Girlhood (and its move into womanhood) is becoming a body that men want to control, that men feel they should control. Among the accusations thrown at Saint Joan of Arc during her trial, the one that surfaces again and again was her dressing in men's clothes. The trial was highly documented: "abandoned women's clothes . . . disregarding the honor due the female sex . . . dressed and armed herself like a man . . . forgetting all feminine decency . . . throwing off the bridle of modesty . . . in all things behaving more like a man than a woman . . . you wear your hair short, cut round above your ears, leaving nothing to indicate the female sex except what nature gave you. . . ."

When she was sentenced to death, Saint Joan of Arc threw herself on the mercy of the court. She promised to wear women's clothes and deny hearing the voice of God. They gave in, sentencing her to life in prison instead. But a day or two later, she was wearing men's clothes again. Then she reasserted that the voice of God was real. Days later, she was tied to a stake in the town square in Chartres and set on fire. She was dangerous. She held enormous power. Her body was a force. She was reckoned with.

That was all a very long time ago. It's easy to feel like progress is a steady march forward. It's not. When you were nine years old, President Trump took office. Forty-eight hours after Trump appointed Jeff Sessions as the Attorney General of the United States, Session requested a stop to the protection of transgender students' access to bathrooms and sports that match their gender identities, which were put into place by the Obama administration. He then went after protections for transgender employees' rights to employment, which were ultimately reversed by the Supreme Court while he was still in office.

The Trump administration then banned transgender soldiers from serving in the military, as if transgender soldiers were something new. There's documentation of at least four hundred cases in which people known as women dressed as men in order to fight in the Civil War. There are likely hundreds more who served without being detected. Most went back to lives in traditional roles for women after the war. But not all.

Albert Cashier fought some of the bloodiest battles in the war, was captured at one point, and then escaped. After the war, on two separate occasions when he was sick, a few people discovered Albert had been thought to be a girl when born. There was a family he was friends with and a doctor who tended to a broken leg. Everyone respected his privacy, telling no one. When he suffered dementia and was sent to a state hospital, the staff put him back into women's clothes. Although the veteran's pension board investigated him for fraud, they decided he deserved his pension and paid it until his death.

In 1915, he was buried in uniform, given an official Grand Army of the Republic funeral, and buried with full military honors, and his name is listed on the wall at Vicksburg National Military Park.

The first visit to the White House by an openly gender-nonconforming person may well have happened in 1886 as part of the Zuni delegation that visited President Grover Cleveland. The Zuni use the word *lhamana* to describe someone who was thought to be male at birth but later took on the clothing and various roles expected of the women in their culture. The most famous lhamana was We'wha, a weaver who was a member of that delegation.

More than one hundred years later, in 2015, President Barack Obama hired the first two openly transgender women to serve in the White House— a staffer who worked as an LBGTQ liaison and a director within the Department of Transportation who's been a commander in the U.S. Navy with twenty years of active duty.

Under President Trump, the Department of Health and Human Services took away protections for transgender patients discriminated against by doctors, health insurance companies, and hospitals. The Trump administration went on to bar trans people from single-sex homeless shelters that align with their gender identities, a rule that sent trans women into all-male homeless shelters. How did they explain how they would tell if someone was male or female? They would check for facial hair, an Adam's apple, and overall height. The Biden administration came in and reversed course, undoing the Trump administration's targeted attacks. But then things kicked up on the state level. In the spring of 2021, Arkansas became the first state to pass a law banning medical treatment for transgender minors. Thirty other bills that would restrict trans-related healthcare to transgender youth were introduced in nineteen other states. Texas introduced five pieces of legislation on this same topic. Some laws were aimed at parents; some threatened doctors with imprisonment. Many were referred to committee or died or failed to pass. The Arkansas law was blocked by a judge before it could take effect, a temporary injunction after the ACLU challenged the law's constitutionality. The far-right also stirred up transphobia around the participation of transgender athletes in high school sports. This is an organized attack.

I fear that one day the knock at the door might no longer be a mistake. It could become law, and then taking transgender children from their homes, their families, would become a regular practice, a matter of course.

One night, when you were twelve years old, you walked into our bedroom and said that you were having scary thoughts. I was wondering if you'd seen a scary movie or read a scary part in a book. I was thinking about how to talk you out of the idea of monsters, goblins, or ghosts.

"What is it?" I asked. "What are you afraid of?"

"I don't know why we're here," you said. In your own way, you went on to explain that your fear was existential.

Part of me would have preferred the simplicity of monsters. I said, "Well, people throughout time have asked this question. It's a great one to ask, to struggle with. Maybe you're a philosopher. In any case, you're in good company."

You are a fascinating kid.

Thinking of Saint Joan of Arc: have you abandoned men's clothes . . . disregarding the honor due the male sex . . . dressed and armed yourself like a woman . . . forgetting all masculine decency . . . taken on the bridle of modesty . . . in all things are you behaving more like a woman than a man . . . wearing your hair long, leaving nothing to indicate the male sex except what nature gave you? All of this—all of it—is how society is coming at you.

Simply put, you are. And then our culture at this moment in history rises up around your body. It tries to make all kinds of claims. It has no right. You claim yourself.

I don't know why we are here. I don't know what *here* is exactly. What is it to be human? If we were made in God's image, then why? We perceive, and in perception, we know pain. We suffer. This is as much the human condition as joy. But why? Why perceive? Why are we given the gift of love and joy? Why, to know love and joy, do we also have to understand their opposites—hate and grief, pain and suffering?

But here's a truth. Like everybody else, you will still have to figure out who you are, who you'll become, and how you want to make your way.

This will be infinitely rich terrain. Yours.

19

AFTER THE CASE AGAINST us was closed, I scanned the families at your school, the ones who'd gotten the note signed by the full faculty. I homed in on a few grandmothers who did pick-up and drop-off. Was it one of them?

I thought back to the people we'd talked to about your change in pronouns. The list wasn't long, but word can travel quickly, erratically.

The neighbors.

It's so middle class to worry about what the neighbors might think. What had become an inside joke now rang like a sick atonal bell. We hadn't worried, not enough.

My thoughts on conformity changed. Conformity in restrictive societies has often been about fear. I understood that. To refuse to conform during the Crusades or the Spanish Inquisition or the rise of Nazi Germany or Communist China or the Puritan colonies could be deadly. If not killed, hanged, burned to death, or killed in concentration camps, you could be excommunicated, and being cast out of a society during most of human history meant you'd most likely die.

American culture says that it celebrates individuality, but that's not really true. Individuality within degrees of variability is more like it. Prince and Bowie and Mae West, for example, are allowed some exaltation, but there are rules for the rest of us.

I don't stand out in a crowd. I have no tattoos, though I think these are so mainstream I'm not sure that they count as standing out anymore. I wore skirts a good bit. My hair is long, often swept away from my face. I'd conformed enough to the South that I usually wore makeup. As a form of respect, I *put my face on* to go out. Jeff is always sporty and athletic looking. No one looked at us and thought, *Renegades*.

And yet we weren't exactly rule followers by southern standards. We had a confident nonchalance about keeping up with the lawn, for example. Our kids, having been raised by Yankees, didn't *ma'am* and *sir* the way some of their peers did. The boys ran around making action movies in the yard. Our daughter went to an arts high school, and our house was full of projects, all in various stages—an ongoing makeshift photography studio, clay pots not yet fired, a puppet costume double the height of an average adult human. We had a busy household, fun and loud. Maybe with our northern accents and our active kids, we represented something to our neighbors that made them uncomfortable. It's hard to say.

Before all of this, I'd thought of conformity as a lack of imagination. Now I saw conformity as an act of fear and self-preservation. I saw it as preemptive, a strong defense. I saw conformity as an outward-facing layer of insulation.

And nonconformity was a luxury we could no longer afford.

I still never know when I might be called upon to defend our family, when I might need to wear a skirt and blazer, put on the strand of pearls handed down from my grandmother, and present some conformed version of myself to the world.

For now, as a family in a typical house on a typical street, we went quiet and still. There had been this breach and with it appeared some torqued version of who we were. We had been mis-seen. We wanted to be seen less. And we did what came naturally. We disappeared, as much as possible, from view. We existed less and less.

―――――

It was around this time that your dad noticed small pink cocoons hanging inside one of our closets. Pink cocoons. In a closet. He showed them to the guy who did our pest control visits; this was the South. Pest control was a big part of our lives. "Why are they pink?" your dad asked him.

"Any wool rugs? Any with some red in them?"

Sure enough, there were a few holes in the wool of the rug in our dining room.

We had an infestation of *pink* cocoons—caterpillars turning into moths within—hiding away *in a closet*.

The symbolism wasn't lost on your father and me. It's the kind of detail that would never work in fiction, the metaphors would be too loud. But you weren't represented by the pink cocoons. You were no longer in the closet. The whole family was now hiding, itching to take flight.

You had to sense our fear. Things had changed. It was around this time when you told me about a bad dream. You had a green button on your chest, and if someone pushed it, you'd turn into a zombie.

"Was it scary?"

"Yes."

"But it's also a really interesting dream," I said, trying to take the dream out of its scary place and just look at it like an object. "No one can push a button and turn someone into a zombie, but sometimes it can feel that way. People telling you how to be."

You listened, quietly, then moved on to something else.

Later, I talked to your dad about the dream. "I think that must be how it feels to have an identity that other people think they can control—with the push of a button or, in real life, the use of a label."

"She'll learn to take the button off her chest, fold it, and put it in her pocket," your dad said. Was this a good thing? I wasn't sure. But it seemed like an important skill to have.

"Or she'll decorate it, make it gilded, and still own it for herself," I said. "She could make art of it. It's part of who she is, but also it's hers to control."

We agreed. Here's the button. Push it. I dare you to try to make me who you think I should be.

That night, I sang to you before bed, as I often did—and I'm sorry for that because I'm not a great singer. As you were getting sleepy, I brushed your hair away from your face and told you about the importance of you having control of who you are.

I was working on getting us to a place that felt safer, a place where you didn't have to be afraid that someone could hit a zombie button on your chest that could make you feel alive but dead.

Even our collie got anxious. He was a rescue abandoned in a parking lot somewhere. Usually a chill dog, he chewed up the cushions of that long yellow sofa, the sofa where Sophie and I had our interviews with the case-worker. It was destroyed.

I asked her what we should do with it. "It has such good bones."

She thought about it. "We should suspend it from the ceiling and attach giant wings to it."

We didn't do it, but I understood the instinct.

———

Though there was no local support group for parents of transgender kids, I found one online and joined in. The internet itself is one of the confluent features of your era that makes transgender progress possible. Suddenly a group of diverse people with a rare commonality could share information, resources, their stories. Geography was no longer a barrier. The parents I met online, and eventually in person, were incredible. And they made certain patterns clear. Where there wasn't much research on transgender kids, suddenly I had access to an enormous trove of anecdotal evidence. We found lots of other families with kids as young as you were. And we heard stories that resonated with our own. We met families who'd had a knock at the door. We weren't alone.

———

We'd never been alone. This was happening in 2011 as well. On Terronska Street in Prague, Czech archaeologists discovered the grave of a male corpse who was buried more than four thousand years ago. Instead of weapons and axes, this corpse was buried with the egg-shaped container at the feet, as women were buried in the era.

———

Even though I didn't return to the transgender support group in town, I stayed in touch with Marguerite. We lived a few blocks away from each other and became friends. She invited me to her wedding. It was a small, quiet event held in her front yard. She and her wife were a same-sex couple, legally married, before same-sex marriages were legal, because her transition to a woman wasn't recognized by the state. In other words, the government-level transphobia embedded in policy had created a weird loophole in which same-sex marriages, which couldn't exist because of homophobia, could exist.

The wedding was beautiful. There was nothing cookie-cutter about it; it was personal and rich and full of love.

The reception was in the backyard, which was enclosed by a short fence. There were hors d'oeuvres and drinks. I was filling my plate when I saw the woman from the support group, the one who had warned me.

I approached her and introduced myself and then jogged her memory. "I'm the one who came to the support group because of my daughter."

"Oh, yes." She smiled a very small smile. "I remember you, of course."

We bullshitted a bit about coming from the same state, those insider home-state jokes. But I also wanted to get to the point. "I want to thank you," I said. "For what you said in the group."

"You're welcome," she said, with a little reserve. She wasn't sure where I was going to go with this, and she struck me as a reserved person in general. She was still not one to gush, but one to tell the truth.

I told her the very short version of what had happened. "You helped me because when the time came, I was prepared. You'd told me that they always blame the mother. So when I was blamed, I didn't have to take it personally. I wasn't as damaged by it. I had some room to see it as part of a pattern, as how these things play out."

"I'm glad it helped."

"It bought me time, in a way. Because I wasn't taking it personally, I had more mental space to think. To strategize. You know what I mean?"

"I think I do, yes."

I think of her sometimes still, when I wonder about how honest I should be in a given moment, when I reflect on all of the tiny invisible stitches that tie us to each other and all of the little ways in which some chance encounter, some stranger, can give you the thing that you might not want but may one day need.

If you've lost something, retrace your steps.

I had lost something.

I hadn't known that I had a contract with the universe until it was broken. My contract was unspoken and had no words. It was vague and somewhat Catholic. The idea was that if I was doing all that I could, thinking of others, being a force for good, then I would be guaranteed certain rights. I'd long since abandoned my right to health, even the health of my children. I'd read the stats on all that could go wrong in pregnancy and labor, the stats on genetic disorders and childhood illnesses. So what was my contract really guaranteeing? What was its reach? I don't know. But it definitely covered not having any of my children taken from me. It was also a contract with my own country and its rights and laws. This contract is a heterosexual, cisgender, able-bodied, middle- and upper-middle-class white woman's contract, as I've touched on already. I didn't believe that I was guaranteed a specific child with specific ways of fitting into our culture, for example, but I was guaranteed something—maybe that my country, my culture would respect and trust my motherhood.

This was what I'd lost—trust. I retraced my steps.

I looked at my calendar in the days leading up to the knock at the door. I looked for the gaps between work and carpool and meetings. I looked at potlucks. I thought back to the people I'd spoken to. I looked at the conversations I'd had. I tried to draw circles, widening out from the few people who knew.

I suspected the older neighbor across the street, a heavyset man who always waved as he drove his riding lawn mower neatly around his yard. One friend reminded me of a guy at work I'd argued with. Someone had forwarded an email that he'd sent around about me; it had been ugly and disturbing. Still, I refused to believe that he'd do this kind of thing, that it would be part of his arsenal. I had it in my head that this was an older woman; I suspected my friends' mothers, people who knew our babysitters, and your classmates' grandparents.

And then my memory fell upon a walk in the neighborhood. A neighbor, a young mother was pushing her baby in a stroller, and we'd chatted. I'd actually walked with her for a bit. Her baby had a beautiful, long name. Yours had just gotten shorter. I explained the change in your pronouns and your new name. She told me that she had a brother who was gay. When he was little, she and her sisters would dress him up sometimes as a girl and he'd loved it. She told me that her mother hadn't ever been accepting and that—here it's a little blurry—maybe the brother, now a grown man, hadn't ever come out to his mother? Or had but was met with rejection? Her mother knew that her son was gay but hadn't been able to meet him where he was. It was a sad story and still a wound for the neighbor, her brother, her family. On this walk, I had also told her the news of my pregnancy.

Also, it hit me. The name we'd never heard of, the one we were supposedly calling you, according to the caseworker, that made-up name was very similar to my neighbor's daughter's name. The two names rhymed.

Some time passed. I'm not sure how long. We were putting the house on the market. I was telling the neighbors, giving them a heads-up in case they knew of anyone looking to buy and explaining to the friends we'd made that we were moving back North—where, exactly, we hadn't yet decided.

I walked over to this neighbor's house. Her husband answered the door. He was very nice, soft-spoken like his wife. He was surprised to see me, glanced over his shoulder. He then opened the screen door, wedging the heavy door shut behind him without really stepping out of the house altogether. He was poised there, in between, suspended almost.

"Is this not a good time?" I asked.

"No, it's fine! It's just that my mother-in-law is here. We're about to sit down to eat. What is it?"

"Oh, I can make this quick." I did make it quick, my heart skittering away. I didn't explain that someone had made a call. But I did say that we were moving North, for various reasons, namely to be closer to family. We were putting the house on the market. "So if you know of anyone. . . ."

"Sure, sure. And congratulations on the pregnancy," he said, smiling.

I hesitated. I didn't know when I'd run into the wife again, and I wouldn't be getting more and more obviously pregnant. I decided to be straightforward about the miscarriage.

He said he was sorry to hear the news, asked if there was anything they could do.

"No, no, we're fine."

He nodded. He was nervous. He was unsettled.

"Have a nice dinner, sorry to interrupt."

"Not a problem! Not a problem at all!"

I walked home.

I don't think about this exchange often, but I do think about his mother-in-law. I wonder if it was her, and I've decided it's better to assume it is because then I can stop wondering. I don't think I ever saw her, even from a distance. And yet I have fully imagined her. This is how I put it earlier: *We*

are built to see faces, to recognize them, to search for signs of love and danger,
to see how they see us. This is, in part, how we come to understand who we
are—by how we're seen.

To learn something, I had to understand the threat. If I was to avoid it in
the future, I had to know what it looked like. I couldn't know, and so my brain
set to work without my consent. I dreamed her up. From a small condo in
a row of small condos, I imagined her into being. I started at her head—as
if this were some kind of birth—her ash-blond hair, dyed to mask the gray,
the soft cut, a puff on the crown, a swoop around her face. I imagined her
small features, her anxious eyes. Next, her narrow shoulders, rounded under
cardigans, so necessary in southern summers when you never know when
you'll go from relentless heat to air-conditioning. And then the rest of her
body, just a slip of a woman—a belly pouch, a cinched butt, thickened ankles sometimes swelling in the endless lurch of sunny days broken only by
pockets of rain that steam up from the streets.

I thought about why she called. Her son had been a feminine boy; she had
to have noticed and worried. A boy among all those sisters, she thought,
he's bound to be a little soft. It had to have scared her. My neighbor was a
good ten years younger than I was. She'd been young during the early years
of the AIDS epidemic, when gay men were dying at a rate higher than American soldiers who'd died in the Vietnam War. Maybe the mother wanted to
protect him. Maybe she made corrections, denigrations, comments about
"those kinds of people" that made it clear how she'd treat a son who came
out. And so he didn't. She might have taken this as a victory.

And here we were, "forcing" our child "to be a homosexual" when all she
could have really heard was that we were using a new name and female pronouns. She'd kept her feminine son from being gay. Our acceptance was a
threat to her way of mothering her son, and so she flipped it—she was going
to save our child from us.

No one is the villain of their own story, and in hers, she was the hero.

Sometimes I think of her on the day she made the call. Why that day? Had
something upset her? Was she feeling a lack of control in some way that
made her want to assert control in another?

Was it a whim?

This is the one that's hardest to take: Was it a whim?

I would have loved to explain the difference between being gay, which is about who one is attracted to and loves, and being transgender, which has to do with gender, not sexuality. I have lots of ways of explaining how the gender that is held deep inside doesn't always match our bodies in the ways we most expect it to, anatomically. I never got to explain this to her, and as a result, a certain calm comes over me when I do have the chance to explain it to someone. She's there in a way, each and every time, hovering in her cardigan.

It's so middle class to worry about what the neighbors might think.

But most of the time, I think of her as a young mother. Like this: Her daughters have dressed up her son. She sees his brightened face, his joy. She's shaken. She fears he'll be beaten up. She's not wrong. And I want to tell her that it's going to be okay. I want to tell her that she can accept that boy. She can love him. She can create space for him. He's grown now. He's hiding his life from her. It doesn't have to be that way. I want to tell her not to be afraid of her own overwhelming love.

What I've realized is that although my brain began imagining her perhaps out of an old instinct to recognize an advancing enemy, I've actually told a story to make her human, to make her real. I invented her. Even if she wasn't the one, I needed *someone* to be the one. Even if she'd never ask for forgiveness, I needed someone to forgive.

As for her daughter and son-in-law, our neighbors, they no longer strolled the baby along the stretch of road where they'd have to pass our house. They avoided us at a few neighborhood get-togethers. I heard that they moved away not long after we did.

20

YOUR FATHER AND I looked at the places where we already had family; we wanted you surrounded by unconditional love. I wanted to move back to my home state. We'd lived there before moving to the South. Our oldest three kids had been born there. My parents still lived there much of the year. I yearned for familiarity. But the state wasn't particularly progressive, and there were no antidiscrimination laws to protect transgender people on the books, yet.

At this point, there were only twelve states in the country that had antidiscrimination laws built to protect you.

We focused on one New England state in particular where my brother and his wife were raising their five kids. We were told that the antidiscrimination act that would be voted on that summer looked very likely to pass; it would add gender identity to the list of protections from discrimination already covered—race, color, sex, religion, national origin, and sexual orientation. We then looked at the communities within that state. We couldn't just rely on a blue state; we needed a blue community within a blue state—we needed a very deep blue.

I interviewed principals all over the state, getting a feel for how different schools were figuring out how to work with transgender students. These were the early days. I heard of one high school where a transgender boy had just transitioned. He'd written a letter that was circulated to the student body, and he was well received. At that same school, ten years later, there would be twelve out transgender and gender-nonconforming students.

We found a principal in a university town who was open and kind. He'd raised two sons, one straight and one gay. He was already actively creating an inclusive LGBTQ+ school environment. With the antidiscrimination laws hanging in the balance, he was willing to forge ahead.

I was honest about my situation with a select group of higher-ups at my university. Two deans emerged to champion a creative way to allow me to move but retain me as faculty—one was Mormon, one was Mexican American, raised in Texas. They were moved by our situation. I wouldn't be able to keep my full-time job, but an arrangement was made. I'd cut back in pay and hours. I'd work long-distance, punctuated with week-long stays. I'd keep my insurance. My career had been on the fast track. I was no longer on any track at all. But I was grateful.

Within eight months of the knock at the door, we were packing up.

I couldn't see it yet, but two years from this moment, in this new town, we would drag a wildly shaped secondhand wingback chair out of a house in New England and onto a sloping yard. It was faded and a little tatty but had regal bones.

We were taking a family photograph.

You sat in the chair on Sophie's lap, and the rest of us stood around you. There were some pictures where we all smiled the usual smiles, but there was a series—the reason why we'd brought out the chair—where we were all very serious.

We looked at the camera, each of us daring someone to step at us.

We'd circled up around you. We were thugs, a family of thugs who protect our own.

You're the only one who didn't listen to the instructions: *serious this time.* You're smiling wryly in the middle of us.

But it's perfect.

Our collective desire to protect you opened up the space for that smile.

I don't know where that photograph is. But it doesn't really matter. It was how we felt in that moment. We'd been shoved around. We were re-creating our lives. This time, we were ready, our bodies as a wall we could build around you.

But I remember this time in our lives as walled. We walled people out, but we also walled ourselves in. That's the thing about walls.

This toughness, these walls aren't the whole truth. Nothing is a whole truth. Throughout all of this, we were happy. We were happy in a way that is enduring. We were shaken. We were angry and grieving. We were full of fear. But we were also, as a result, tougher, more thankful, and full of hope. We bounce. That's what we learned. Our family can bounce.

It wasn't easy. Sophie would miss out on her senior year. At first, she scrambled to find a way to stay, but she knew she never could watch the rest of us go on without her, especially not you. She says of it now, "I was mad that I couldn't be mad." She knew it was the right thing to do. When we were trying to unload furniture before moving, she threw down about that oddly shaped secondhand wingback, insisting, tearfully, that we bring it with us. (It's still with us.)

Isaac remembers being angry about how he was told. "You acted like you wanted us to weigh in. I remember saying to Dad one night in the playroom, 'You're not asking us. You're telling us and making it seem like we have a say.'" The hardest part for him was leaving the uber-Christian girlfriend he was still crazy about.

He lobbied that she could come with us on a trip North to visit my parents. Jeff and I gave in. This was going to be hard, and it felt like the right concession. In the lead-up, he had to tell her that you were trans, and before that, I'd have to explain it to her mother. There would be evidence of your previous boyhood; some folks might still slip on the pronouns; we could easily run into people who had no idea of the change.

I set up a lunch with the mother first. I wasn't so sure about her. The family smiled easily, had treated Isaac with so much generosity, but their Christianity was mysterious to me, and I worried that it was linked up with far-right political ideology. This might be rough.

I invited the girl's mother to an outdoor café. This way, if it went badly, I wouldn't have to make an awkward exit out of a crowded restaurant. I was anxious about it all and, to be honest, still a bit raw. We'd been through a lot, and I hadn't really begun to process it.

We had sweet tea and ordered lunch. We chatted about the kids. She had a blond bob and soft bangs, a heart-shaped face. She was one of those people who you assumed had never gone through an unattractive phase. She'd so obviously been a pretty baby who would be a pretty old woman one day.

Before the food came, I decided to just go ahead. I started at the very beginning. In fact, I probably sounded like I was narrating about the Dawn of Time. I was so anxious in those days that my lead-ups were long and windy. I was stalling. Did I use the terms *gender fluid*, *gender creative*? I doubt I would have said *transgender*. I worried about how much freight that word carried. In any case, I explained things and told her why I wanted her daughter to know. "When we're at my parents, there may be people who remember her or even refer to her as a boy, but of course, she's a girl."

I choked up. It was unplanned. I was messy at this point, vulnerable.

"Oh," she said. "Well, you've been such good parents!" I can still see her face, how it went from mirroring my emotion to trying to buoy me. She was lovely, warm, and accepting. She had no concerns whatsoever.

Isaac was then free to tell his new girlfriend, and like her mother, she was completely understanding.

This is the thing that keeps surprising me. You never know who will condemn and who will buoy.

Unlike the older kids, Tate was excited to move. It was tinged with the disappointment of having to drop out of his soccer teams, but he was itching to go to a big public school. He wanted to take up skiing. As much as he'd loved being a southerner, he was ready to see what it was like to live where it snowed.

Each of the kids felt like they'd have to prove themselves all over again in a new place. Your dad had to leave his coaching and his own team, which was still playing tournaments in his age bracket. We'd have to leave our friends—all those people who'd stopped everything to write on our behalf—and the private school where each person on the faculty and staff had signed that letter. You'd have to leave your school with your teachers wearing the Styrofoam necklaces you'd made for them. And you'd have to say good-bye to the G.

While we got ready to go, we remained happy in our own particular way. The kids excelled at darkly comedic one-liners. We let each other be jerks. We forgave each other like it cost nothing because it costs nothing.

But I wondered, once we'd moved, if we would have more to give or less. I knew we'd have more to prove. And I could see how we were already changing in dynamic ways.

But still, without the knock and all that followed, wouldn't we have changed anyway? We were, after all, living with you, and with a graceful organic assuredness, you were asserting your true self in the world. And that had an effect.

We'd gotten you some flight attendant wings, and you pinned them to your cousin's hand-me-down Easter blazer.

Eventually, we bought you your first diary with its little lock. You asked me if you should write that you're transgender. This means to me that you'd absorbed our fears.

"You can write whatever you want," I said.

You showed me your first entry: *We built a house.* (We'd bought a doll-house kit and put it together.) *I am transjendr.*

Sometimes, when it comes to authenticity—what we're willing to risk and fight for to be our true selves in all of the large and small ways—I think that most people have more in common with those who don't come out than those who do. While you were living it, we were witnessing your journey. Once you've fought to be who you are in a world that is openly hostile to your existence, why compromise? Each of us came into ourselves with more honesty and ferocity. How could we not?

Tolstoy's opening of *Anna Karenina* is one of the most famous lines in literature. "Happy families are all alike; every unhappy family is unhappy in its own way." He hit on something that seemed so true to so many people that there now exists the Anna Karenina Principle. (Aristotle got to this concept first; Tolstoy made it more personal.)

But Tolstoy was wrong about families. Unhappy families seem to fail in the same ways over and over again—they don't love the person who stands before them unconditionally; they don't accept the person for who they truly are. Maybe they choose not to love their own, or maybe they don't know how, having been denied that love in their own childhoods.

But happy families are not all alike. Each must invent ways in order to survive with their happiness intact. We invented ourselves, individually, and as an organism, as a whole. And we survived.

———

Maybe, one day, you'll think we were wrong. You'll wonder what it would have been like if we'd stayed. Maybe you'll think we should have stayed. You might become the kind of person who refuses to leave. In Ireland, I'd come to love the story of my relatives who'd stayed, how it countered the pervasive American narrative of striking out, of manifest destiny, of bravely charting a course to find new land or fortune or yourself. This is a bedtime story that the dominant American culture tells itself in order to deny the genocide of Native people and slavery and, as they've had to twist it, the anti-immigration laws that ripped apart families at our borders. It's the bedtime story that allows them to fall asleep into the American dream. It's fitful, this sleep. No peace in it. Keep an eye out for that story in all of its forms. (It erases you too.)

Years later, we would visit friends in this southern state. At the end of the first day, you said, "It's not so bad. I mean, it's normal here."

The way we'd made it seem, you'd been expecting—what? Violence in the streets? Gunshots ringing out through the night? Nothing obvious. In fact, the opposite. Everyone was friendly. People smiled and said hello on the street. (I would miss all of that outward gentility and friendliness.)

The lead-up to the move coincided with the "It gets better campaign." Every day, there were new promotional videos of gay and lesbian celebrities telling the younger generation to hang in there. And each time I saw a video, I thought, "Yes, but in some places, it's already better." We moved to that better future.

Now when I think of the term *Bible Belt*, I imagine a belt used to beat a child. This is how gay and lesbian, transgender, or queer children and teens have been dealt with. And worse. Far worse.

It was summer when we packed up. Your father was with Tate in a truck. You and Sophie and Isaac and I were pulling an extra U-Haul. A few miles south of the Mason-Dixon Line late at night, we hit a storm. There was heat lightning and jagged bolts at the same time, along with heavy deafening rain, pounding windshield wipers, cracks of thunder. We were bleary. We pulled off the highway to wait it out. After the storm eased up, we made it the rest of the way. When I woke up in a place that felt good and safe, I was so deeply relieved that I started crying before I even got out of bed. It was as if we'd put something behind us.

When I get scared, really scared, in an immediate sense, I fight. It's not a great instinct, especially for someone small like me. I don't freeze. I don't run. Your sister too. Let's say I taught you to run. Not to fight. I'm good with that. It's hard to know when to stay, when to fight, when to freeze, when to leave. Maybe I just want to say: you'll know what to do. You'll have an instinct, and you should go with that. Instincts are another way of saying that we know what to do even when we don't know that we know.

Part III

AFTER

21

MIGRATION ALONE TAKES ITS toll. The Red Knot is a migratory bird that weighs around 220 grams, less than half of a pound. The Red Knot breeds in Siberia and migrates to the west coast of Africa in winter, with some traveling as far as South Africa. Its migration isn't easy. En route, it loses almost half of its body weight. Our own migration north took a toll on us. It hit each of the kids in different ways. It stripped us down a little, but we landed.

Years have passed since all of this. A breathless blur of them.

Things got better for us, all in all. During the Trump years, things got worse all around. Or maybe America has simply been exposed for what it's always been.

While writing this book, there have been moments of such sharp disconnect. For example, you were on the sun porch sewing a dress for a Mrs. Maisel–inspired photo shoot that you dreamed up while people were filing lawsuits and protesting and honoring the trans people who have been murdered this year.

How do I explain to you the firestorm around your body?

How do I explain that and yet also protect you and your body?

I'm still figuring things out. This landing would give me time to process what had happened and to try to begin to understand gender, its place within us, and its artful presentation—from its gimmickry to its rules and how they are sometimes brutally enforced to its liberated expression—and how gender plays out everywhere, all the time. It is relentless.

What follows will be fractured and messy. But that fractured messiness is how form meets function. It is the most honest way to say what I have to say. How I'm going to tell the rest is a reflection of how I cannot make sense of this for you, how I cannot put it in order, how I cannot find the overarching narrative that holds it all.

The only thing that I am sure of is you.

And here, in this new place, you could be an ordinary girl, whatever that means. I could say, "You fit in with the other girls."

But you were also very you. I remember around this time, you were playing with your Thomas the Train set with its wooden tracks and magnetized train cars in the upstairs playroom. After a while, you found me and your father in the kitchen. You showed us what you'd made. You'd taped two wooden bridge pieces to your feet with clear mailing tape, fashioning a pair of high heels. This was genius of course; we knew genius when we saw it.

Another time, you walked into my office holding a drawing. "I drew a picture of Lady Gaga with Martin Luther King shoes," you told me.

I looked at the drawing. The shoes were a cross between ballet toe shoes and hooves, with no heels. "I think you mean Alexander McQueen, not Martin Luther King."

You did. We stuck the drawing to the fridge with a magnet.

And you had a budding sense of your transness. You woke me up one morning and announced, "I'm going to be the first girl president."

It was a few years before the 2016 election. I said, "I don't know. Hillary Clinton might get there first."

You accepted this but came back a few minutes later. "I'm going to be the first transgender girl president."

"Now that you've got a shot at."

What I mean is this: Here, no one outside of our family had to know that you were trans. We'd faced a very specific set of issues when you transitioned. But living in a place where people didn't know that you'd been assigned male at birth ushered in a whole new set of issues.

One word that kept surfacing for me was *assimilation*. In this case, my use of the term is inherently discriminatory. How can one assimilate into their true gender? They simply are who they are. It's as problematic as the term *passing*. It's problematic in many different contexts. I apologize for it. But also, the word is powerful. It echoes through history. There are parallels to be drawn and to be cautious about. It is a massive field of study. I need better ways to express how American culture demands assimilation—in race, religion, ethnicity, and ability. One December, I was in a public school library in Texas with a giant Christmas tree display. A teacher explained that they weren't allowed to call it a *Christmas* tree; it was just a pine tree with decorations and presents. We need to have a better way to talk about how America fails to be inclusive.

While trans people have existed throughout history and cultures, I had to try to imagine a future for a new trans generation. You are a minority at a moment in history in which the confluence of technology, science, and medicine enables you to choose to remain part of that minority or assimilate. (How can I not think of works like *Black No More* by Harlem Renaissance writer George Schuyler?) You can blend in with other girls and women in ways that were more difficult for previous generations. The internet made it possible to find each other, to build community, to share resources. Simultaneously, cultural views around LGBTQ+ rights were changing swiftly. The stalled momentum for trans rights buckled and gave, and things changed.

In the documentary *Disclosure*, Sandra Caldwell, an actress who came out as trans late in her career, talks about what she lost. "I would never think for a moment that I was the only one. And you want to go and you want to say, 'Girl, ain't we somethin'?' But, nah, you just let it alone." There's a slight pause. "I wish I could've. Man, wouldn't that have been good." Her smile fades so quickly. In an instant, she's hit by the sadness of that isolation.

It would have been good. So deeply good.

Not everyone in your generation will have this choice to blend in. Some will be denied access to healthcare. Some will have to fight for it. These things will break down on all the old lines—like poverty and race.

Some will choose not to assimilate for political and personal reasons.

Some will take up the middle space, rejecting both genders or embracing the nonbinary or perhaps fluidly moving between genders.

Some will never identify as transgender at all. They'll simply identify in the way that their gender was made clear to them—as girls or boys, women or men.

I've met parents who have thought deeply about this and believe that their trans child doesn't have to identify as trans at all. They can simply be a girl or a boy—as they truly *are*. I agree. A friend who's raising a trans daughter put it this way: "Being out as trans might make you visible only in terms of gender and invisible in every other way. Being invisibly trans might allow you to be visible in other ways. I guess it's about that: we're all already picking what we want to be visible and invisible about ourselves."

A friend of mine who transitioned in her fifties and who speaks elo-
quently about how important it is for her to be seen for who she truly is
once remarked that if you were to come out, you might risk being seen less
fully. Meaning your transness might be the new lens that your friends see
you through. A blurrier instead of a clearer lens.

When Zeke Smith was outed on the television show *Survivor*, he said, "I
didn't want to be the trans *Survivor* player. I wanted to be Zeke the *Survivor*
player." His being trans and not out was framed as a deception, a lie. And
if you are out as trans, then you are often perceived through your transness
first with unwieldy prejudices. Again, this quickly becomes familiar to other
minority groups.

Try as I may, I fall short of doing the topic justice; my disadvantage as a
parent of a trans daughter is my cisness. I don't have my own stories to hand
down to you. This is why you need that larger queer family; you need the
stories that they alone can hand down about coming out and not, what is
gained and what is lost.

I'm afraid of assimilation. I'm afraid of its erasure of a group of people
and its potential erasure of you—in your fullest, most realized sense of self.
Sometimes I think: If you live in a culture that doesn't want you to exist, why
give them what they want? Does your blending in put those who can't blend
in at greater risk? How can you resist giving them what they want while getting what you need?

Your grandfather's work in genealogy from many generations back shows
that one of our ancestors came from a small town in France that was nearly
100 percent Jewish. There's little chance our ancestor was not Jewish and
yet, in America, he left that identity behind. What did we lose as a result?

I'm afraid of these fissures in a small community. I worry about dividing
lines, how you'll have to work hard to keep each other close, to fight for each
other.

I'm afraid of the way blending-in might demand guilt.

Your childhood is marked by acculturation. It's so pervasive we only know
it when it's broken by a brilliant flair—Nicole Maines playing the first transgender superhero on TV. Or a fleeting glimpse—the stunning young trans
woman working the pocketbook section at Bergdorf Goodman's. And ordinary moments—the genderqueer person who sold you a new bike, helping
you find the right bell. The liberated beauty in all of it.

You'll have to know your heroes. In her speech at the 1973 Christopher Street Liberation Day Rally, Sylvia Rivera put it this way: "We have to be visible. We should not be ashamed of who we are. We have to show the world that we are numerous."

I'm not saying you have to be out. Who you're out to and why and under what circumstances is always your own call. Always. But here's my worry: What if so many transgender kids of your generation become invisible in a new way?

The old way was to never transition at all, to live a life without ever having been fully alive in your own skin. The new way is to transition into that body, to leave that old label from birth behind and to never associate with the transgender community.

In many stories of assimilation, someone has to choose to leave behind their culture, language, food, and customs, prayers and songs, their communities, their people, brothers and sisters, mothers and fathers. . . . You're being raised by a family in the majority in a household that isn't queer. We're also white with our college educations and our nice house in its safe neighborhood—or as Sylvia might have put it, we're part of the "white, middle-class, white club." Sylvia was Puerto Rican and Venezuelan; Marsha P. Johnson was Black; both were raised in poverty. All of these things matter. Being transgender is to be part of our complex culture—its white supremacy, poverty, capitalism, sexism, misogyny, homophobia, transphobia, pathologization, ableism. . . . There are many kinds of oppression.

You won't have to choose between the dominant culture and your family, because we are the dominant culture. By being stealth, you get (almost) all of the privileges of that culture. You have to be aware of those privileges.

I have options here. I can tell you that you can detach yourself from the past. I can afford it, literally; I can pay for you to slip into the world as a girl who becomes a woman. I can say, "Just skate on. Just keep going forward." Being a girl who becomes a woman is hard enough.

But if I give you freedom from this history—and it is a burden, it has a weight, it will be heavy—then I also deny you another family, a fierce community, a rich and beautiful heritage, a coalition that's got your back. There's a larger family for you with all of their hard-earned pride and love and fight.

I'm afraid of the way assimilation might exact a heavy toll. I'm afraid that the toll might be a deep sense of isolation and lonesomeness.

When I was twenty and leaving the country on my own for the first time, my father hugged me and whispered, "Don't forget who you are and where you come from." I know now that this is the parents' fear. It means, *Don't forget us. Don't forget me.*

I'm not speaking now on behalf of the family you were born into, *this us.* I'm talking about *your larger queer family*, the ones who created this present moment for you to exist in, who fought for your rights, stood up against oppression, rioted and marched, and were jailed and beaten, who put down their lives for you.

You come from a big, beautiful group of human beings. When you look at the history of the gay liberation movement, you'll find transgender people there, always on the front lines.

Why were they always on the front lines? I hear this question in your voice now.

Because they had nothing to lose.

Why did they have nothing to lose? you ask.

They'd usually lost everything already.

A gay man hanging out at the Stonewall Inn one hot muggy night in July of 1969 could go to work the next day without anyone knowing he was gay unless, of course, he was arrested and his name was printed in the paper. Transgender people living their lives as themselves didn't usually move seamlessly through the world. They were out. They were at risk all the time.

All over the world, there are transgender people still at risk all the time.

Listen to me.

Your immediate family is here for you. And your big, beautiful queer family is here for you too. And as I write this, I can hear them whispering, *Don't forget us. Don't forget.*

In truth, I don't know who your people will be. Not really. They might be environmentalists, fashion designers, entrepreneurs, comedians . . . *influencers?* You are, after all, growing up in your own specific generation.

You will find your people. You will have many people. You will choose how you're seen and when you want to be seen wholly—and what that wholeness means.

––––––––

I'm writing one narrative line here. You are at the center. This is the story of our lives in orbit around you. But I could also tell the story of our lives in orbit around each of the kids. Your story has shifted all of us in the most obvious ways, but you were not our sole focus. Like me, you're the baby of the family, the youngest of four. The youngest has to be smart and adorable, has to know when to glide under the radar and when to pop up. By the time the youngest comes along, the parents have been through a lot of wear and tear. They're broken in. The youngest is a tagalong, if they don't get left behind altogether. Within the group, day to day, the youngest isn't the center of attention. We're easily dismissed and sidelined. The older kids are louder, more exciting, and more demanding.

As the older kids head out into the world, the youngest gets to take up a little more space. But the moment an older child comes back home, it's a whirlwind. No matter what, the returning child is prodigal.

Also, I love my work. I don't cordon it off by unseen boundaries; I carry it with me wherever I go. Our houses have varied, but my desk remains the same. It's often situated in the corner of the bedroom. I'm always in earshot. Much of what I've written here isn't because of research and thinking I've done about you, but about human beings and the world that I've then connected to you.

Even the story of the knock at the door is about you, but not. In so many ways, we put you in a bubble within our own family. I couldn't create that bubble for the rest of the kids; they were too old and knew too much.

The stories that follow will give the impression that your transness was ever-present, was our sole focus. In truth, your transness would come up when least expected and demand attention. But, day in and day out, your transness was largely unremarkable.

Your older siblings were still doing everything for the first time—getting jobs, making and breaking curfews, choosing colleges, figuring out what they wanted to study, traveling farther and farther away and back again, moving in and out of dorms and apartments, bringing home boyfriends and girlfriends, going to proms and concerts and graduations, voting for the first time, racking up parking tickets . . . the on and on of growing up.

In all of this mayhem, you were the easy one. When you were in third grade, your dad told me that he'd heard the other parents complaining about a boy in the class who kept having outbursts, a chair-thrower. You hadn't mentioned any of this.

When you were having your after-school snack, I said, "I heard there's someone in your class having a hard time. Maybe even getting really wild and angry?"

"Are you okay?" your dad asked.

You smiled as if looking back fondly on a favorite bedtime story. "Yeah," you said, "it's great. Sometimes we get evacuated, and it's always nice to have a break. And sometimes we just keep on working. He's really creative. He has a real sense of flare."

You were the kid who laughed easily, didn't take things personally, and didn't get that riled up. You cried so rarely that when you did, it was taken very seriously. "Who's upset the baby? Who made her cry?"

I'm not saying that you don't run a little anxious. That's a double inheritance from both sides of your family. But you're steady and deep. And within the chaos of our family, you are the moment of calm.

22

AND SO I'LL BEGIN with us.

These portraits will be reductions. They won't truly capture your siblings or the feel of our house, with all of our heartbeats pounding away within it. But let me try to distill.

First, Sophie.

The summer we moved, Sophie had been heading into her senior year. She'd been attending an arts charter high school where the lead history teacher talked about his days in Vietnam and extolled the virtues of wheatgrass shots. The health teacher, by law, wasn't allowed to teach any sex ed and referred to the kids as "tight mama" and "tight daddy," for reasons we never really understood. A photography teacher once had a breakdown and rocked under his desk during class. None of the kids reported it. "It just seemed so valid," Sophie said.

In the halls of her new public high school, overachieving was a basic expectation. There was an obsession with college entrance applications, SAT test prep, and the importance of a solid list of extracurriculars. The guidance counselors' office was decorated with pennants from all of the colleges the students had attended over the years, including each and every ivy league school.

It should have been a welcome change, but Sophie read the whole experience as hyper-privileged. In this crisp turtleneck town with its women all wearing comfortable flex-sole clogs, panting their ivy-league educations, she felt out of place.

Then she realized she could graduate online in one semester, and she jumped at the opportunity. By winter, she was free to volunteer at various LGBTQ+ support groups. She gave talks to the faculty and staff at an elementary school about supporting transgender and gender-nonconforming youth and helped health teachers integrate more LGBTQ+-inclusive sex education.

And she made art. I recall vividly the obsessive beauty of it all. In retrospect, I can see that she was still grieving the loss of the pregnancy from the previous fall, the child she'd already imagined and loved. I hadn't realized how hard it was on her until we finally arrived and settled in. I didn't have answers. Miscarriages are such strange hardships. We don't have rituals for this kind of mourning. Now, looking back, I wish I'd invented rituals around the loss. I didn't want to dwell on the pain or anger. I allowed myself to be overwhelmed by the demands of our new life here. This was a missed opportunity to teach the kids how to try to process loss.

When spring rolled around and her class was graduating from the arts charter high school in the South, she asked to speak at graduation, and someone okayed it. Early on in the speech, she told the audience to stand, to look at each other—students and the people who'd supported them, who loved them. And she asked if the four years of hard work was worth this moment of appreciation.

The crowd was with her. Yes, they seemed to say. It was.

Here, she took a hard turn.

She told the audience that it wasn't worth it. That high school wasn't about getting to this moment. It was about taking this moment and moving forward into the future with it. It was about having this moment push you forward, out, onto something else, something you'd have to make or build for yourself. She told them that it would be hard.

Without knowing it, she was talking about what happened to us, the love that rode in for us, buoyed us as we built something for ourselves in a new place.

Isaac, on the other hand, flourished from the start.

He pined for his girlfriend but also thrived.

One night he came home with a five-foot trophy, having won something called the Man Pageant at his high school. His talent was stand-up that ended in a lip-sync battle with a knee-glide toward the audience.

Your brother Isaac is your brother Isaac. One can claim that it wasn't having you as a sister that changed the course of his life, but the move from one area of the country to another, which is just a logistical result. But that's not it. His college essay is, in part, about you.

It begins, "When I hit puberty, my little brother started wearing dresses. . . . That little brother is now my sister, and her transition changed my family's life and has had a great impact on my worldview. Because of a backlash incident to my sister's transition—an anonymous threat. . . ." *A backlash incident*—this was the phrase we used as a family. We rarely spoke of it beyond this. He went on, "We moved when I was fifteen, and I couldn't talk about why we'd moved. I learned that you never know what people are dealing with."

He then segues to talk about a kid at school who rubbed people the wrong way but who, most of all, seemed lonely. "I knew from my sister's experience that everyone has a story, and that sometimes they can't share it or express it. Sometimes it's too painful. Sometimes they don't even understand the story or they choose to keep it to themselves. No matter what, everybody's got one. I decided . . . that I couldn't judge him until I really knew him. And so I worked on getting to know him. For me, that has to be a conscious decision that you make every day. It's not about being selfless but other-people-full."

———

Tate had gone to the same small private school since pre-K. Now a rising seventh grader, he was dying to go to a big public middle school. He adapted well—in school and with friends and soccer teams. He started his own business, weeding yards for elderly neighbors. In high school, he called landlords to negotiate lawn services for blocks of real estate all over town. He was the kid to negotiate free gym time in exchange for cleaning the gym at night.

He, too, had left behind a girlfriend—a sporty girl a foot taller than he was. He quickly had a new girlfriend. She, too, was sporty. She had two moms. We rented a sabbatical home from a lesbian couple. A few of your good friends had two moms or two dads. It wasn't unusual here.

In many ways, Jeff and I were raising a bro. But he had another life too. He went with us to the transgender health conference and babysat so that parents could attend workshops. When the governor of North Carolina passed the discriminatory anti-trans bathroom bill, Tate wrote letters to universities in North Carolina, telling them he wouldn't be applying. He wasn't going to live in a state that rejected his sister's most basic rights. While Sophie made it to D.C. to the Women's March after Trump's inauguration, we stayed local. Tate and a friend of his marched for women's rights and girls' rights. He was marching for you.

When Tate was in eighth grade, you were thinking about coming out. I asked Tate how he felt about the idea of you being out in middle school. Would you be safe? Could it work?

"It would be hard," he said, making a sandwich.

"How?"

"It's like a little knife. The kids would all have one. And they could cut her with it, anytime they wanted."

I never forgot it. A little knife.

In one moment, I'll think it might be safer for you to be out. We've chosen to live in places where that feels more possible. And yet, why would anyone hand out little knives to middle schoolers, to teens, to strangers?

And you. At five years old, a kindergartner, you were riding the bus to school, confident if a little quiet. You were the wide-eyed type, taking it all in. Your hair was long and curly. Sometimes your sister braided it for you and then, when the braids were undone, your hair had dynamic frizz.

The law that protected you in the public school system had in fact passed through the state legislature and had been signed into law. We were waiting for guidance from the Department of Education to see how they would interpret the new antidiscrimination law on the ground. Nate, the principal, wasn't worried about it. We met with him to decide who on staff would be informed that you were transgender. This included the school nurse, who was very kind. You were allowed to go to visit him anytime you needed to, even if just to have a quiet moment. But you'd get to know him over the years because you were prone to bloody noses, something you've outgrown.

It also included your teacher, Mrs. H. She was Japanese American and had been teaching for decades. Her classroom was unlike any I'd ever been in before or since. It was peaceful. The children had energy but also seemed grounded. Her own daughters were now fully grown, and by the time you graduated, she was a grandmother. As you made your way through the grades, you visited her for lunch sometimes. And now that we've moved away, you still keep in touch. It is the sweetest of friendships.

Halfway through the year, long before Tate told me about the little knives of middle schoolers, I asked you if you would ever consider telling your class that you're transgender. I wanted to keep these options open.

"It would be okay," you told me, "except for five kids."

"Which five?"

You rattled off their names and why each would be problematic—these three would be mean, that one would only be silly, and this other kid just wouldn't understand. I realized that you'd been clocking every kid in that class, sizing them up from the start. I'd been worried that my question would catch you off guard. Meanwhile, you were living your life as a trans person. At five years old, you were already adept at reading those around you.

You decided to come out to your best friend, the little girl who lived next door. We'll call her Meredith. Her father was a MacArthur genius with far-left politics. Her mother had lived all over the world, an individual with an oddball exuberance for life. A former cheerleader, she'd sometimes do high kicks when the bus pulled up at the end of the day. Despite the fact that they seemed to be outsmarted daily by their Labrador retriever, who was widely despised in the neighborhood for his trash-digging, humping, and bounding through our yards where he left behind heedless poops, they seemed like they'd get it.

Meredith was thoughtful and imaginative, a great playmate.

I found a quiet moment to talk to her mom. We'd become friends too. What I wanted to get across was the difference between privacy and a secret. It seemed important that I not give the impression that you had a secret. Secrets hold too much power. Instead, I wanted to make clear that being trans was special and it was private. At this point, the difference between private and secret felt crucial. A secret could intimate shame. Privacy is a right.

We were in their living room with their white couches, armchairs, and fireplace. Meredith's mother was constantly rearranging the furniture, and this was a new constellation. I started by explaining things as straightforwardly as I could, but it wasn't straightforward at all. I rewound back to the beginning. "Well, as you know, I had a daughter, then two sons, then I thought I'd had a third son, but I was wrong." I finally made my way, clumsily, to the word *transgender*.

"I don't understand," Meredith's mother said.

"What don't you understand?"

"I mean, she has XX chromosomes, though. I mean, she's actually a girl."

"She has XY chromosomes. In every way, at her birth, she presented as a baby boy."

"Really?"

"Really."

"But she just is such a girl."

"I know," I said. "She wants to tell Meredith."

The mother thought this was a lovely idea. I can't remember whether we decided to do this later that same day or another day. You were anxious to tell Meredith, so we didn't put it off too long.

We were, once again, in the neighbor's house. You were excited and agitated. Meredith's mother called her daughter into the living room, back to the white sofas. You wanted me to tell her without you there, so you started to leave but then you ran back to me. "I want to hear this."

"That's fine," I said.

But then you tugged on Meredith's elbow and said, "When you hear this, you have to still like me. You have to be my friend."

I remember this moment so precisely. Your whisper, your face. Her expression, confused.

I hadn't known, until that moment, that you understood what was at stake. You understood that telling someone this truth about who you are could change the way they felt about you, could make them turn against you. You knew that this could mean the loss of a friend.

But how did you know that? It wasn't something that we'd ever really discussed in front of you. Surely, it was in the air. It was a fear that we had, one we hadn't hidden well enough.

When you hear this, you have to still like me. You have to be my friend.

You were telling her your fears and what you needed from her.

Before I started talking about babies being born, I said, "There's a difference between secret and private." How did I explain this to a five-year-old?

What distinctions was I making? I don't know. I went on, "It's important that you don't share something that's private with other people." And then I moved to the explanation of your birth and getting the label wrong, and I ended by saying, "Being transgender is special."

We waited. The moment seemed to expand. I had faith in this child. I assumed she'd say the right thing. I was recalculating that now. Why did I trust a five-year-old? How could I let so much ride on this moment for you?

She glanced among us. She didn't really realize that we'd finished. She was a very bright and kind kid. I had every right to trust her. She said, "Okay."

And then she turned to her mother. An only child used to praise, she asked, "What's the private thing that makes me special?"

This was no longer my scene. I bowed out.

But it was a beautiful experience, an important one. You'd chosen a good person. You knew what was at stake. You knew what you stood to lose. You took that risk, and she didn't turn away from you.

This seemingly small moment was huge. I realized that this wasn't an isolated event, that you would spend your life arriving at these moments again and again. You'll have to let loose this beautiful and delicate truth with hope and trust. And moments will yawn open before you and relationships will teeter. And some will change—for the better, for the worse, in ways that are hard to define.

Years later, you were in middle school and you'd had a bad day. You walked around with more anxiety because of your gender. You had more at stake than I had as a girl, more to fear, more to lose. You worried about someone finding out. We would sometimes role-play what to do if something like that happened—how to distract, deny, how to excuse yourself and get some help. On this particular day, I confessed that the difference between something being secret and private wasn't really helpful. "Either way, you don't want people to know. And that's hard no matter what you call it."

I believe in words, but I also believe they can be flimsy.

With children, it has usually gone easily like it had with Meredith. As you get older, it will get more complex. It will not always go this easily with adults.

It turns out that when you give a little knife to a kid, they usually don't use it. And, if they do, it can only cut you a little bit.

But when you give a little knife to an adult, they have the power to do real damage.

———————

Your father.

He would drive into the gymnastics parking lot, and you'd be nervous, every time. He'd assure you, "Once you get going, you'll love it. You always do."

It was a ritual. You'd say you were ready. Once inside, there was the usual scene—the mad rush of kids getting ready, the crowded waiting room with its fungal stink, the bustle of the other parents, mothers mostly.

Your dad was in charge of your hair. At first, he struggled. The ponytails were off-centered or lumpy, too high or too low. But over time, he became an expert in pulling back the curls, sweeping everything up into a high ponytail. You stood in front of him, barefoot, dressed in your leotard (your favorite was red and sparkly) and shorts, wearing your necklace with two Catholic medals, gifts from your grandmother.

Your dad was aware of the way the mothers would look at him. A gaze of how-adorable and good-for-you.

Good for you for what? Taking on what's traditionally a woman's role? Overcoming his fear of being perceived as less masculine?

What they didn't know was how masculine your father saw the work. He was trusted not to pull a strand the wrong way, knowing he could do it right and that he could make the ponytail pretty. Their gazes and smiles were congratulatory and condescending. He took the condescension because he doesn't mind a little congratulations.

None of them knew you were transgender, that there was more complexity to this moment—to a lot of moments in the lives of this father and daughter.

Your father comes back to this moment because he's surprised, even now, by the force of his pride. This quiet moment usually reserved for mothers and daughters—a girl's hair—taken on by a father and his trans daughter. He was preparing you, dressed in your shiny outfit, for this fierce and exacting sport. A sport that's not about the ball or a goal but about the body. Its strength and power, its defiance of gravity.

He'd run errands during your class, and sometimes, if he was back early, he'd watch you fly through the circuit. Graceful and strong. A bounding boundless girl.

———————

Your father and me?

We quickly realized that because you weren't out, we weren't out. It's not just the transgender child who is stealth. It's the whole family.

Jeff and I were at a picnic in the side yard of our neighbors' house. They lived in a peach-colored house not far from ours. They were professors, mostly, with young kids.

Someone asked the inevitable question: "So why'd you move here?"

We'd practiced our answers, but somehow we were always caught off guard. It was the simplest, most mundane question. It rattled us.

There was no obvious answer. We'd moved from the South to the North and landed in a town where we had no immediate family, no job (my job was two plane rides away), and no actual ties.

Jeff and I stumbled through our regular responses. It was a mélange.

"I arranged a deal with my university so that I could teach from any-where," I said. "The schools here are great."

"And we wanted to move closer to family, but not too close," Jeff said. We'd learned that just saying "we wanted to move closer to family" was followed by *So you have family in town?* And we'd have to explain that some were an hour away, other sets were two hours away. It didn't quite answer why *here*.

Sometimes Jeff would say, "We missed the Northeast. I was raised here."

New Englanders accept that someone would want out of the South.

But there was a woman at the picnic. She'd been raised in New York City and now worked in the psychology department at one of the nearby uni-versities. She kept asking questions, running us through our Rolodex of an-swers until we ran out.

She stared at us. "No," she said, bluntly. "That's not all there is to it."

I was impressed, but we blew past it, smiled and shrugged. We compli-mented the host on the food.

Jeff and I would struggle to make friends in this town. When we'd ar-rived in the South, we'd been inundated with invitations to potlucks and church events (galore) and fundraisers. A walk in the neighborhood always included long talks with neighbors in their yards. Not here. Much of this was logistical. Neither of us would have friends from work. The older kids were moving into the upper grades where parental involvement recedes. But there are the cultural elements. Strangers in the South talk to each other. In the North, they really tend not to.

I missed many things about the South, mainly the loving community, all those people who knew us and knew us well. I now had the time and space to realize what we'd given up.

While you and your brothers were acclimating quickly, Sophie, your dad, and I struggled. Like many families who immigrate, the kids seemed to be fluent in a matter of months, leaving us behind as foreigners in a foreign land, still struggling with the language.

Your dad and I felt the overwhelming need to protect the family. In your father, the need manifested itself physically. He got in the best shape of his life, and he also started volunteering to speak at schools and on panels and to run workshops for dads of transgender kids. All of this was done somewhat privately with first names, without outing you.

And me? I was trying to connect what I was feeling with where I was, like tracking down a new language inside of my own body and hoping to find correlations to the outside world. I found myself in situations again and again that I wasn't prepared for. No, let me edit that. I put myself in situations again and again that I wasn't prepared for. I was learning to swim by repeated drownings.

We worried that what the psychologist at the picnic was frank enough to say aloud—her suspicion that we were holding back—was something more people felt, even if subconsciously. After what we'd been through, we were more guarded. My desire to be a family of tanks was something they could read, even if they didn't really understand it. And we were suspicious of them. We didn't want to make another mistake. We still lived in fear of a knock at the door.

We always would.

I should note that the definition of *us* is growing. I talk about the larger queer community as a family, but there is another more immediate extended family we've built by hand. Jeff and I went to trans health conferences and met other families like ours. You now have a group of trans girls (and their little brothers) who are like cousins. Their parents are extra aunts and uncles.

We also found a cousin who's a trans man, an artist, living on the West Coast. We connected on Facebook, having recognized the common ground. Finding him was deeply emotional in ways that I can't articulate. Why should it matter that there's another trans person in the family? It's another way of hearing that you're not alone. *We have to be visible*, Sylvia told us back in 1973. He became visible. He appeared. And you appeared for him. You two have never met, and yet there is this tie that connects you. A bright beautiful thread.

And in addition to your godparents, you also have an extra godmother, a trans woman I've been friends with for many years, since before she transitioned. She visits. She sends you gifties. She offers me wise counsel and is part of our family. She watches you grow up with tenderness and awe. And what does it mean for you to have her in our lives? Talking with such casual brilliance about food or language or politics or the human condition, she's quite simply living a life that she's carved out for herself with beauty and hard-won freedom—and very cool shoes, always. She is a living, breathing gift just by being.

The idea of family is expansive. Little kids play house. They make another home within their home—pillow forts and tents made of bedsheets. I want you to have homes within homes within homes. Families within families within families.

You attended a day camp when you were around seven years old. The counselors knew that you were transgender. One of the counselors was a young trans man, home from college for the summer. The director had told me this, to contextualize the camp's comfort level. I hadn't met the counselor, but one day you came home and explained that one of your counselors was transgender.

"How do you know?" I asked.

"He told me."

"How did it come up?"

"We were walking behind the others, and he said, 'I'm trans too. When I was little, my parents thought I was a girl, but I was a boy.'"

"And that was it?"

"Yep. He just said it. He was happy."

Up until this moment, our way of telling someone that you were transgender was protracted and painful. It was a holdover script informed by the lawyer who explained how we'd be perceived in the courtroom. This script made sure to hit the right notes—we'd been surprised, we'd sought professional advice, it was a steep learning curve. We showed our fear. We showed our concern. We sometimes mentioned a backlash incident but didn't go into details.

What we'd forgotten was that it could also be simple and joyful.

The way this camp counselor came out to you ("He just said it. He was happy.") was profound.

This young man was letting you know that he existed, not telling everyone. Just you. *We have to be visible*, Sylvia said. In this crucial moment, he was making himself visible to you. So you knew you weren't alone.

One day, you might be out, completely and utterly.

And also, one day, you might tell us that we can't share with anyone that you're transgender. Each of us would accept that, without question.

But it would be hard for each of us to try to figure out how to tell our own stories without telling yours. Ours don't make sense without yours. *That's not all there is to it*, the psychologist at the picnic said. Having you in our family has changed our family—its trajectory, its migratory patterns, its routes. It has changed each of our internal landscapes. Tate is not this exact Tate without you. Isaac isn't the same Isaac without you. Sophie is certainly not this Sophie without you. Your father and I are who we are because of you.

The stories of who we are rely on your story.

The flip is also true. You are who you are because of Sophie and Isaac and Tate and your father and me. As this organism, the family. And as individuals.

We make each other. Stories of how we were made aside, here are each of us, formed and reformed.

Our house is a place to belong, but we don't belong to each other. And here I'm going to quote George Michael. You know his music because I'm incapable of cleaning without a soundtrack. His coming-out song "Freedom" is beautifully pained. He starts with a promise: he won't let us down or give us up. But he asks for the same—that we don't give him up. He tells us about his boyhood, that he didn't know what he wanted to be. And then he comes out a bit more, that there's something inside of him, someone else he has to be. His line about clothes not making the man is ecstatic, joyful. He's out.

But each time he announces his freedom, a parenthetical of fear circles back to the beginning. He sings his freedom and tells us again he won't let us down. He sings his freedom and tells us he won't give us up. He sings his freedom and pleads that we don't give him up.

He also carves out his own life. He tells us that we must see that we don't belong to each other, that we don't own each other; we are each our own.

23

I REMEMBER THE VOICE of the representative for our health insurance company. He was soft-spoken, young, cordial. I was calling to figure out how your transgender healthcare coverage would work. We were going to be heading to a gender clinic, one of the most respected in the country. I wasn't sure how my employer's plan would work. There would be intakes, endocrine care, gender specialists, and recommendations for best practices. We'd heard rumors that costs could run high, very high. Sophie was in college by now; the boys were on their way. I was anxious. I explained our situation and said, "I'm just trying to get a feel for the overall plan as it relates to trans health."

He excused himself to look up the plan. When he came back, he said, "I've found the exclusion."

"Oh, okay. Can you read it to me?"

He paused and then read directly from the policy. I could tell he was deeply uncomfortable. It was a blanket exclusion, covering all trans-related healthcare.

The exclusion didn't use the word *transgender*. It didn't use the words *gender dysphoria* or *gender identity disorder*.

The words used were *psychosexual deviance*.

You were ten years old.

Psychosexual deviance.

I wasn't sure what to say. I was stunned. "She still believes in Santa Claus. She's just learning how to knit." I don't know why the knitting was relevant. "I think it's a little early to make that call. Don't you?"

"Yes."

Let's pause here for a moment. This is you at age ten.

We were living in an old farmhouse near town. It had five small bedrooms and floors that sloped so jaggedly that we couldn't replace the hardwoods; the whole house had been shifting for a century or more. The playroom was upstairs. We filled it with toys and a fat L-shaped IKEA sofa, perfect for your flips. You were going to dance classes and gymnastics and taekwondo. (Taekwondo was short-lived. A kid with asthma barfed on a mat, and the whole endeavor lost its charm.)

One of your friends had moved into a wrecked mansion not far away. Her parents were in the middle of flipping it. You loved that old place, how good it was for hide-and-seek—all of these different floors, its long heavy drapes and big old Victorian bathtubs. It even had a widow's walk.

For your tenth birthday party, you requested Godiva chocolates instead of cupcakes, and I made up one of my elaborate scavenger hunts, running in and out of our house, following a series of clues.

This was, as you put it, "at the height of your Lego years," and you remember putting together a Lego yacht while Isaac, a recovering Lego fan himself, weighed in with tips.

Tate got grounded that summer. For a while, he wasn't allowed any screen time except *Cheers* reruns after five o'clock. We'd watch them together as a family. Why *Cheers*? I prefer punishments that make my life better. Once Tate's punishment was over, you and I kept going with the show. Over the next few years, we'd work our way through the entire series—275 half-hour episodes.

Isaac went off to college in Chicago, and Sophie graduated from art school. You rode her shoulders at her graduation and walked across the stage when she got her degree, holding her hand and gazing out at the crowd, wearing a pair of bright yellow Doc Martens.

But what I remember most clearly is that your father built another swing out of PVC pipe and attached it to a grand old oak in the backyard. You spent hours on end there, swinging and spinning and dreaming.

On the phone with the representative at the health insurance company, I explained that this exclusion couldn't have anything to do with my daughter. It made no sense. It didn't use any of the right words. Plus, those were terms abandoned in the 1960s. "Who says *psychosexual deviance* anymore?"

"I understand," he said, and I had a feeling he might actually understand.

"Isn't there another section that's more suited to her actual situation?"

"Ma'am," he said, and it was so gentle, it was so incredibly heartbreakingly gentle, "this is the section that applies to your daughter." The way he said it was clear: This is the truth, the awful truth. This is the reality for your daughter. This is how she's seen. He wasn't on the insurance company's side. It was personal for him. He was on our side.

Of course, I could be wrong. I talked to a lot of insurance people after him—denial after denial, discussion upon discussion, appeals, and faxing. None of them were rude, but for this young man, it was different. He was telling me a truth. He was saying, *Yes. Yes. This is where you are now. Here.*

I felt like he knew this place, was no stranger to it.

There's documentation of girls in 1500s Spain who transitioned to male identities, living the lives of men.

In Neapolitan culture, the term for trans women is *femminielli.*

The Maori call trans women *whakawahine* and trans men *tangata ira tane.* The first means *like a woman*, but the second quite simply translates to *human man.*

In the eighteenth and nineteenth centuries, the indigenous Itelmans of Siberia named trans women *koekchuch.*

None of this is new.

When you were in first grade, you told your friend Emma that you're transgender. You were playing at her house after school.

Emma said, "Did Mother Nature make you a girl?"

"No," you said, "I made myself a girl."

"Did you just find out?" Emma asked.

"No," you said, "it's something you know inside yourself."

We call it a sense of self.

A sense.

We have far more than five senses. It's now understood that we have a sense of gravity. We know that our relationship with gravity when we're walking is different from when we're swimming up from the bottom of a silty lake.

Our kinesthetic sense gives information on our movements, where the parts of our body are at a given moment. Imagine the articulation of a girl's body in a full sprint across a field.

Spatial perception relies on both the sense of our bodies and the environment around that body—objects and people and elements. We can sense someone who is too close, who is invading our space. We're aware of the hand that suddenly is a pinky's brush from our own. And at night on a dark street, we sense the distance between us and the man who's one streetlight away. We're heightened by every small movement within the confines of an elevator.

I had an intro to psychology class where the professor asked us to imagine what it would be like to circle the Statue of Liberty from the point of view of a helicopter. It was easy, almost immediate. I wasn't even really trying, and yet there she was and I could imagine her, in the round. This sense of spatial perception allows us this ability to hold things in our mind and to turn them and to turn ourselves.

We have a muscular sense as well—how much something will weigh, how to counterbalance weight. We have a sense of balance too. We know when it's messed with, how the world tilts and pitches us from our footing.

We have a sense of pain, which is far more complex than touch and is distinct from the cutaneous receptors in our skin, which are part of another sense. They respond to touch, yes, but also vibrations, pressure, and heat. I know when I've said too much and my cheeks are flooded with blood into a full blush.

We can sense ultraviolet radiation and know when we've taken in too much sun. We have the sense of hunger and, through a separate system, thirst. We have the sense of suffocation—that sudden need for more air, how quickly we start to claw for it.

Butterflies, bees, mole rats, whales, and migratory birds navigate, in part, by way of their sense of the earth's magnetic fields. Preliminary studies show that it's possible for humans to have this sense too, probably because of our nomadic genes.

Our senses allow us to be arranged in the world, to perceive that world, its motions set against our own motions.

We take so many of our senses for granted. Before I was tasked with imagining the Statue of Liberty in a college psychology class, I'd imagined and remembered and held things in my head and turned them around and turned myself around millions of times. I just wasn't aware of that ability.

I also have a self-concept. It exists in the past—how I once was, that ever-shifting version of my child self, teen self, young-to-middle-aged self, and this ever-burgeoning self. My self-concept holds future versions of my self, ideas of the person I could become, some cautionary, some Iris-Apfel aspirational. I hold that self aloft in my mind too. She is ever-changing. She's far more difficult to hold in place and circle than the Statue of Liberty.

You are arranged in the world, and you arrange yourself in your mind, moving through the world. And your sense of self is one of your senses.

Just as I'd never considered so many of the senses beyond the five I'd been taught as a child—sight, sound, touch, taste, smell—I didn't really consider my sense of gender. But it was there. It was clear—a bell that rang in my ribs, a bright and constant note. So constant that it is absorbed into everything else.

Unlike most people, your sense of your girlness is keener. It was a bright and constant note, but you were made aware of it early because it wasn't absorbed into the culture around it; it bounced off of it. Many people aren't very aware of their girlness, their boyness, their womanness, or manness.

I've become more aware of my girlness and my womanness because of you. It is something that now takes up space within me. I can *feel* it.

Some definitions of gender identity use the word *sense. Merriam-Webster* puts it this way: "a person's internal sense of being male, female, some combination of male and female, or neither male nor female."

The *Oxford English Dictionary* also uses the word *sense* in its definition of *transgender.* "Designating a person whose sense of personal identity and gender does not correspond to that person's sex at birth, or which does not otherwise conform to conventional notions of sex and gender."

What does it mean to be a girl swimming to the sunstruck surface of a lake? What does it mean to be the girl sprinting across a field? What does it mean to be a self, moving and thinking and dreaming and spinning and breathing through a life?

What does it mean to have a girlhood?

Didn't your father and I help create a girlhood for your sister and boyhoods for your brothers? Shouldn't we just be done with it and say childhoods instead of making the delineations? Yes and no.

We can't ignore the delineations. We can't claim to be gender-blind. Ignoring the issues, even when trying to dismantle them, seems to do more harm than good.

We were conscious of raising Sophie as a girl in a world in which it's not easy to be a girl, and how it was different than raising Isaac. But the expectations put on boys by our violent culture were also damning. Then we had Tate, who was a different kind of boy wanting a different kind of boyhood. (Boyhoods are a wreck in our culture—violent, cruel, and dangerous. Our collective boys-will-be-boys response is a dereliction of duty. It's merciless. As they reenact our viciousness on their smaller stages, we so often refuse to step in and offer a different way, to see our own ugliness and address it.)

Maybe I don't believe that any girlhood or boyhood is truly conventional. I'm reminded of a John Irving quote: "People who complain that my books are bizarre haven't been paying attention to real life." (Irving has paid attention to those who've moved across gender identities.) If someone thinks that they had a conventional girlhood, isn't it possible that they simply weren't paying close enough attention? Girlhoods are individual, uniquely textured, frayed in ways that show the wear and tear of one person's distinctive life. Only one. Each our own.

And so this is a warning, an incomplete sampling of some of the ways people will treat you, in no particular order:

As illustrated above, people will pathologize you. Don't let them. You'll need what you need from doctors, like all of us do at some point in our lives, but there's nothing wrong with you. There's a long and hideous history of LGBTQ+ people being viewed as diseased. It is ongoing. Don't believe it.

People will be openly hostile, and at the same time, people will have good intentions. The openly hostile ones announce themselves, all bluster and froth. Beware the well-intentioned progressive, beware the well-meaning oftentimes white and oftentimes women who work in offices, who oversee human resources and hold administrative posts. They'll be very, very concerned for you and they will sympathize, and then their inaction will speak for itself. They disappear so suddenly.

Beware of even some of those folks who pride themselves on supporting civil rights and yet refuse to see any correlation to the civil rights of transgender folks. Their selective blindness is astonishing—how can some-one so smart choose to be so dumb?

People will think they can openly discuss your body. Nope. This is an act of objectification, even when it's disguised as progressiveness. It's closely tied to the history of transgender women, which is the history of having few options, of living on the outside of society, the fringes. The history of prostitution and sex work is inextricably tied to the American story of being a trans woman. We should always tread gently here, as gentleness is long overdue.

People will try to dehumanize you. Don't let them.

People will question your relationship with God. They have no business getting between you and God.

People will treat you as a hero; they'll talk about your *bravery*. Lizzo has spoken about this. Showing her beautiful, ample body has been called brave, again and again. What's brave about showing her beauty as another woman would? Nothing. She refuses what's supposed to be a compliment but is really a subtextual message: *Here's what you should be feeling—shame.* "If you saw Anne Hathaway in a bikini on a billboard, you wouldn't call her brave," Lizzo said. "I don't like it when people think it's hard for me to see myself as beautiful." Close to this talk of bravery is the idea that you're someone's cause. A true ally is helpful and listens to what you actually need. Beware of the fixers, those who need to help you more than you need to be helped.

People will see what they want to see, what they need to see. Humans are adept at projection. Some will need to make you someone to fear. This will help them in many ways. For some women, this act of vilifying you allows them to remain victims, which can be crucial to their understanding of self and their position of power in our culture (especially dangerous are trans-exclusionary radical feminists, or TERFs).

People will dismiss and diminish your experiences and encounters with transphobia—people you love will do this, people who love you. (Don't let them do this; don't let *me* do this.) It will be confusing. It will take vigilance.

There's more. Things I don't know. Things only you will know.

My goal here is simple. I want you to know what might be coming at you so that when it appears you aren't surprised. You can say, "Oh, yeah. I was warned about this. And here it is." My hope is a moment of detachment. "This is the form it took, huh" as opposed to being sucker punched. This was the true gift given to me by the woman in the transgender support group—*They'll blame you; they always blame the mother.*

Some people will disagree with my approach. They'll say I'm priming you for an experience, laying the groundwork for a self-fulfilling prophecy. This is no prophecy. Some of these things have already happened to you; it's just that, so far, I've been able to protect you from them. I won't always be there. And I want you to be prepared. I want you to be able to see someone telegraph their moves, to read them like a pugilist who sees a punch winding up long before it has a chance to land. (You're already getting skilled at this.) I hate the metaphors of sucker punches and boxers. But I won't change it. Why would I? To make all of this sweeter?

As I write this, I know the futility of it—and the hubris. I will never be able to begin to foresee the forms of aggression and discrimination that you'll face.

But now I have to do the opposite of protection. I'll have to hand over the stories I've hidden from you. They belong to you.

24

THOSE WORDS — *PSYCHOSEXUAL DEVIANCE*.

I was lucky because I got to absorb that blow. I thought of all the transgender people who'd made that call themselves. They were read that exclusion. They had to take the blow to the heart, directly.

This is the thing about transgender people: they take blows to the heart. And some have grown so strong of heart that they take blows for the rest of the community. In 2015, young Gavin Grimm in Virginia started fighting, publicly, in court, for his basic right to use the bathroom and locker rooms in his high school. Speakers at a school board meeting called him a freak, compared him to a dog. The school retrofitted some broom closets as bathrooms for him to use. Closets. He refused, metaphorically and literally. He opted for the nurse's bathroom. He won his case in 2018, a year *after* graduating. He took blows to the heart. (I hope that one day Gloucester High School is named after him.)

Born well over a hundred years before Gavin Grimm, Lucy Hicks Anderson, a Black transgender woman, fought for her right to live as a woman. Look her up. She took blows to the heart.

Sylvia Rivera comes to mind again, storming the stage, charging the gays and lesbians with abandonment, really, for silencing and ignoring their transgender brothers and sisters in jail. "Y'all better quiet down." That's how she starts her speech.

And that's what I hear in my head as I write this. *Y'all better quiet down.*

No one is allowed to call my child a deviant. No one.

My child is beautiful and brilliant.

This has been going on for too long.

That's it. No one gets to write a policy—a policy?—calling other human beings deviants.

Sylvia yelled into the mic because they were still loud. She talked about the organization she created with Marsha P. Johnson, taking in transgender people who had nowhere else to go. They did this even though they were broke, even though they got kicked out of their apartments. They kept starting over. "The people [at the organization] are trying to do something for all of us, and not men and women that belong to a white middle-class white club. And that's what you all belong to!"

She was speaking to me. She was telling me to quiet down. She was talking to me as part of that white middle-class white club.

She'd lost everything. She named her losses. "I have been beaten. I have had my nose broken. I have been thrown in jail. I have lost my job. I have lost my apartment for gay liberation, and you all treat me this way?"

Blows to her heart.

Blows to her body.

But I think of her lungs. "Listen," the poet Mary Oliver wrote, "are you breathing just a little, and calling it a life?"

Listen to Sylvia's voice, her whole body bringing forth that voice. Her lungs expanding. She wasn't breathing just a little and calling it a life. She was full of life. Each of her breaths was more of a life than some people will ever live.

Each breath.

Y'all better quiet down because she came to speak, to be heard, to draw in life, to live.

Ta-Nehesi Coates writes, " 'Good intention' is a hall pass through history, a sleeping pill that ensures the Dream."

I used to eat nachos and drink margaritas every few weeks at the same little bistro with a friend of mine, a psychologist who's Black and raising two biracial kids. We used to argue about good intentions. She'd learned to mistrust them and then eventually to despise them.

I was still optimistic. "But I'll take good intentions over the other options, if those options are things like hostility, open hatred, degradation . . . murder. I'll take them."

She shook her head and said, "Okay, see how that goes. Get back to me."

That first phone call with my health insurance company marked the beginning of a long, unending battle, filled with the well intentioned.

I started making calls, writing emails, working my way through my university's HR department, talking to deans and union reps and eventually those higher up the academic power structure. I explained over and over that the antidiscrimination policy includes gender identity. *How can you state that policy, in good faith, and then deny coverage to transgender people for transgender healthcare?* The emails and calls with the well intentioned were lovely, warm. They got it. They were deeply sympathetic. Again and again, they couldn't do anything themselves. Their hands were tied! What a frustrating policy. No luck!

And they passed me along . . . to the next well-intentioned person.

This went on, in fits and starts, for a couple of years.

Eventually, it was summer and a higher-up had an idea. She wrote me an email.

She explained that there was no good news from the foundation about fundraising for trans healthcare coverage, "which means that we can likely only work on a GoFundMe campaign or the like."

I read it, and read it again.

Wait, what?

I reread it.

I read it to Jeff.

He said, "She's actually suggesting a GoFundMe campaign."

We had to say this out loud in order to believe it.

"She's suggesting a GoFundMe campaign to cover our child's health-care when I have a health insurance policy that is part of my compensation package," I said, "in a workplace that has an antidiscrimination policy that includes gender identity."

This was the back-and-forth. Stating facts. Confirming them. Restating them.

A GoFundMe campaign.

Who was this "we"? Did it include me? Would I take my work time to create and promote it? While outing my own child?

A GoFundMe campaign, started by someone who was fully insured, asking for help from friends and family and their friends and family in order to cover what the insurance company was legally required to cover—which would be a gift to the massively wealthy insurance company, letting them off the hook financially and ethically?

How to explain that this is not how healthcare works? This is not how discrimination is fixed—with charity.

But that was not the most troubling part of the email.

Or at least not to me.

She then asked me for names. "If you could send me a list of names of those you've contacted, a petition of sorts, I may be able to make some progress with that in hand."

A list of names. Those I've contacted—about my daughter's healthcare coverage? Colleagues' names? Union representatives? People outside of academe?

A petition of sorts. There'd been no petition of any sort. I keep my daughter's gender identity close; this administrator knew it was confidential. I'd stated that already.

So she would begin working on this GoFundMe campaign by reaching out to people I know? Without me? Or . . .

None of it made sense.

Jeff and I were floored.

I sent the email to Sophie, who was furious. I sent it to your grandfather, who called it outrageous. I sent it to your aunt, my oldest sister, who does advocacy for her son with special needs. She went off on your behalf with expletive-fueled artistry.

I didn't respond for weeks. I let it sit. I collected myself.

Eventually, this was what I told her.

I was not going to launch a GoFundMe campaign. I believe it would stir up substantial backlash. It could be seen as akin to suggesting that an African American faculty member create a GoFundMe campaign for his child's sickle cell anemia treatments if the treatments were being denied by insurers on the basis of race; or suggesting a Jewish colleague create a GoFundMe campaign for her infant, denied coverage for Tay-Sachs care because of the disease's Jewish genetic links. Taxpayers might be frustrated because healthcare is part of our compensation, and so asking everyday taxpayers to pay for that twice, while letting the insurance company off the hook, ends up supporting a systemic transphobic practice. These are just a few reasons.

What I've found is that people do not always like it when I draw parallels within history. It creates context. They've constructed a version of themselves as a person who wouldn't have let blatant 1950s-style racism stand, for example. They've watched the movies and identified with all the good guys. They'd have been the brave voice, setting the wrongs right. They like that version, of course, and this is why pointing out parallels to racism, for example, makes them feel like blown glass. Like a figurine. Like something that is beginning to shatter.

I've been that person. I haven't particularly relished being called out on my own bullshit. But especially now that I'm older, I prefer it to being a person with more bullshit.

Here's what I have to say about my own sexism and racism, my own homophobia and transphobia, all of the ways in which I do not stop and take in the full humanity of the person who stands next to me: First, I try to know it's there. I try not to think that it defines all of my humanity. I'm not bad because of it. I'm not good for a lack of it. I'm human, and I pass people by every single day without truly seeing them, without fully trying to understand them, without empathy and grace. If I overreact to my own stupidity, my own narrowness and shoving of people into boxes, I'm not seeing clearly. I need to see clearly. Then I can start to address. I'll always be addressing.

Good intentions that go nowhere—I can hate those acts. And I do. And now when I start to hear a familiar pattern of speech from a person situated in a position of power, I take note. I prepare myself for what might come. I have to still come at people with love. Again and again.

Sometimes love works. Sometimes it is this act of listening, of meeting someone where they are, and of forgiveness, that expresses humanity. And that humanity can be hard to ignore. My faith operates on the premise of love, and so I have to try.

There is only one kind of hate that you truly have power over, and that's your own.

And there is one form of hate that is the most dangerous. I've noted it before; it's an internalized, deep down self-hatred, transphobia from within. It seems impossible. We position ourselves in a culture. That culture positions us. The boundaries of self bleed into that culture. That culture bleeds into us. Don't hide your own feelings from yourself. That hiding only causes more fissures. Let these feelings out. Give them air. They should squawk while batting around the living room for a while, a bunch of loose parakeets— in the open air, where you can see them.

When I came back to my friend over nachos and margaritas to report on how things had gone with all of my belief in good intentions, I admitted defeat. She was right. It didn't go well. The thing about good intentions is that they require no action. In fact, while "paving the road to hell," they waste an enormous amount of time. It's a rope-a-dope technique, except it feels so earnest. And while you're spending all of that fuel connecting with people who want to help—*How can I help? What can I do?*—there is no progress, and that can have a cost. Especially in healthcare. That cost can be deadly. Good intentions are a promise to worry, to fret, to feel sorry for you, maybe even to feel guilty. But that's it. She won the argument, hands down. She and Ta-Nehesi Coates were right.

But I still can't quit good intentions. Because every once in a while, somebody comes through.

Back when you were in kindergarten, we kept waiting for guidance from the Department of Education on how the laws, passed that summer, would be interpreted. Fall came and went. Winter too. We were a little worried, but meanwhile you had all of the rights we wanted you to have. Principal Nate had delivered. You could use the girls' bathroom. Everyone referred to you with female pronouns. You were called by your preferred name, not what was on official records. The official records didn't show up in the system. This way, you wouldn't be outed by a substitute reading a print-out roster.

And then one Friday in March, the last day before spring break, the state's Department of Education released the guidelines, very quietly.

They were terrific, everything we could have hoped for and things we'd never thought of. In addition to the rights we expected, they explained how young some kids are when they understand that their gender identity doesn't match what they were assigned at birth. They illustrated some of the points with examples, little bits of storytelling. They stipulated funds for teacher education on gender identity and expression and that any new construction plans for schools should include more single-occupant unisex bathrooms. They explained that if a student had an issue with a transgender student using the bathroom that matched their gender, the student with the complaint would be provided an alternative—not the trans student. I've used the guidelines as model guidelines, sending them to parents and educators and administrators in states where guidelines don't yet exist.

The detractors came out and voiced their opinions, but they didn't gather any real momentum.

Toward the end of the year, your dad and I had a meeting with Nate. As we were wrapping up, your dad remarked about how great the guidelines were.

"Yes," Nate said, "we weren't sure how they were going to go."

"Really?" I said.

"It was quiet for a long time, and the lawyers for the district heard that I was already granting your daughter the rights that I felt should be included." His smile was weary. "They were telling me that I didn't have the right to make those interpretations, that the guidelines might go in lots of directions." He looked at us then, his eyes filled with tears. "I told them they'd have to fire me. I'd never take away her rights."

We'd had no idea the pressure he'd been under, no idea that he was undeterred by it. He'd been willing to fight for you, and he'd been willing to lose that fight.

A year after you'd left the school, you and your dad were back in town. We'd promised to swing by when we were in the state visiting family. He arranged a visit day at your old school.

Your dad was heading out of the building after dropping you off and ran into Nate, one last time. They were standing in the hallway with its old worn floors and walls covered in kid art. The two of them were moving in opposite directions so their bodies passed and then turned—a slow revolution of planets. Your dad was telling him how thankful we were, for everything he'd done for us.

Because it's true. We needed a place to take us in. We needed a refuge. And this school became that refuge.

Nate said, "Are you kidding me? You were the best family I've ever worked with."

It was the kind of thing a principal might say to every family. He was not one to play favorites. But this time, both men choked up. They turned that slow rotation. And your dad couldn't say anything. His voice was locked. He nodded and Nate nodded back. And that was all that was needed.

This is the thing about people. They are sometimes quietly stunning. You can't give up on them.

Another meeting was called at the university. I was put on the phone with . . . were they lobbyists? I recall the words *legislative liaisons*. I believe they were somewhat in charge of messaging.

There's this expression, *Don't bring a knife to a gunfight*. Well, I'd brought the equivalent of a basket of cucumber sandwiches because I'd been expecting a picnic. I knew things were going badly very early on. I was introducing myself, explaining my background, how I came to advocacy by way of my daughter, and giving some information about the current healthcare issues when I was stopped.

The woman who would do most of the talking said, "I don't want to be part of something that is anger-fueled. That's not going to work for me."

I was confused. When running through things like background and policy, my tone tends to be pretty flat. "I'm so sorry if you heard any anger in my tone," I said. "I might have been speaking quickly just to get everyone up to speed as fast as possible and it came off as abrupt."

She begged off, "No, no, you don't sound angry at all. I was just saying . . ." I wasn't sure what she was saying.

She continued to interrupt me throughout the call. Maybe that was just her nature, or maybe it was strategic. Probably both.

I found myself saying over and over, "I appreciate that correction . . ." and "Oh, thank you, that's important to note . . ." and "Huh, that surprises me. That's not the data that I'm familiar with . . ."

Eventually I said, "If nothing else really comes of this, I'd like to have at least raised awareness."

"You might not think you've had impact," she said, "but I know who you are and have had conversations about you on every level. You've caused lots of conversation."

Was this supposed to be a compliment? It didn't feel like one.

"Well," I said, "HR struggles to use the word *transgender* and needs help in—"

Again, I was cut off. She asked me who in HR struggles.

I didn't have any names at the ready.

"I can't support that kind of language against a group of people," she said. "No one likes to be painted with a broad brush. You shouldn't say all of HR."

No irony. No awareness or recognition of the fact that I was there for the broad-stroke claim that all transgender people were psychosexual deviants.

I apologized and amended my comment. "*From my experience*, people in human resources simply didn't know that trans people weren't covered and that they should be a resource able to answer questions for those who aren't yet in our healthcare system—new employees, for example." I was treading water but knew that I was sinking.

At one point, the woman who did most of the talking patiently explained that not everything is covered by insurance, even one of her husband's eye procedures wasn't covered.

I did not ask the obvious follow-up: Oh, was that denial also on the basis of psychosexual deviance?

That's called self-restraint.

I started to predict the corrections and preempted a comment by saying, "Look, I'm not an expert—"

And another voice on the call cut me off. It was one I hadn't heard before, another woman. She said, "That's right. You're a mom."

Ah, yes, but I wasn't on this call because I happened to be someone's mother. I was on this call because I was a colleague and this was my place of employment. They weren't fielding calls from random mothers.

And I *am* an expert. I can talk to anyone about these issues, from a pediatric endocrinologist to an ACLU lawyer to a gerontologist. (I had questions about gender identity in the elderly.) I can spend days in a research library, shuttling between information in this area of specialization and information in another area of specialization, trying to piece together research from all different kinds of doctors.

But I know that if I really want an answer to something, my best bet is another mother. Usually a mother with a trans daughter just a few years older than you. But not much older. Things are changing so fast that even someone five years older than you is a completely different generation.

I let the mom comment go, for the time being, even though deep down, I thought, *You have no idea the advantage I have as a mother. You're in this meeting because it's your job. You can give up. I won't, not ever.* Her comment was meant to put me in my place, but what it revealed was a profound misreading of motherhood as well as the institution of the American family. (I'll get to that later.)

The hardest part of the call to take was the rah-rah LGBTQ+ rights talk that would suddenly buzz in like a low-flying airplane crop-dusting a field. I had to thank them for it. "That's great! Yes, I really appreciate all of the support."

Sometimes I wonder how much I would have pushed if I were advocating for myself, if I were a trans person. I wonder if I'd have taken too many direct blows to the heart and decided I couldn't keep pushing. How much, on my own behalf, could I have withstood? The acts of courage from the trans community, their refusal to give up or give in, and their toughness are astonishing. We owe them a debt of gratitude. They paved the way and keep pressing on.

When I finally sent the email to the woman who'd suggested the Go-FundMe campaign, I ended it this way: "From every corner of the university, I've heard the desire to make this right. This is heartening. If we rely on the state legislature or the courts to make change, however, it could take years. My hope is that, in the meantime, the university is actively seeking a solution to align its actions with its own strongly held beliefs about equality, here, within its own walls."

And that's the crazy part. It didn't take years. I wrote that email in the summer of 2019. The very next summer a case was pending in the Supreme Court. I wasn't tracking it too closely; I didn't want to get my hopes up.

Aimee Stephens was working at a funeral home in Michigan when in 2013, at the age of fifty-two, she decided to transition. Her bosses had known her as a man. She wrote them a letter, kindly informing them she'd be dressing as a woman when she returned from her vacation, after surgery, and her attire would be in keeping with the dress-code policy. She was fired shortly thereafter. Aimee took it to the courts. She died of complications related to liver failure in 2020, one month before she won the case, a landmark victory, with a conservative judge writing the decision. The Supreme Court ruling confirms that the 1964 Civil Rights Act protects gay, lesbian, and transgender employees from discrimination based on sex. The ruling makes it clear that the university is responsible for any discrimination against its employees; they can't say their hands are tied. They have to change. They haven't changed yet. But you can probably guess that I enjoyed following up with a few people with the good news.

The legislative liaisons have not responded.

But Aimee. She'd been an embalmer and a funeral director. She knew what death was. She wanted to live. She transitioned and became fully alive in her own skin.

I can hear Mary Oliver again, asking, "Listen, are you breathing just a little, and calling it a life?"

Aimee chose to breathe, to have a life.

And she took blows to the heart.

YOUR DAD AND I were at a birthday party for an old friend of ours. We were in a large sunny living room, or maybe it was a porch, but one with such lush furniture it felt like part of the main house. The host was the head of a boarding school; the house wasn't his and neither was the amazing art. Everything belonged to the school. Even the hors d'oeuvres, I'm guessing, fell under some kind of allowance.

I saw Jeff from across the room, talking to the president of a women's college. She was a trim woman with straight pale hair. Her outfit held a politician's stiff blandness. She was smiling. But Jeff was looking back at me in a way that I'd never really seen before. I get jangled at these kinds of parties—too observational, too candid—but your father is good at them. So I was confused by his expression. I read it as a distress signal. I walked over.

He introduced me to the president.

She shook my hand. "Your husband and I were just talking about your daughter. A girl with a penis!"

This phrase had recently become popular among the educated for reasons I don't understand. What a weird asterisk. You're a girl, except for this one thing? The emphasis felt very wrong. The trans girl appears in our imagination and everyone is thinking now only about her genitalia?

At this point in the conversation, I wanted to hit pause. You just brought up the genitalia of one of my children? Upon first meeting me?

She went on, "She'll have to attend . . ." and named her prestigious all-women's college.

I was trying to process what was happening. Jeff had gone mute. How had it come up in the first place? I trusted that there was an important reason. Was she trying to say, "I get it, I'm hip, I'm comfortable with the new terminology"? Did this phrase also become popular because it proved to the listener, *Look at me, unafraid of saying the word* penis?

She was talking about her own family now. She had grown daughters. I wanted to stop her and say, "So what do your daughters-with-vaginas do for work now? What are they up to these days?" But I wasn't really saying anything at all.

She insisted again that you'd have to attend her college one day. "Yes, yes, let's make that happen!" I said while backing away as if I had important business with the cheese platter. Was Jeff still there? Had he already headed for the cheese platter? I don't remember.

Shortly after this, the college was under fire because they didn't have clear policies on admitting trans women. They'd denied the application of a transgender high school senior because she didn't provide a proper birth certificate, which is nearly impossible to change in certain states.

The issue with this venerable women's college was its alumni body of older staunch feminists. You'd think feminists would be deeply sympathetic to the cause of trans women. But the history is hideous, actually, and feminist hostility to trans women can still be hateful.

I followed up with the president, explaining that you'd be denied admission if you were applying today and that their "show us your papers" approach was more restrictive than the state guidelines for kids in the public schools. She hastily handed me off to the VP of enrollment, who, after some back and forth, replied with "Thank you for writing and for your continued interest in [the name of the college]."

I was no longer interested in the college.

What surprised me about the little knives, as Tate put it, was the way they were wielded by feminists and progressives on the left. I'd gotten so used to the way knives were brandished by those on the far right in the Bible Belt. When we first landed in the progressive Northeast, the little knives that started swinging in from the left landed so much harder because I'd let my guard down, leaving too much flank exposed. Not anymore.

I've already discussed the phrase "gender is a social construct." For some, this idea is essential to understanding who they are. We need those conversations about the harm that's caused by rigid rules about gender and its expression and expectations, and violent ways in which women suffer under those rules and expectations.

But often other people's concepts of the social construct of gender place obstacles in my road. I might have to mess with what someone once found mind-blowing in college. If the person is a woman one generation senior to me, I might be interfering with their sense of feminism, their battles with our culture, both personal and political. And if you want to do a little research, you'll find that radical feminists—transgender exclusive radical feminists, or TERFs, in particular—have been some of the cruelest, nastiest, most consistent transphobic bigots around. They've done so much harm.

Robin Tran, a comedian and trans woman, encapsulates the irrational fears some TERFs might have. "I'm afraid I'm going to be the first transgender woman in history to . . . progress the trans movement forward while setting the women's movement back fifty years at the same time by . . . transitioning into a horrible stereotype of a woman. Being like 'Oh my God, can someone open this bottle for me? It's so hard to open. Oh my God, guys. Someone open that door for me right now.' " It's funny because Robin Tran isn't a threat. She can't move the women's movement back fifty years by asking someone to open a door for her. It's one of those fears—like your father thinking that your transness was his weakness made manifest—that, once said aloud, disintegrates or, in her case, becomes immediately comedic.

What's actually happening in the women's movement is a broadening of the definition of feminism. Roxane Gay, a writer who is Haitian American and bisexual, was asked this question, *How can a woman like Beyoncé balance being sexy and very feminine with feeling strong and empowered?* She answered this way, "Women need to realize that femininity and being strong and empowered are not opposites: They go hand in hand." Robin Tran can dress with femininity. She can like it when someone opens a door for her, and she can see herself as a feminist at the same time if she wants. Roxane Gay goes on to say, "We have to stop viewing strength as something not feminine because I think strength is extraordinarily feminine."

So many people, on the left and right, think they can talk about your body as if it's up for public discussion. For ages, when a transgender woman was being interviewed on a talk show, the journalist or daytime host—often another woman—would seem compelled to ask about the transgender woman's genitals. I can think of no other kind of interview in which an interviewer would feel like it was completely fine and within their rights to ask this kind of personal question. At the start of 2014, Katie Couric asked model Carmen Carrera about her body. "Your private parts are completely different now, aren't they?"

Carmen literally shushes her. "I don't want to talk about it because it's really personal . . . [I want to show] people that after the transition there's still life to live. . . . I still have my career going, I still have my family. . . . I want to have more kids. I want to focus on that rather than what's down here because that's been spoken about so many times. . . . Other interviews with other trans people, they always focus on either the transition or the genitalia. And there is more to trans people than just that."

After the interview, Couric was taken to task by Laverne Cox; the two are friends. Couric apologized and threw herself into the work, creating the documentary *Gender Revolution.*

Sophie's gotten these questions too. She was visiting her college roommate's parents. They were getting ready to leave the house; in fact, she was walking out the door. Unknown to Sophie, the daughter had told her mother that you're trans. So all of this caught Sophie off guard. The mother asked, "How's your sister doing?"

"She's good!" Sophie said.

"How old is she now?"

"She's ten."

"Oh!" the mother said. "Is she showing signs of going through puberty?"

Sophie has always been the master of the non sequitur. She smiled and laughed like the mother had said something so clever. "Aren't we all!" Sophie said. "See you later!"

My parents, in their mid-eighties now, have had to prepare responses too. They've practiced what to say about your body when someone asks about medications and surgeries. "We don't discuss the private medical information of our grandchildren. But Carolyn and Jeff are doing a lovely job."

In the South, femininity and frilliness were the norm. Sophie and I balked at it. Sophie especially. She was drawn to heavy boots instead of ballet flats. Other girls on the soccer team came to practice in full hair and makeup. They rolled their shorts to make them short-shorts. Sophie hated all of this and refused to be part of it.

Now we found ourselves on the other side of the argument. Having never been fans of the pervasive hypermasculine and hyperfeminine expectations of the South, we were now in a place that had done away with them, where men and women could be somewhat free of those expectations, and that felt liberating. Rare were tight skirts and spiked heels and baby girls in bow-covered headbands that left little dents on the sides of their heads. In fact, babies were often dressed in gender-neutral shades.

The problem was that a new rigidity slipped in. Soon, we realized that buying Barbies for your daughter was an act of sexism and indoctrination into a culture that was antiwoman. That your glittery, spangled, bright pink outfit choices were seen as a failure of my parenting, an acquiescence to a disastrously misogynistic society.

When Sophie wore light makeup to school in those early days when she was still attending, she got looks. When I rode a bike in platforms and a skirt that summer, two different neighbors stopped me, worried that my heels made biking unsafe. "How do you bike wearing those shoes?"

"Fine?" I said. "Without incident?"

It was tricky. We were suddenly defending the pinkest edges of the feminine side of a slider scale that had shifted on us.

The problem is when the policing of each other's expressions creeps in. Sophie and I had been judgy in the South. But now, on the receiving end and while watching you grow up, we knew that there had to be room for all expressions of gender. As RuPaul famously put it, "We're all born naked, and the rest is drag." We had to be open to everyone's gender expression, including those who play at the edges, those who mix and match in between, those who keep it androgynous—all of us in our various acts of daily drag.

26

LET'S TALK ABOUT ERASURE.

A few years after we'd moved, we made a new friend. She was a mother of three children, one of whom had fairly pronounced autism. Her son and Isaac had a sweet relationship, having met in theater performances. She'd fought for her son to participate in those school functions, which was his right by law. We decided to confide in her. I can still see her, standing in the doorway to our kitchen. I was the one to explain. Jeff was getting something to drink.

She said, "Oh, I had no idea. But around here . . ." She made a gesture—raising her hand to her mouth. "It's like, big yawn, right?"

We had moved to this town because gender wasn't something that caused distress or led to allegations and knocks at the door. But I wasn't prepared for a "big yawn."

Also, this was a woman who had to live in fear for her son's life. He was tall and broad. We'd seen him on a walk near their house. He was flapping his arms. His gait was erratic. He could be misunderstood, feared. People could call the cops. What then? Could her son follow the police instructions?

I couldn't begin to understand her fears for her son. But big yawn felt like a dismissal. It felt . . . white and northern and privileged, all of which she was. But maybe also accurate. And yet, at the same time, my health insurance policy was calling you a psychosexual deviant. I felt trapped between two poles. But they both had something in common. Neither particularly cared about your transness, but for opposite reasons. How do both of these things exist at the same time within the same country? (America is really lots of little countries held loosely together by the idea of a country.) How do you tread water between these poles? What if I treated everything that I think about gender and violence and the future and this country as a big yawn?

I didn't know what to do with this seemingly woke indifference.

She wasn't in any way trying to be mean. She was saying that we'd found the right place. We were safe here. *Big yawn.* I was stunned by her inability to draw parallels. Both of our children were living in different worlds than we were. They were dangerous. They were seen as threats.

Big yawn—it was so quick that it felt knee-jerk, almost primal. What did she gain by dismissing your experience so quickly and with such finality?

Actually, I think she had a lot to gain.

When you tell someone a story about discrimination or someone's transphobia or bizarre behavior around your body, your gender, there will be people who diminish it. What I've found is that these reactions usually come from my cisgender and straight and white family and friends—people you love very much and people who love you, unconditionally.

My friends of color or those raising children of color or children with disabilities or children who are transgender, for example, usually get quieter as I tell a story like this. They seem to know what's coming before the story finds its pivot. They nod along like this is a song they know well. They'll vent for me sometimes, as if they know I'm too weary to vent for myself. They'll get real, if I need it, offering very specific advice. Sometimes they'll ask what I need.

Why do cisgender, straight, white people often find this so hard to do? Why do they move so quickly to make excuses for the person who's done you wrong? Why do they look for holes in your story? Why do they diminish and dismiss?

One evening, I texted a short version of a transphobic experience you and I had just experienced to one of my closest friends. She's white, cis, and straight, and able-bodied, and she knows personally how hard it is to tell a story like this. She has survived violence.

She first wrote, "What's wrong with people?" And then quickly added, "But there are good people in the world too," as if I'd forgotten good people, as if in telling this story I was indicting good people all over the world or negating them. Why would she feel the need to remind me of all the other "good people" while I'm telling the story of one specific person? Was she trying to give me hope? Was she trying to defend her own goodness? She didn't need to. I know her goodness and love. Why did this response surface so quickly?

Do some people simply not like conflict? Do they want nicer stories?

Do they choose to believe that something was just a misunderstanding because they don't want to admit to the immorality of humanity? If there's less acknowledged evil in the world, is this a form of magical thinking that there's less actual evil? That's not how evil works. It works in the opposite way. If ignored, it grows stronger.

Was my friend, in that moment, acting as a survivor of violence? Was she triggered by the story, and, in reminding me of the goodness of others, was she reminding herself? Is this how trauma operates on some level? Do we need to keep believing and reminding each other of goodness in order to make it through our days intact?

I love this friend so much that this is where I want to land.

But I can't—not completely. When someone diminishes the story, they are trying to spare the person they love from something awful that has happened to them. By denying it, by poking holes in it, they are trying to erase it. If they can shift your perception of it, then they think they can make it go away.

But having someone deny your experience or diminish it or poke holes in it or make excuses for those who've done awful things, all of this isolates the person who's experienced this awfulness. It can send the message that they're crazy or whiny or unreliable or overly dramatic. It can make them doubt what they know to be true. It can make them doubt themselves. It can definitely make them resent the person who's doing this to them. It can make them shut down to this person who loves them, whom they love.

There is no question that this dear friend of mine is truly an auntie, full of love for you. This is why it's all the more important. When this kind of thing comes from someone you love and who loves you, you should call them on it. When they do it to someone else in your presence, you should call them on it. That's what love needs.

They're so fleeting, these little moments, that it's easy to let them go. I'm guilty of it. But they can accumulate and get in the way of love.

This is what we do for those we love. We tell our stories. We listen. We mess up. We do better.

SO, THE OBVIOUS: YOUR father and I can't know what it's like to live the transgender experience. We can't begin to know what we don't know and how differently we might parent if we were transgender ourselves.

As a result, we're often caught off guard by the ways in which transgender issues suddenly appear. As you well know, the fact that you're transgender is usually just not part of an ordinary day. Tennis lessons, a Zoom dance class, your dog-walking job, playing cards with your grandmother, getting bubble tea with friends. . . . But then, when least expected, there it is.

Like this: You came home from a seventh-grade field trip to a Holocaust museum where you met Izydor Einziger, a 101-year-old Holocaust survivor. I remind you that we very likely have Jewish ancestry—a man who immigrated to America in the 1800s from France. If he is our ancestor, he left behind his Jewish identity, and I wonder now, at what cost? Was it liberating or lonesome or both?

I asked you if the museum guide mentioned the pink triangles that gay, lesbian, transgender, and queer people had to pin to their coats. I hadn't yet taught you this part of history.

"Uh-huh," you said.

I explained that in Berlin in the lead-up to Hitler's rise, a man named Magnus Hirschfeld created the Institute for Sexology, a library and archive that also offered counseling. More than twenty thousand people visited the institute every year. Hirschfeld hired transgender staff and promoted tolerance and basic rights for LGBTQ+ people. He built relationships with law enforcement, getting them to stop harassing people who were dressing against gender norms. He coined the term *transsexual*.

But then came the Nazis. "There's a famous picture of Nazis burning books," I told you. "In the foreground, there's the bust of a man thrown into the fire. That's a statue of Hirschfeld himself. And the books are those from his library. The burning was carried out by kids—the Nazi youth brigades. They burned the books and archival materials in a pyre in the street."

What I didn't tell you: Hirschfeld's institute had lists of clients, including their addresses. The list was used to round people up, send them to death camps, or kill them—some executions were part of the Night of the Long Knives.

(It's not just Hitler. It's the playbook of every despot and wannabe authoritarian. Look up Franco, Pinochet, the Spanish conquistadors. Look at the moves of the Trump administration, the first act of Jeff Sessions when he was appointed to the Department of Justice. It's always the same.)

When Obama was president, the federal government allowed for a change of gender markers on passports. We went through the process for you. But then the Trump administration took over. Their turn on transgender rights was swift. We'd been planning on going through the process to change your name and gender on your birth certificate but decided not to go through with it. I became more afraid of the list.

By making the change to your passport, did we voluntarily sign you up on a national registry of transgender people? Did we add your name to a list like Hirschfield's?

Your assignment following the field trip was to write a thank-you letter to the Holocaust survivor. While you were thinking about what to say, you told me the way Izadore Einziger explained how it happened. "The government took these small steps and then—pow!—everything changed. It all went so fast."

You read your thank-you letter to me. "I wish more people could hear your story, especially about the small steps and then how fast things changed. I think it would change a lot of people's minds today."

During the four years of the Trump presidency, I saw the small steps. I saw them being taken all the time. We were a nation tripping forward, falling—an accumulation of quick steps, some messy, some insanely precise.

When the Biden administration took office, I felt some peace, but I'm still migratory. Some part of me will always be looking for safe places for us to land. I recognize this instinct in me as the same instinct that my immigrant ancestors felt.

A field trip. A beautiful and painful gift from a Holocaust survivor sharing his story. It landed differently in this household. It landed differently on you. I can't measure that weight. I can't know how it will be a memory that comes back to you, changed by time and perspective. I can only open up this space and hold it for you.

Or like this:

It was a boring day. We were on the sofa with our feet kicked up on the ottoman. We teed up the trailer for *Rat Race*. "The older kids loved this movie when they were your age."

During the two-and-a-half-minute trailer, there are not one but two transphobic jokes.

Cuba Gooding Jr.'s character orders a drink. "Miss, can I have another one of these?"

The bartender, who's sporting a vest and a short haircut, turns around.

"Oh sorry, I thought you were a woman," Gooding's character says. This actually makes no sense because, especially from behind, this person could be mistaken for a man.

"I am a woman," the bartender says.

This is supposedly hilarious. Why? Gooding's face falters. Are we laughing at Gooding's character making a mistake? Or at the bartender who doesn't conform to the expression of gender that we expect?

Seconds later, a Lucille Ball impersonator complains to Gooding, who's now driving a bus full of Lucille Ball impersonators, that the bathroom door is broken. "Anyone could come in."

"You ain't got nothing the other Lucys haven't seen already," Gooding says. Again, this joke is off because it's something one would usually say to a man, not a woman. Women's privacy in bathrooms is a given. Even in a single-occupant bathroom, there's nothing to see. It's the absence not a presence of a penis.

Lucy's voice drops to bass. "Not necessarily."

Gooding screams in pure terror, horrified by this confession. He yanks the wheel, and the bus veers off dangerously.

After the trailer, we were quiet.

"Well, that was pretty transphobic," I finally said.

"Yeah."

These moments are impersonal—flashing across the screen, piped in by the speaker—and yet they're little knives. They come at you with no warning. They cut. And, at the same time, they dole out little knives to anyone who sees these scenes, teaching fear.

I circled back to the trailer later that night, as you were getting ready for bed. "What did you think about the transphobic jokes?"

You shrugged.

I explained why they seemed awful. I asked how they made you feel.

But you didn't want to talk about it.

I don't know where these things go—is there a vault inside of you? Do these things pile up?

One night while watching old *3rd Rock from the Sun* episodes on TV, we saw one where Sally is mistaken for a trans woman and starts dating a man who finds out she has typical female anatomy and rejects her. It's a twist. "For the time period," you said, "it wasn't as bad as it could have been." For a twelve-year-old, it was a keen observation.

I know not to let you watch *South Park*, which has offered up some of the most grotesque and brutal antitransgender stuff on television—and, most of all, lazy comedy. The sin of lazy comedy is hard to forgive in our household. There are so many reasons not to watch *Ace Ventura Pet Detective*, in addition to the transphobia, that it's easy to ward off.

You've seen *Tootsie*. I told you what it was about first. You wanted to watch it. You enjoyed it and saw no connection to your own life. Why should you? He's not trans. I recently asked you if you remembered the movie, and you said, "The one about the woman with the little girl. Jessica Lange, right?" The omission of the main plot was noted.

What will you think of *Some Like It Hot* and *The Bird Cage*? Will you seek out the heartbreak of films like *Boys Don't Cry*, *The Crying Game*, *Dallas Buyer's Club*, *The Danish Girl*, or *Welcome Back to the Five and Dime, Jimmy Dean*? What about the horror films in which the psychotic killer is a man dressed as a woman or trans or . . . the gender identity isn't clear because they weren't really thinking of that character as truly human? Some films like *Paris Is Burning* will announce themselves. (It's beautiful and heart-wrecking and inspiring.)

But you won't always get a warning. How do I parent you to brace yourself and yet not live your life bracing?

I hope for more shows like *Orange Is the New Black* and *Pose* in which trans women are finally playing trans women. And *Mrs. Fletcher*, where the trans character's transness is—and also beautifully isn't—part of the plot. I want you to see someone like yourself in film and television and in books, to see that you're not alone. But I don't want you to stop at trans representation. Look at portrayals of women and people of color and people with disabilities and gay, lesbian, bisexual, and queer people—and all of the people who, in one way or another, are treated as other.

You adore Melissa McCarthy. How many times does she get hit by cars, tumble downstairs, fall from great heights? Why is her body treated like she is less human than the bodies of skinny actors?

Our culture doesn't treat all bodies equally, especially bodies that are not white and able and sanctioned. There are consequences to how people are portrayed: the murder of Black people by people who are supposed to protect and serve—Tamir Rice, Philando Castile, Trayvon Martin, George Floyd, Breonna Taylor, Michael Brown, and Tony McDade, who was both Black and transgender, to name just a few. Why did George Zimmerman feel like it was his right to kill Trayvon Martin? And the history of lynchings . . . Black bodies hanging from trees. Why hang them from trees? Why leave Michael Brown's body in the street for four hours, except to further terrorize a community?

This violence, this aggression, it's unpredictable. You never know when it's coming or what form it will take or how swiftly it mutates. Hatred of the other, once practiced, is easily transferrable. If someone has practiced hatred for Black people, it's easy for them to direct that hatred at Asians or Jews or Muslims or lesbians or transgender people—whatever event, in a given moment, provides an occasion for their rage and fear and repositions them in a place of power, power they feel the need to protect in every way.

The Human Rights Commission Foundation reports on violence against transgender people each year. Like the American Medical Association, they have labeled it an epidemic. Being Black and transgender and a woman in this country are seen as multiple comorbidities—or multiple morbidities. *Morbidities* mean having a disease or symptom of a disease, or the overall number of those with diseases in a specific population. *Mortality* is the term used when discussing someone's risk of dying. Morbidities, if unchecked, can increase the risk of mortality. Being Black, transgender, and a woman are not medical issues. It's our society that is diseased with racism, transphobia, and sexism. These diseased ways of thinking are what leads to violence, suicide, death, and murder.

How do I walk the line? How do I explain the world out there while not terrifying you, while in fact encouraging you to claim your place within it?

Your cousins started it. Instead of listening to noise cancellation or relaxation tapes or rain sounds to fall asleep, they played Harry Potter audiobooks. They became a bedtime story that wound into their dreams. Sophie started doing it, and now you do too.

In the summer of 2020, Americans—and allies around the world—took to the streets to protest police brutality in the wake of the murder of George Floyd, an unarmed Black man killed by a policeman, Derek Chauvin—during a worldwide pandemic causing massive unemployment and financial losses and a rising death toll. Officer Chauvin bore down on Floyd with his knee on Floyd's neck for eight minutes and forty-six seconds while Floyd begged for his life and other cops stood by, witnessing his murder. As the Black Lives Matter movement became a force, the author of the Harry Potter books, J. K. Rowling, was tweeting her bigoted opinions about transgender people.

Her tweets aren't worth repeating. But in some, she was disguising her bigotry as concern for trans kids who are getting excellent medical care from gender-identity experts—as if kids with this level of support and medical access are in need of . . . *her*? Meanwhile the trans community begs her to stop.

To me, it's about preserving her own identity as a victim. Meanwhile, she's empowering TERFs (trans-exclusionary radical feminists) who rail against trans women, whom they see as men in disguise as women and therefore as threats. This isn't rational. They don't know you. It's not about you. Except it is. Rowling is a powerful voice, leading the charge against your rights. This is where the far left meets the far right and they work in unison.

There's a lot of power in being a victim. Never underestimate the ways in which someone, especially someone from the dominant culture, will cling to victimhood.

The timing of Rowling's rants against trans people is curious. Why divert attention from the Black Lives Matter movement? Was she avoiding a confrontation with her own racism—an area where she cannot claim to be a victim in any way? Was it a way around facing the devastating and urgent issues of Black people—in America but also around the world—by drawing attention to a group that she finds threatening? In railing against trans people, she reclaimed herself as a victim. The idea is that victims aren't perpetrators; victims remain innocent; victims deserve our love and support. Why does Rowling so desperately need love and support? I have no idea. Why is she going about it in this seemingly self-destructive way? Unclear. But Rowling is a piece of work, and she has become a vocal leader for a larger demographic, one that is troubled and troubling.

And also a group that is often well educated. But remember, intellect can close the heart as quickly as ignorance can. With ignorance, you can hope that knowledge will lead to new understanding. This is unlikely when the intellectual has already built a fortress of bigoted ideology.

What keeps surprising me is how hard it is to predict who will get it and who won't. This often falls on political and religious lines, on generational lines, and on gender lines—but not always. Friends who've stepped up for us include a retired New York City cop and an evangelical minister in Texas.

So, do we ban Rowling in our house, the author of these books that we love? How do we reject the maker but hold onto the gift?

Luckily we have Daniel Radcliffe. While playing Harry Potter during his formative years, he seems to have absorbed the greater truths of Rowling's books, the ones lost on her. While she caterwauls into hatred and misinformation, he's rock solid. He stated unequivocally, "Transgender women are women." And then he explained this: "If these books taught you that love is the strongest force in the universe, capable of overcoming anything; if they taught you that strength is found in diversity, and that dogmatic ideas of pureness lead to the oppression of vulnerable groups; if you believe that a particular character is trans, nonbinary, or gender fluid, or that they are gay or bisexual; if you found anything in these stories that resonated with you and helped you at any time in your life—then that is between you and the book that you read, and it is sacred."

As someone who's not transgender raising someone who is, I see your gifts, ones I never had.

First of all, you developed a sense of self far ahead of other kids whose senses of self fit more tidily within the culture around them. Your sense of self is heightened. How could it not be?

And your sense of everyone in your environment is heightened too. You've been practicing something the other kids haven't been.

When I introduce you to people, you nod, but you don't offer to shake hands. You're quiet. You eye them. You pay attention. You know what I never do? I never tell you to be warmer. I never tell you to shake hands. I never tell you to smile. I prefer your nod, your quiet watchful eye.

Your ability to see people who are like you is heightened too. You once saw a kid who'd recently transitioned at your school look at you from across a crowded cafeteria—you immediately knew by that look that he'd been told you were transgender. By the time he gathered his courage to ask you about it on the bus on the way home, you were ready with an answer that confused him and diffused the moment. It bought you time to make a plan, and we did.

You've been operating on a different plane for as long as you can remember. Your superpowers are senses that science doesn't really fully understand yet. They're so much a part of who you are that you take them for granted.

And while you're reading everyone in a room, you can be nearly invisible. You have an uncanny ability to blend in. But your ability to go unseen is only matched by your ability to stand out when you want to.

The second gift might be that you understand that you have a kind of superpower.

While we lived in this New England college town, your transness was like a secret identity. I suddenly realized that children's literature and media are full of characters with secret identities. Because I was raising you, I was more aware of what we show others, what we keep to ourselves, and how a secret identity can also be a very authentic one.

We noticed secret identities everywhere—*Hannah Montana*, *The Witches of Waverly Place*, *K. C. Undercover*, *Kid Danger*, *The Incredibles*—and almost every other superhero story. Harry Potter had a secret identity that he himself didn't know about or understand until he was invited to Hogwarts, where he found his people. You went through your *Charmed* and *Buffy the Vampire Slayer* phases with great devotion. These obsessions have always been there in our culture—*My Favorite Martian*, *Three's Company*, *I Dream of Jeannie*, *The Count of Monte Christo*, *Ethan Frome*, *Back to the Future*, so much of Shakespeare, throughout mythology and the New Testament and the Old Testament. Who do we reveal our true selves to and under what circumstances?

And *Shrek*! Fiona has a version of herself thought to be ugly by society. She's hiding it. But she's loved by Shrek as a whole, and that love and acceptance allow the hidden self to become the true self.

"She's never the old her again," you told me once. "She's the new her forever."

In kids' shows, the main character usually has to tell a friend about their true identity. It's a big deal. This friend has to react the right way. And they always do. They are now in this together.

As we created a circle of people who would have our back if things went wrong, you continued to tell a few friends.

But then you stopped. Friendship dynamics changed—not because you came out, but because friendship dynamics change as a matter of course. You regretted telling those people. By third grade, you realized that you couldn't unring a bell.

This regret was one reason you stopped. But there was another.

"When I tell people, they don't get it," you confided.

"What don't they get?" I asked.

"They don't get that it makes me special."

Exactly. You don't want someone to react with anger or hostility, but you also don't want someone to react with a shrug. You were receiving the innocent kidlike version of the big yawn.

People will say that you're asking too much by not wanting to get beaten up but also not wanting someone to shrug at you. Some might think that the LGBTQ+ community should be happy just to *not* get beaten up. They should see the shrug as progress and shut the hell up. (Some LGBTQ+ folks are being raised in an unreadable rotation of being beaten up, shrugged at, and being told to shut the hell up.)

You can't control how people can react, but it is a gift that you see your identity as something special. We all have complex inner selves. To love that inner self, to know you're special, is something some people never experience.

And this brings me to the complexities of beauty. I see this, too, as one of your gifts, your understanding of beauty, from the inside out.

When I was younger, I hated it when the boys in high school and grown men, strangers, told me to smile. I'm not alone in this. Sometimes the suggestion was more pointed: *You're prettier when you smile.*

Usually, I ignored them, but when I was sick of it, I'd say, "You want me to smile? Earn it."

This seemed to confuse them. They'd already earned it—they were men. I was supposed to want to be pretty and to please them. "What?" they'd say.

And I'd explain the function of smiling. "Smiling is the response to something funny. Say something funny, and we'll see if it makes me smile."

Nothing much ever followed this. Some awkwardness, some uncomfortable shifting around. Occasionally a bad joke. Stone-faced, I'd move on.

Well, there was one other thing I'd do sometimes. The comment was usually said while the guy was watching people walk by. It was more catcall than conversational. So sometimes, I'd turn back around and flash the ugliest, most terrifying smile I could deliver. A stiffened grimace, jaggedly asymmetrical and pained. I'd whip back around before hearing their reaction.

Here's the thing. You're pretty. You've got those big blue eyes, thick slightly curly hair, this perfect nose—no idea where that nose came from. You're sometimes glam. You're always put together.

At a transgender conference, I was talking to a friend of mine. We were watching you and her daughter and two other girls chatting and laughing.

I said, "They're pretty. Each of them. It makes me nervous. Other girls get jealous. Will it make them more of a target?"

My friend turned to me. "Pretty is always easier. Always."

In an episode of the BBC show *Sherlock*, Holmes and Dr. Watson are drunkenly playing a game of forehead detective. Watson has a sticky note scrawled with *Madonna* stuck to his forehead. Trying to guess his own identity, he asks, "Am I pretty?"

Sherlock answers, "Beauty is a construct based entirely on childhood impressions, influences, and role models."

Sherlock is right—but not completely. Sometimes people have to fight childhood impressions and influences. They haven't had role models for their kind of beauty and have to forge the path themselves.

Take Lizzo for example. She's forging her own path. Her expression of her beauty, the way she claims it, doesn't just make her freer. She's freeing others. After you saw her in the orange ruffled Valentino dress she wore to the American Music Awards, you bought material and re-created it without a pattern. You painted a purple Barbie purse white to match Lizzo's iconic tiny purse. So now she has become a childhood impression and influence, a role model for all kinds of beauty.

Beauty and identity are inextricably bound.

That summer before you transitioned, you used these words: "When you say I'm beautiful, say *she, she* is beautiful." If I saw you as beautiful but as a beautiful boy, that didn't work. It was broken. You needed to be seen for your beauty and as a girl. Both.

Laverne Cox talks about her beauty this way: "It took me years to internalize that someone could look at me and tell that I am transgender—that is not only OK, that is beautiful. Trans is beautiful. All the things that make me uniquely and beautifully trans, my big hands, my big feet, my wide shoulders, my deep voice, are beautiful."

Laverne came to our New England town to speak at the university. The only two people in our family who could make it were your brothers. Isaac came home and told us how intellectual the talk was. "She's a genius."

Tate talked about the crowd. "It was packed. There had to be over a thousand people there," he said. "All those people who'd come to see her, they loved her. It made me feel better." That adoring crowd made him feel like you were safer than he thought. I wonder what you would have thought of her. What would you have needed to see?

Ian Harvie, a comedian and trans man, has a fantastic TED Talk. In it, he says, "No one inside this room and no one outside this room feels one hundred percent okay about [their] body in direct relationship to [their] masculinity, [their] femininity, and [their] gender; and if you do then you're the weirdo."

Gender and beauty are social constructs. But they're also inner truths. They belong to us. Each of us. They are ours. Beauty isn't just how we're perceived. It's about who we are. When a southerner says, "Don't be ugly," they aren't talking about looks. Just as when we say, "This is a beautiful person, a beautiful human being," we aren't talking about their appearance.

Watson doesn't accept Sherlock's answer. "Yeah," he says, "but am I a pretty lady?"

A pretty lady. Who gets to say?

What I'm driving at is that beauty and gender reside at the collision of the demands put on women, both transgender and not, by a sexist, misogynistic culture and the center of your being. They are the trappings—from the outside in—and they run deep—from the inside out.

Your father and I are raising you, not just you as a transgender kid but specifically *you*. And so we get to see things in a new way, questioning what, before, we simply allowed or didn't see or didn't have the courage to acknowledge that we saw. We now get to walk through this world with our senses attuned to so much more than we ever imagined.

You are radical, through no choice of your own. But sometimes the most radical thing anyone can do is express joy, pride, beauty, and ugliness, an uncustomary way of living a life, a creation of happiness.

And sometimes you simply have to take care of yourself. Audre Lorde wrote in *A Burst of Light*, "Caring for myself is not self-indulgence, it is self-preservation, and that is an act of political warfare."

Some of us are handed a life and accept it. No questions asked.

Some of us are built to ask questions.

Some are handed a life and—with so many questions—make art from it.

DURING ALL OF THIS, I felt unbelievable pressure to make money, mistakenly deciding that money had saved us and could continue to keep us safe. As Jeff was working out and getting fit (and seemingly younger), I was sleepless with worry. I was the sole breadwinner. We'd waded into two college tuition payments for the older kids, and Tate was starting his senior year of high school. My fears about not making enough money, and working harder as a result, were some of the most obvious manifestations of my need to protect the family.

I'd been pulled back to half-time at my old job in the South as part of the deal to continue to work from afar. I applied for other jobs and got some of them. Part of the job search was about finding work that would get better health insurance coverage from those northern states where it's illegal to discriminate in health insurance against trans people. Some of those jobs were labor-intensive. I was moving between institutions and cultures. In addition to my commute that took two plane rides to get back to that southern town to work in person at different times throughout the year, I was commuting to a job a few days a week that was an hour away. By the time you were in fourth grade, I was working at a job that was two and a half hours away. I spent the night there a couple of days a week.

That fall was a disaster. Sophie went to a postgraduate program back in the state we'd left. She quickly learned that they didn't have the facilities she needed to do the work she'd proposed. While she was packing up to come home, she got bit by a loose dog. She had to start a series of rabies shots. Isaac, who'd previously been doing well in his college in Chicago, was quietly tanking. We'd learn about it at Christmas when he came home to tell us that he wanted to quit college altogether. Meanwhile, that was the fall when Tate got sick.

It was a lucky turn, in retrospect, that Sophie's postgrad program had gone badly. While we were at the hospital with Tate, she watched over you.

It was a scary time. You and Sophie turned your bedroom into a sewing room. You made a tent for your bedroom, a pair of bright-yellow overalls, and the surreal costumes of your favorite Japanese pop star. She kept you busy and focused. By the time Tate came home, you'd created a show, making a giant shadow version of yourself, casting it onto a sheet as the music started up for your grand entrance. It was exactly what we needed.

Afterward, I went back to commuting and juggling jobs and workloads. I was also still working on my own projects, and I'd volunteered to be the intake coordinator at the organization that had helped us so much when we were in crisis. People would leave messages that would come to an email address. I'd call them back, ask questions, offer resources.

I was trained by a woman who was the grandmother of a trans boy on the West Coast. She'd been the single intake coordinator for more than ten years. This was a time when there was very little research on transgender kids. (There still isn't a wealth of research.) She was a resource beyond measure. She knew the most common ways that trans girls transitioned versus trans boys. (Your assertion of your gender identity at such a young age was more typical of trans girls. Her theory was that transgender boys can sometimes exist comfortably under the tomboy umbrella, whereas trans girls aren't as protected and have to fight to be who they are at an earlier age. But often the trans boys' transitions were urgent and seemed sudden to their parents, when their bodies betrayed them in puberty.) She was, I'd argue, one of the most important researchers in the country, though she didn't think of herself as a researcher. Her anecdotal evidence was massive. She'd interviewed hundreds, maybe thousands, of transgender kids' parents and was the sole keeper of the data, data she'd absorbed. I took notes. I told her to write it all down too, to keep it, maybe one day to find a way to share it.

Now when I google her name, which isn't common or uncommon, she isn't to be found. If I google her name and the word transgender, nothing comes up. Her work is completely invisible.

There are a number of women out there like her. The internet was born, and people who once felt completely alone could find others facing similar issues. Listservs, group chats, and Facebook groups emerged. Friendships and alliances. Things began to change.

What I've discovered over time is that there are secret societies. When I had my first miscarriage after Sophie and Isaac were born, women I'd known all my life told me that they'd been through it too. Unlike loud, rabid Red Sox fans, these secret societies function quietly around certain forms of loss and grief and illness and love and advocacy and mutual support.

The parents of transgender kids who show up at the conferences, who show up for their kids, whom we've become friends with are some of the best humans I know.

I think you'll find this to be true. A specialist once told me that being trans works like a miner sifting for gold. You might lose some people along the way, but not the golden ones.

When the intake coordinator was handing off the job to me, she said, "I get fewer criers now. When we first started, mothers—it's almost always mothers—would just break down. But it's getting better." She was hopeful.

She was also the keeper of a secret list. The list, crowdsourced from transgender families throughout the country, was of pediatricians who would care for transgender kids and provide resources and information. We were never to give the entire list to anyone, but we could dole out names of doctors in certain areas of the country to people who lived there. And we could grow the list. The fear was that if the list were to become public, doctors, especially those in certain regions, would be retaliated against.

I was daunted by the job. But calls came in and I started the work. I talked to parents—again, almost always mothers—about their gender-nonconforming and transgender kids. I talked to people all over the country—military families, deeply religious families, and progressive families. I talked to parents of children of different ethnicities, races, and religions; parents of children who had underlying chronic conditions; who were on the autism spectrum; or who were so intellectually advanced that they were skipping ahead in their grades, their educations barely able to keep pace with them. I seemed to be on the parents' side, but everything I said to those parents was for their children. This work was meaningful and overwhelming. I'm not sure exactly how long I did it—six months to a year, I think.

I will say that the need for this organization was dwindling. Resources were popping up all over the place. The very idea of a transgender child, which had been so baffling just a few years earlier, was now clearly established. There were conferences and guidelines and supports from major medical institutions. Health conferences about transgender care and rights popped up all over the country, and they now included a track for families.

We were living in the fourth and final house over the course of what would be six years in that town. We'd sold the house we'd bought because we were planning to move farther north once Tate graduated, to live closer to the job that was two and half hours away. This was a rental. Its exterior seemed Soviet Bloc–inspired. In the spring, when the ice and snow melted, the playroom flooded wildly. The inside was chopped up with short flights of stairs leading here and there. The fireplace was blocked by a piece of plywood painted bright red. Squirrels would get trapped there, and we'd have to let them loose in the house with all of the doors wide open. After skittering and banging around, they'd find their way back to the wild. In watching them go, it seemed they were the lucky ones.

Having become addicted to the idea of flight, we tried to live as if able to pick up and leave at any moment. We were getting ready to move, but we wouldn't end up where we thought we were headed.

One morning, I woke up in the on-campus housing that was provided for me at my new job. It was a small but stately Victorian, sparsely furnished. The heat was unreliable, and I brought a space heater with me each week. I wouldn't run it during the night, for fear it would start a fire. So I woke up in a chilly bedroom.

This particular fall morning, there was a text from Jeff. *I'm so sorry. I saw the message. Are you okay?*

I had no idea what he meant. I started to flip through my various messages. I found one. A student had written to tell me that her partner had died by suicide. I hadn't met her partner, but I knew she was a trans woman.

The student who wrote the message was in shock. She wrote few details. She didn't need to. I knew the statistics around suicide attempt rates within the transgender community. Like so many parents of transgender kids, I knew that this was the greatest health risk to my own child. This tragedy demanded a moment of grace. I did what I could to help, to comfort. I didn't do enough.

Later that day, I was scheduled to teach a five-hour class. Everyone in that small class knew the woman who had died. I told them that I had sad news. I told them of the death.

There was shock and sadness.

"Of course, each of you is welcome to go home and process this," I said. "We do not have to have class today at all. But I've found, weirdly, that having to focus on something else is helpful. The work we do here could hold us for a little while. I'm willing to do that. If it would be helpful to any of you, you can stay."

Remarkably, they stayed. We spent those hours together, protected by the work at hand. We sat at the long table, talking about words and images and how people navigate small moments of their lives. We stayed together for those hours, each of us there for the others.

———

The death of my student's partner shook me, but I didn't want to talk about it.

Jeff was surprised by my avoidance. "You always want to talk through things."

"I'm Greatest-Generationing this," I told him. I Greatest-Generationed as much as I could that fall. I'd never imagined the power in not talking through. But now, as I see it looking back, I felt so helpless, so out of control that my not talking was a way to maintain some measure of control. I worked harder. I buried myself in my work. Toward the end of that semester, Jeff was worried about me. "Are you sure you're okay?"

I had this recurring daydream. "It plays out like this," I told him. "I'm talking to a student or a colleague and my arm falls off."

"Like onto the floor?"

"No, it just becomes detached, but here's the disturbing part."

"Your arm becoming detached isn't the disturbing part?"

"I just lift it and shove it back into place, and I say, 'Oh, sorry. Never mind that. You were saying?'"

"That's definitely not good."

I went to a therapist. She'd been raised ultra-Catholic. She got me.

———

What I realized:

This job wasn't right for me.

I needed to stop working so hard.

Though it had helped, money hadn't saved us.

The truth is that the people you love save you.

You save the people you love.

Sometimes that love allows you to try to do for others.

Sometimes that's enough. Sometimes there is no *enough*.

I wanted to go home, to be nearer to my own parents, my old friends, to live in a place I once knew.

Part IV

NOW

29

WE MOVED AGAIN. THIS time back to my home state, which is technically the North but very close to the South. In fact, we live so close to the Mason-Dixon Line, we seem to teeter on it. This is where we'd lived when your dad and I were first married. Your siblings were born here and remember some of their early childhoods in a house just around the corner from where we live now. We left long before you were born. Our bedroom windows on the second floor look out at trees, and on summer nights like these, the fireflies are vivid and magnificent. They seem huge in the darkness, each sending up an urgent flare.

This is now—quiet and still with urgent flares.

We weren't sure that we were going to land in my home state for good. It was as if the epigenetics of migration, the need for it in order to survive, had been pulled to the surface of my DNA and become a way of life. We were in motion again.

My parents spend much of the fall in the mountains, and so their house was going to be empty. We decided to use it as a home base. I still had my job in the South but also lined up speaking engagements to help make up for the loss of money from the other job I'd left behind. You and your dad traveled with me. We took your education on the road.

Moving from hotel room to hotel room, in those small spaces, you used the objects around you to make art. You found a large bead that had fallen off a necklace, and stringing it on a piece of dental floss that you hooked over one ear, you re-created Vermeer's *Girl with a Pearl Earring*. Using the plastic zipper bags used to store those fuzzy hotel blankets, you created a large see-through headdress that sat, regal and nouveau, on your head. You took two of the wooden hangers from the closet, and using one of your belts, you fashioned a pair of steampunk wings. This is your way of looking at the world—for moments of transformation, adornment. Just last night you picked up an empty overturned laundry basket and said, "If I cut a hole in the bottom and stepped into it, I could make a kind of square hoop skirt, and then hang laundry from it—socks and dresses."

Your on-the-road education also had the traditional aspects. We kept up with math and science. We built history curriculum around the places we landed. It lasted for a couple of months, but each time we came back to our home base, we settled in a bit more. Your father was asked to teach a course or two at the local university and to help out with a nonprofit. I felt of use being near my aging parents, and I'd missed them while we were living so far away. Your dad and I were closer to old friends and family again.

But things weren't ideal for you. Here were a few clues. You were excited about visiting with your grandparents' elderly friends. You looked forward to seeing Meryl's collection of souvenirs from her travels in Japan. You'd sing lyrics to '80s songs while walking the dogs. Your Halloween costume ideas were actors all the rage in the 1930s and '40s. In short, you needed friends your own age. You needed besties and mean girls and kids talking about crushes. You needed slang and gossip and access to teachers who actually knew how to teach math.

We sent you to the small progressive school Sophie and Isaac had gone to before we moved South. You were not their first transgender student. It turned out to be an excellent fit.

We found a house that suited us. We bought it and moved in before Christmas. We hosted the family holiday party with all the generations, aunts and uncles and cousins. It was rowdy and fun.

A friend of mine said, "Sometimes it's nice to be in a place where you know all the roads."

For the first time in years, I felt rooted, like we might just stay here for a long while.

STILL, NOWHERE IS PERFECT. This is what I had to accept. Leaving and leaving and leaving wasn't going to save us.

When we arrived, you were starting sixth grade. This started a three-year clock to figure out high school. I got in touch with all kinds of high schools—private, public, charter, and Catholic. I asked people at the various high schools if they had experience with transgender students and if they had policies in place. Would you be allowed to use the girls' bathroom, wear the girls' uniform, play in girls' sports (though sports weren't your thing), have the right name on transcripts, the yearbook, your diploma; have teachers and staff address you with the right pronouns, not the ones that might be found in a school-wide system. . . .

Most of your education had been in the public school system. But I wasn't ready to send you to the big public high school in town. Its reputation had gotten rougher over the years. The charter schools—only one of which seemed like a fit, educationally—were nearly impossible to get into, either not quite in our district or using a lotto system for entrance with very few available spots for incoming ninth graders. The nonreligious private schools would cost almost $100,000 for your four years. After seeing your older siblings through college tuitions, we needed to focus on saving for your undergrad experience.

This left the Catholic schools, which, by and large, were significantly less expensive. In this area, there are a lot of them.

Was I really considering a Catholic school for my transgender daughter?

Keep in mind that my main concern going forward is boys and boys turning into men. When you come home from school, you're frustrated by the boys—the things they say, what they do, their immaturity. But what's worse is how the girls have started to gravitate to them, giggle at their mean jokes, get giddy and flirty. You've started to notice how girls betray other girls, how they don't stand up for each other.

What's school like for you? Now, in middle school, there are tough days, as is true of almost every middle school experience. One night, as you were getting ready for bed, I asked you how often you used to be aware that you're trans when you were in elementary school. "Did it ever just appear in your head that you were different in this way?"

"Yes," you said. "Maybe once a week."

"What about now?"

You didn't have to think long. "A few times a day."

The drumbeat is getting louder and faster, harder to ignore—more intrusive.

Your school doesn't put up with bullying, but when the teachers aren't around, you still hear the words boys use to taunt each other. You don't like those taunts, and you don't giggle at the boys' dumb jokes the way your all-girl circle of friends sometimes does. And the boys like a giggly audience. You're annoyed when the girls allow the boys to treat them badly. You hate when the girls don't stick up for each other. In this way, your girlhood and mine are pretty similar; I was annoyed by these dynamics, and I still am—they are a recurring theme. You'd prefer it if there was a little more Beyoncé-in-formation. In fact, I'd say that your main concerns are feminist.

You want to tell the boys off sometimes, but you're still working on your big voice.

As boys turn into men, my fears are greater than just teasing and friends who don't back you up. You're also always the smallest kid in your class, like your father and I usually were. You come from petite stock. It was hard to imagine you in high school at all.

I was stunned to find myself not just considering a Catholic high school; I was considering something I would have never considered for myself or for Sophie—an all-girls Catholic high school. Surprising but true.

Your dad and I set up a visit at one of the all-girls Catholic high schools. We were buzzed in through a locked gate. On a grassy lawn, some of the girls were in gym class. They were laughing and joking and throwing a ball around. There was so much less of that pressurized energy and scrutiny, the mandate of coolness.

The meeting was with two women—one from admissions, one from counseling. They were supportive. They wanted to be ready. They'd had students transition after graduation. They had people to talk to, people above them. They explained how they were tied to the diocese but also had some freedom. They understood why this would be a good place for you, and they understood our fears about safety. In this, we weren't alone. Most of their parents were drawn to the school because it felt safer than others.

People tend to love your father in these meetings. He doesn't like conflict, and somehow he gets this message across. He sets them at ease. He makes a few light jokes. He creates this atmosphere in which everything's going to be okay. He's a natural cajoler. I'm not as good at this. I'm a little too leaned in, too intense. His energy counterbalances mine.

The admissions person and the counselor couldn't say yes, absolutely, that they would admit a trans girl, but they definitely weren't saying no. If you got in, you'd be the first, as far as they knew.

I could see you on that grassy field, throwing a ball around. What was the sport? I couldn't even tell. I wanted you to have that freedom from fear, that opened-up space to learn and breathe and be.

It seemed like a crazy idea, but your dad saw it too. "It could work for her," he said. "It really could."

———

A little background.

The priest who officiated our wedding baptized me and then all four of you kids. He was brilliant and kind. While he was living in a retirement home, my mother told him during one visit what was happening to us in, as she put it, the Bible Belt. "A place that refers to itself as the Bible Belt should be the most accepting place of all," he said. The priests and nuns in our lives have been gentle souls, and I realize how lucky we are to have had that experience.

I went to Catholic school from sixth grade through college. Nuns taught me about God and humility, sacrifice, comedy, tragedy, and also feminism. The order that ran my middle school didn't exist within a parish, which allowed them far more autonomy than many other Catholic schools. They worked the land themselves. You would see them on tractors, veils flapping, as they tilled the fields surrounding the school.

I chose Saint Joan of Arc as my confirmation name. Not Joan. No. The full name: Joan of Arc. It's why she appears a few times in these pages already. I was fiery and uncompromising. As my father used to say, "Snots [his nickname for me], you're intolerant of intolerance." This was a trait that the nuns appreciated. In fact, my middle school principal took me to speech contests and encouraged me to be a little fierce and uncompromising in front of audiences.

Do you remember meeting her? After your grandmother's knee surgery, she came to the house with another sister. You served them cookies on tea trays. She'd known you from birth and so knew you were transgender. She didn't have to check with Vatican dogma. She loved and accepted you without question.

In some ways, the clergy of my childhood prepared me for the transgender experience. The nuns followed the tradition of St. Francis de Sales. Two of his quotes remain with me. The first is, "All through love, nothing through force." We refused to force you into boys' clothes or to play with boys' toys. We weren't going to buzz cut you into masculinity. In being led by love, we were led by you.

All through love is also how I've had to work as an advocate. My lack of power makes it hard to achieve anything by force.

The second quote is, "Be who you are and be that well." You do this naturally. In being beside you on this journey, I've been forced to look at who I am, to question my own authenticity—what I'm willing to sacrifice in order to be who I am and rise to the challenge of *being that well.*

The Catholic Church also prepared me for the transgender experience when it comes to the body and how we adorn it. Look, I'm not the first to make these connections. At the Met Exhibit *The Catholic Imagination*, you saw the regalia of vestments for bishops and popes. The priests of my Catholic church growing up wore colors and clothes that no other men of that time were allowed to wear and remain within gender norms. The priests wore long robes of bright purples and crimsons.

At the same time, the nuns at my school only showed their faces and hands. One way we know gender is by how hair is styled and cut. Theirs was hidden. They wore no makeup, of course. Their habits were full-length and layered. It was all very woolen, even in summer. Their shoes were practical. Aside from their faces and hands—or perhaps because they stood out in such sharp relief—the rest of their bodies seemed to exist formlessly, within their habits. This choice to step out of the demands of feminine identity was profound, as was the choice to become a priest, which meant departing from the norms of more common masculine attire and moving into a space with flare usually reserved for women. These are radical acts disguised as traditional ones.

I visited my middle school principal when I was in my mid-thirties. She'd been assigned to a squat brick school built in the 1950s. She charged through the halls, as I'd always known her to, in the habit she'd always worn. When we got to her office, she confided in me one of the greatest surprises of her life. "I had no idea that I would be considered countercultural."

Make no mistake, I'm not upholding the Church. I'm certainly not condoning the Church's history, including the present moment, which is one of immeasurable suffering. They have inflicted incredible pain on people, in particular the LGBTQ+ community. Their belief that your body belongs to the Church is firmly entrenched in the Catholic identity. Catholics are obsessed with bodies, often on the strange and invasive grounds of fertility. It's tied to the vow of celibacy; the most honored among us—those called to be priests and nuns—have to sacrifice sex. Therefore, sexuality becomes the purview of the Church—who has it, who doesn't, under what circumstances, and for what purpose. Representatives of the Church often reduce and pervert our bodies. It is their gaze that is the perversion, not our bodies. They have done this at the expense of the soul.

They're not alone. You see this power structure again and again: one group believes they control another, that they have dominion over their bodies.

Our nation's history is a bloody one. Just look at the Edmund Pettus Bridge in Selma, Alabama, on March 7, 1965. Troopers beating peaceful demonstrators with nightsticks, coming at them on horses, firing tear gas. Pain and suffering and blood and split flesh and fractured bones—the Black men and women and even people your age trying to march across that bridge risked their lives for the right to vote. This violence and the courage in the face of it forced the president to send a voting rights bill to Congress.

That courage inspired others. One hot night in August, a year later, in the Tenderloin district of San Francisco, cops were harassing trans women who were eating and talking in a corner diner called Compton's Cafeteria. The police tried to make an arrest. Being in police custody put these women at risk of being beaten and raped. The woman threw coffee in a cop's face. This started a brawl that poured out into the street. Trans women and drag queens fought back. Chairs and dishes went flying. The plate-glass store-front window was smashed. A newsstand was lit on fire. More cops were called in. A paddy wagon showed up. The cops filled it. The next night more people from the LGBTQ+ community showed up to picket the cafeteria, which had banned trans people.

This Compton Cafeteria Riot predates the Stonewall Riots by three years. It was discovered and brought to light by historian Susan Stryker, a trans woman. So much trans history is hidden away. But, again, trans people have always been with us.

Whenever you're looking at corollaries between racial discrimination and transgender discrimination, it's important to start with respect for Black Americans when it comes to the fight for equality in this country. In *The 1619 Project*, Nikole Hannah-Jones puts it this way, "For the most part, black Americans fought back alone. Yet we never fought only for ourselves. The bloody freedom struggles of the civil rights movement laid the foundation for every other modern rights struggle," and that includes the struggle for the rights of trans people. John Lewis walked across that bridge in Selma in the spring of 1965. A cop fractured his skull with a billy club. In the summer of 2016, he led the sit-in for gun control on the floor of the House after a gunman opened fire in a gay nightclub, killing forty-nine people. When the Trump administration first proposed to ban trans soldiers from military service, John Lewis said, "I have fought too long and hard to end discrimination based on race and color to allow discrimination based on gender identity to be considered acceptable."

In her hushed office, Sister confided that she was surprised she'd become countercultural. This is something you two have in common. You don't yet fully know it, but your body is countercultural. Your body is radical. Your body is also good and healthy. It carries your beautiful soul.

Jesus was and will always be countercultural. His body was and will always be radical.

The bigoted Catholic doctrine around gender identity and sexual orientation has been costly. There is a human toll, deaths by violence and suicide. Their doctrine creates shame. It is created with shame at its center. This is intentional. Doctrine is created in order to silence and hurt and erase. They know what their doctrine does. They are aware that it means that our sons and daughters, our brothers and sisters, our aunts and uncles and mothers and fathers will kill themselves. They preside over their funerals and blame them for their deaths by suicide with merciless condemnation and eternal damnation. They have left a body count in their wake and all the grief that follows.

I remember how you told me once that you didn't need to talk about being a girl because you were you in your own land. How many have died in their own land, unable to share the existence of that land with someone else?

The numbers are untold, unknowable, and massive.

Eunuchs existed four thousand years ago in China.

And they're in the Bible. In the Book of Matthew, you'll find this: "There are eunuchs who were born that way," Jesus says, "and there are eunuchs who have been made eunuchs by others—and there are eunuchs who choose to live like eunuchs for the sake of the kingdom of heaven." (*Born this way.* Lady Gaga wasn't saying anything new.) Does this include those born intersex *and* those born, as accepted in other cultures at the time, in the body of one gender but lived as another? And the eunuchs who chose to be eunuchs—how did that make them more likely to enter the kingdom of heaven? Jesus adds, "The one who can accept this should accept this." It's almost as if he knows that not everyone will understand. I can hear the sigh in his voice.

After all of my questions and calls, your father and I were finally directed to the diocese itself. We made an appointment with the superintendent. We were nervous. We didn't have any idea what level of understanding or acceptance we'd be met with.

But there we were, sitting in the office of the superintendent of the diocese. It too was hushed, carpeted, and unadorned. It seemed almost perfectly preserved from the 1950s.

The superintendent was around my age or slightly older. He was short and rounded, a man without edges. As it is with some people, it was very easy to see him as the little kid he'd once been. It wasn't so much his looks but his demeanor. He'd been one of those earnest altar boys who took the role seriously. He spoke with a heavy accent that tied him to this area. He'd invited a youth pastor who had thick dark hair and wore an earring. I assumed that the youth pastor had been invited because he was more in touch with the younger generation, which is more accepting of trans people, by and large.

The conversation was more theological than your father and I had prepared for, but it was also gracious and open. We gave some background about transgender kids in general and briefly went over your clarity on your gender identity. The superintendent asked about bathrooms, locker rooms, sleepovers. We ranged from passports and gender markers to sacraments and baptismal records.

He conceded, "The Church's theology and science and medicine haven't really caught up with each other. The Church is very slow; that's one thing I know. It moves slowly."

The theme that recurred in various ways was the soul and the body. I leaned toward the importance of the soul. They kept veering back to the body.

We finally got to a spot in the conversation when I turned to the youth pastor, who'd been so quiet. I asked him if he had any questions.

He did. It was hard for him to find the right phrasing. He was apologetic.

"It's fine," I said. "Keep going."

The youth pastor wanted to talk about your body. He was concerned about your fertility. I won't go into that here. But I gave him some medical updates regarding fertility preservation. I explained that you'd likely be able to have biological kids of your own, if you wanted to, as well as adopt children. You had options.

He explained the Church's stance against all forms of fertility treatments.

My head was cluttered with arguments. Not all people are fertile, but they're still granted Catholic education. Not all people who attend Catholic schools are Catholic and therefore don't follow doctrine. Not all Catholics who attend Catholic schools follow all Catholic doctrine. Those called to join the clergy take a vow of celibacy, so why this fixation on procreation? Many Catholics undergo fertility treatments; many children in Catholic schools were born because of those interventions. I wanted to ask, "Do you educate the children who were born as a result of, say, in vitro fertilization?"

I wish I'd simply said, "I don't think we need to worry about my daughter's future decisions about having children. She's twelve, and we're talking about high school admissions."

The youth pastor expressed his concerns about how he'd teach classes about sex ed and relationships within the teachings of Christ to a trans student, so this was really about sexual orientation, not gender identity—or so I thought. I did some presuming, played to the better angels of his nature.

"I'm sure that you feel completely comfortable the way you teach it now," I said. "You look at a classroom full of children and know some of those children are gay and lesbian, and it's your job to explain the Catholic doctrine and then to support them. I'm sure that you've figured out how to do that very well so that they can feel aligned with their faith and with who they truly are, so that they're able to live wonderful fulfilling lives and have great relationships. It would be no different if our daughter was sitting in that class or not."

As a Catholic, I know how to navigate Church teachings in the context of how things actually work in the world, as my mother did for me, as all of my Catholic friends have done for each other. We know some de-escalation and deprogramming skills. Look, 98 percent of Catholic women of child-bearing age who are experienced with sex have used birth control other than the natural family-planning method sanctioned by the Catholic Church, so no one is hanging on the youth pastor's every word when it comes to marriage and sex.

The superintendent proudly brought up the fact that they now allowed students to buy tickets for prom however they wanted, allowing same-sex couples to attend together.

See?

It was going so well.

At one point, Jeff showed them your class picture. He wanted you to be seen for who you are before being discussed further in the abstract. "Just so you know who we're talking about," he said.

"Oh," the superintendent said, "well, if I were a principal and this was the kid who came in and you just marked *female* on the forms, I'd never have to know."

Without being aware of it, he'd revived the long-standing Don't Ask, Don't Tell policy of the U.S. military, which was mercifully repealed in 2010. I explained why that would be ultimately dangerous. It also wouldn't work for the kids who transitioned in school or who were out as transgender. It presumed a closet and, arguably, that the students weren't visibly trans.

Your dad and I were meeting the two men where they were. We were lean-ing into their good will and receiving their questions and comments with good will in return. It wasn't easy, but we knew it was important. Not just for you.

We dove deeper into the conversation. They knew by now that you were choosing not to tell others that you're transgender, opting for privacy. This might change during your high school years, by choice or by outing, but at present, this was your position.

The youth pastor had one more question. Actually, it was more of a scenario. He was nervous and edged toward it slowly. We gave him time. He asked about the dating situation in which someone—he assumed a boy—discovered that you were transgender, taking the boy by surprise. He was worried about the boy, how disturbing this would be.

I told him in a very reassuring voice, "I understand completely. We wouldn't want this situation to come up either. We don't want anyone to be caught off guard. Our main concern is that our daughter could be beaten to death."

This is one way to reorient a room of men. The youth pastor's fears about a young man's fragility were immediately reframed in light of the fears that a transgender person faces: being murdered.

When I went to Transgender Day of Remembrance, the cause of death that lodged fixedly in my mind was beaten to death. This is the brutal truth. This is something I've been afraid to say. These are the words that I am try-ing to dislodge. When we were thinking of where to move, way back when, I had a system. I'd imagine a headline. *Transgender Woman Beaten to Death in* . . . and I'd insert the name of a city. If my reaction to that headline was, *Well, no surprise there*, then I would never live in that city. Never. I'd never even have my grown daughter visit me in that city.

After this jagged turn, we righted the conversation and ended, well, I'd say *warmly*. As the superintendent was walking us back to the reception area, he confessed that he'd been nervous about the meeting. He was sure he was going to face angry parents who'd yell at him. Again, he struck me as that altar boy he most certainly once was.

We confessed we'd been nervous too. We still held a kind of adrenaline-spiked energy.

And then, in what may have been a spur-of-the-moment idea, he asked me if I'd write something to explain the transgender experience, within the context of Catholic doctrine. This was the pressing point, *doctrine*.

"Uh-huh." I was surprised.

He went on to explain that he'd need help bridging the gap to priests and nuns.

"Of course," I said. "I'd be happy to."

And with that, we were sent off, assignment in hand, with the promise of meeting again soon.

31

HERE'S HOW IT STARTS. Education. Imagine the transgender student who feels like they can't transition or they've transitioned but can't come out or they've come out but are bullied. There's the basic level of discomfort in the bodies of transgender kids, and then there's being called the wrong name, referred to by the wrong pronouns, being mis-seen and unseen for who they are—or living in fear of being outed or bullied or laughed at or attacked—and all of this while trying to navigate schoolwork. With that level of distraction and fear, it's very hard to concentrate.

If they transition, they face high rates of bullying, cruelty, and violence. Some are kicked off of their sports teams, denied the right uniform, the right bathroom . . .

Some are also facing hostile situations at home. Some are kicked out of their homes. Some run away for their own safety. Some self-medicate.

If someone isn't given a shot at a solid education, they are at far greater risk of unemployment, homelessness, violence, and murder.

At the first trans health conference I ever attended, a parent asked about long-term health risks for people taking hormones. The doctor gave a full assessment of issues that trans men face; many of them mimic the risks that would be inherited from father to son if they'd been born male, now that testosterone is a factor.

"What about trans women?" another parent asked.

The doctor took a deep breath. "Those outcomes are murkier. Because trans women are so discriminated against, they're at far greater risk for issues like alcoholism, poverty, homelessness, and lack of access to good healthcare. All of these issues impact their overall health so much that it's hard to gather data on what their health outcomes would be if these issues weren't present."

This was stunning—a group of people is treated so badly by our culture that we can't clearly study their health. The burden of this abuse is that substantial and pervasive. Your generation will be healthier. The signs are already there.

The thing we don't really talk about is what so many trans women who are murdered have in common: they were denied the right to a safe and equal education.

You will get an education, of course. But there are so many trans people who have to choose between trying to get an education and self-preservation.

And I mean that both ways—in terms of physical safety and protecting the self on the deepest level.

When I'm pushing for your rights (and I keep pushing, in all kinds of ways), I hope I'm paving a way for the next family. Because I know we owe a debt to all those who pushed before us.

I took the assignment from the superintendent seriously. I felt like I'd been given an opportunity to create real change. If I did it right, if I was smart enough and loving enough and thorough enough, I could make a difference, couldn't I?

It didn't take me long to find the Vatican's stance. It had come out just the summer before, under the title " 'Male and Female He Created Them': Toward a Path of Dialogue on the Question of Gender Theory in Education." I'm here to report that things have gotten better since the time of Joan of Arc. And I'm also here to warn you: never let any religion tell you who you are or give their take on why and what you should do about it. Never.

The document is just over thirty pages long. It is complete with footnotes. The paragraphs are numbered like a legal document or Bible verses.

In my first read, I had only one goal: to find moments of openness, kindness, and love. I found enough of them to get my footing.

Next, I looked for any common ground I could find. There was an obvious one—gender theory. The document isn't really about gender theory, but the Vatican takes issue with it as it relates to gender-nonconforming and transgender students. And so do I, but for different reasons. I've already warned you about the ways in which the concept that "gender is a social construct" isn't helpful when it comes to understanding the depth of gender identity.

But what was their stance? They accept neurology, endocrinology, and genetics in forming gender identity but only take the science as far as it's useful to their argument. They drop it when it gets complex, and therefore rich and dynamic and mysterious—in other words, when it really shines with the artistry of God's design. In Matthew there's a moment when Jesus says, "Blessed are you, Simon son of Jonah! For flesh and blood has not revealed this to you, but my Father in heaven." I'm not sure why some people want to simplify gender to flesh and blood. You know gender in a way that was never just flesh and blood but a deeply held sense of self, so deeply held that it resides in that territory of the soul. I have more to say about all of this, so much more, and I'll get to it—but you know this: There is God in you, and you are proof of God's intricate, complex, rich, and beautiful design. We all are. (Even those fire ants that you were so sure that God had gotten wrong.)

Some people get rigidly fixed on the binary of gender because they like simplicity—male or female. To be reductive about God's design, for me, is to ignore the astounding, awe-inspiring beauty of His work. It's snubbing God.

In our house, we don't snub God.

The Vatican's document is confusing because they're confused. They sometimes seem to deny the very existence of transgender and gender-nonconforming people in general, while also—and this is truly helpful—they defer to doctors in terms of care.

The document was worthwhile, not just because I found moments of love and respect to help build a bridge to the diocese but also because it exposed some of the assumptions and fears that will get thrown at you.

Here's a section that needs a lot of unpacking: "This oscillation between male and female becomes, at the end of the day, only a 'provocative' display against so-called 'traditional frameworks,' and one which, in fact, ignores the suffering of those who have to live situations of sexual indeterminancy." By "sexual indeterminancy," I believe they mean those born intersex.

So, as you know, the majority of transgender people don't oscillate between male and female. Most are clearly one gender or the other and are as fixed in their definition and expression as their more "typical" peers. There are those who are gender fluid. And I've found that once a cisgender person understands that the binary can flip, they can start to understand that it can blur and shift. Think of the way the sun strikes a tree full of leaves, reflecting light.

But this oscillation is also, possibly, a misread on the Vatican's part. It's not unusual, especially in young transgender people, to feel bold enough to be who they are during some periods and to have to shut that down for their own safety during other periods. This could be perceived as oscillation in their identity; instead, it's usually a reaction to oscillation of support, given and taken away.

But let's talk about the next accusation here, which is not oscillation but "being provocative."

Here's what people misunderstand. If someone—and by *someone* I mostly mean a man, in this case—finds a woman to be beautiful, the man assumes that this was the woman's intention, a provocation. They take her beauty personally, as if it's an invitation. To what? To claim the woman's body.

Likewise, if someone is provoked by a transgender person's presence, that person assumes this was the transgender person's intention. By someone, in this case, I mean the Vatican. But think about how dangerous this is. If one is provoked, then their reaction to provocation can be easily rationalized. "I didn't mean to get violent; I was provoked." This is called the "gay panic defense" used by people who've murdered gay men and the "transgender panic defense" when someone has murdered a trans person. It has a lot in common with George Zimmerman's defense, in fact. He saw a Black boy in his neighborhood, chased him down, and shot him. Zimmerman felt provoked simply by the presence of that boy's body.

The idea that transgender and gender-nonconforming people are, by and large, provocateurs would be ridiculous if, again, it weren't such a dangerous idea. Yes, activists have been forced to stand up and be seen and heard. Sometimes provocation is a tool. But the vast majority of transgender people do not want to provoke anyone; research proves quite the opposite. They want to live their lives quietly and simply, free from gender scrutiny. Many go to great lengths to blend in. And whether they blend in or not, they live their lives. You can find transgender people in all walks of ordinary life: lawyer, judge, dentist, professor, army medical doctor, poet, novelist, politician, minister. . . . Deciding to keep their medical history private or to tell people is usually a matter of safety.

The final accusation is really damning—that the transgender community is, by their very presence, ignoring someone else's suffering. I've found transgender folks to have an enormous capacity for empathy and love. To quote transgender memoirist Nick Krieger, "I wish someone had told me, not that my life would be hard, but that it would be phenomenally rich. I wish someone had told me that through my own self-inquiry and my own unique experience, my empathy would deepen, my compassion would expand, my gratitude for being alive would be huge."

Let me tell you this: Your life will, in fact, be rich. It already is. Your empathy will only deepen. Your compassion will be expansive. And your gratitude for life is already vibrant and exhilarating and huge. And raising you has deepened our empathy and expanded our compassion and gratitude for being alive.

When our gazes have gone steely, when our hearts get cinched in our chests, tightened into cold fists, when we seal ourselves up and hide from one another the truth of who we are, we need to be softened, unclenched, unsealed; we need to stop hiding; we need the truth of our humanity—even when and especially when that truth is complex.

My response was six pages long, more than 3,400 words, broken into sections: Introduction; On Gender Theory; On Science and Medicine: Genetics, Endocrinology, and Neurology; Developing Strategies; On Fear; and In Conclusion.

Before I sent it, I shared it with Catholic friends to critique, ones who are much more Catholic than I am. They gave notes, but overall, they said it was moving and powerful. I gave it to my father too. I was crafting an argument, and I wanted his legal eye. I collected notes and revised.

I ended my response by discussing the title of the Vatican's document. This was where it got interesting, where I really got to talk about God. The title again: " 'Male and Female He Created Them': Toward a Path of Dialogue on the Question of Gender Theory in Education." It comes from Genesis 1:27. If you take your focus, for a moment, off of the options for us and you focus on God's own image, you quickly notice the use of "male and female." I'm not the first person to point this out. Isn't this saying that God is both male and female? The Bible doesn't say "male *or* female God created them." *And* is a conjunction here that, as defined by the *Oxford Pocket Dictionary of Current English*, is "used to connect words . . . that are to be taken jointly."

What about the Holy Spirit? Is the Holy Spirit male or female? Male and female? Can a spirit be gendered?

A while back, I got to know the transgender Jewish writer and memoirist Joy Ladin. In her memoir, *Through the Door of Life*, she breaks down this passage and goes on to write, "When I look in the mirror, I see the mystery of God's creation. Look at what makes me so hard to look at. If you can see the image of God in me, you'll see God everywhere."

This is what I've been driving at all along. Because of you, I see God everywhere. Not because there is something that makes you hard to look at. Just the opposite. It's because I adore looking at you. Loving you is so easy. Looking at you—your deep abiding grace—has changed the way I look at others.

When things were hard in the South, around the time of the knock at the door, your father heard a song that he'd heard many times before, but this time it was different. It's a Pete Townsend song about love. It's written to someone who feels like everything is over, surrounded by people who are unkind. It's an invitation, someone asking to open the door to your heart. When your dad listened this time, he started to cry, and the song still chokes him up. Your love had opened the door to his heart. You'd kicked those doors wide open.

(That's what having a child is—it's saying yes to having the door to your heart kicked open.)

When we look at the world this way, with our hearts laid bare, we see God. We can't help it. We can't not.

(It's the kind of love that can set you free.)

I sent my response to the superintendent before Christmas.

At that same time, the principal whom I loved and adored, who'd meant so much to me throughout my life, was dying. Sister had Alzheimer's. I'd visited her earlier that fall. The school and convent were now surrounded by some remaining fields, a housing development, a crop of solar panels, and the old cemetery.

We sat in the parlor and shared stories. I marveled at the moments when she became less self-conscious, less attached to the meanings of words, and told a story. Words connected to images, spinning away from meaning, but beauty rode in. The story rose up from the ordinary and existed, poetically, on some more heightened realm.

When in doubt, she returned to what rooted her. "God is good." This was her mooring.

Now, she was resting peacefully in a bedroom on the first floor of the convent. She was no longer able to speak. But at one point, she did laugh. I thought of you, laughing in your sleep. How that became precious, something that I needed to protect. This primal joy. It was in her. It had been protected. It endured.

I was asked to speak at her funeral. It was a passage from the Book of Hosea about being married to God, *espoused*—and it is passionate. "Thus says the Lord: I will allure her; I will lead her into the desert and speak to her heart." And then there's the shift to direct address; the voice becomes intimate. "I will espouse you to me forever: I will espouse you in right and in justice, in love and in mercy; I will espouse you in fidelity, and you shall know the Lord."

I read this passage at her funeral, in a school gymnasium, with her coffin nearby. The crowd was made up of former students, friends and family, and all of the nuns who'd lived with her in the convent on school grounds, these women who had become espoused to God—*in love and in mercy*.

Love, mercy.

32

MY OWN GIRLHOOD.

Well, first off, I should note that one of my most vivid childhood memories is of being misgendered. In kindergarten, my parents went on a trip. My grandparents came to take care of us. One afternoon, my oldest sister and her best friend decided to give me a pixie haircut for picture day. I hated the haircut—and my sister and her friend. On picture day, my grandmother put me in a horrible green dress with a little girl stitched on the front. The little girl had long yarn braids. The result is a deeply forlorn kindergarten photo. A few days later, I was back in jeans and a t-shirt. The man who organized all the newspaper boys in town was dumping stacks of papers on the corner. "Hey sonny!" he said to me, kindly.

Sonny. It was the stupid haircut.

I turned away and ran home, crying.

I never really thought much of the memory until you transitioned. I wasn't all that invested in being girly, but still that moment came as a crushing blow. Why? Because gender runs deep, in all of us.

I was lucky though because, in general, no one cared if I was pretty or tidy or girly or not. My parents weren't personally invested in my existence being a reflection of them. And also, they delighted in me. They thought I was funny and smart. I don't think that anyone imagined I'd be pretty one day but, overall, beauty wasn't stressed as a crucial attribute. The nuns, with no makeup, no fancy hair, wearing their simple habits, didn't care about prettiness either. In retrospect, all of this was a relief.

My mother was worried about men. Men were dangerous. We lived near a park, and I wasn't ever allowed to go alone or with other kids. I remember going when I was learning tennis from a woman who lived in the neighborhood. Parks were places where perverts hung out, waiting for children. I wasn't allowed to walk past the stop sign. I wasn't allowed to ride my bike away from our cul-de-sac.

My mother told me cautionary tales. Not about little girls in red coats and forests and wolves. No. She told me real stories about rape and attempted rape and violence. She explained that men could be abusive, including her own father. He never hurt her, but he was violent with my grandmother.

These were things that I wouldn't have understood, not really, if not for her stories. She'd chosen my father who is gentle and good and smart. His father, a man who also struggled with alcoholism, died when my father was five years old. My father was raised by his mother, who worked, and his unmarried aunt, who stayed home. He was the middle child between his two sisters. Being raised among women served him well.

When I got to high school, stories would circulate. What had happened later that night, when the party was almost over. What had happened in the swimming pool or in a car or in a basement. What had happened when there was a group of guys and only one girl. What happened to the girl in the frat house. What happened to the girl in her own house . . . among her own family. . . .

As much as I was taught fear within my family, I wasn't handed down much shame, thankfully. I learned from the outside world that I should be ashamed of my body, that women's bodies were disgusting on the one hand and objectified on the other. One of my earliest and most vivid lessons about how women are perceived and treated by men came from having to listen to Howard Stern on the car radio in high school, when the dial wasn't in my control. Howard Stern's treatment of women on that show made me sick to my stomach. To hear a woman, the cohost, Robin Quivers, laughing along and rarely giving any pushback was a betrayal. It seemed so obvious to me in my teens that Howard had been the ugly gawky boy in middle and high school who now hid behind his flanks of hair and his mic to get back at women who'd never paid him the attention he felt he deserved. I hated Howard Stern, and I could tell by the way he spoke to women and to men about women that he hated me. Most of all I remember how the boys in my high school loved him and thought he was funny. And in watching them laugh, I understood what they really thought of girls and women, of me. I understood that they all believed they deserved more attention and that attractive women made them feel like little boys—embarrassed by their lust and afraid—and they all wanted to get some revenge because of it. And if a woman wasn't attractive, she was a waste of their time or, worse, their lack of attractiveness was, again, taken personally. Didn't women want to be found attractive by them? Wasn't that our goal? If we were failing to please them with our looks, then we weren't trying hard enough or we didn't care. And if we didn't care about how they felt and what they needed, then we were ... the enemy?

Obviously, it wasn't just Howard Stern. It wasn't even the love of Stern. He was a blip. There were *endless* places for me to learn about what it meant to be a girl and a woman. I took in the Madonna-whore complex and the slut-prude version of it, which was built for high school purposes—that there was no way around these stark labels. I felt lucky to be flat-chested and fairly curveless. I knew that this made me safer and that it made it easier to simply walk down a street and have a conversation and be taken more seriously.

I was shocked when I went from being a scrawny messy little girl who went largely ignored in public to suddenly feeling watched by men as I grew up. It felt like a disruption of the hierarchy. Men being at the top of the power structure seemed to want something from me. It was strangely powerful, and deeply confusing. Confusing because it feels like power, but it's not real power. It's an ask, sometimes a demand, for something in return for that attention. Sometimes it's stolen by assault or rape. If it's not given or blamelessly taken, sometimes there is retribution in other ways.

I've promised to protect you so that you can have a girlhood. But there is nothing simple here. Girlhood isn't simple. I won't sugarcoat what has already been sugarcoated by our culture. Girlhood isn't sweet. It requires vigilance, toughness, and a clear sense of your own power.

Did I know what happened to kids who were different like you? I think we all got the message. In retrospect, it was everywhere. In my fourth-grade class, three of us would always arrive early to homeroom, before the teacher. It became my job to talk this one boy out of beating up this other softer boy, every morning. This was the inner-city public school I went to before the nuns. What happened on the days I wasn't there to diffuse it all?

In some ways, I'm haunted by the era of my own childhood. If you'd grown up just one generation earlier, just ten years earlier, even five, your life would have been much more complicated. Would we have listened to you? Would we have been more afraid of the dangers of the outside world pressing in? I'm a staunch protector, and I'd like to think I would have been that way in any era. But what does a staunch protector look like in my own girlhood? There were transgender kids then too. They just weren't out. Weren't some of their mothers staunch protectors?

How would I have ever known this you? This amazing and incredible you? What would have happened to the real you? Where would she have gone? She wouldn't have gone away. I know that. What toll would it have taken on you? How much damage?

I realize that my mother's fears imprinted on me. If my girlhood was marked by the frank truth and I feel like those frank truths helped keep me safe, then this is in large part why I feel the need to do what I'm doing here. The blueprint of what I'm writing to you—how and why—exists within those conversations with my own mother, for better and for worse.

In my youth, I was watching out for the guys who seemed to have certain tendencies, who were erratic, who seemed like the kinds of boys who'd stay too long at the party when there was only one girl left, too drunk to go home.

I'm not saying that I don't have a few stories to tell. I didn't escape my girlhood, my teen and college years, without incident. But none of them escalated too quickly or too violently. I wasn't unscathed, but I also wasn't scarred.

I was still simply lucky. Because what I've learned is that you can't always tell what kind of boy is that kind of boy. The wolf isn't always clearly a wolf.

This is what fuels some of the fear around trans people—that they are wolves in women's clothing. Isn't that what the wolf in *Little Red Ridinghood* does when disguising himself as a granny? Isn't this one of the earliest fairy tales that a child hears? It's really about the fear of someone stepping out of their gender, disguising himself as a woman in order to devour an innocent little girl. We're inundated with stereotypes of the trans person as someone to fear or ridicule.

I have a Halloween photo that I've always loved of Sophie at five years old, wearing a red cape and kerchief. She's holding a basket. Her mouth is caught in a shocked O. Isaac is beside her. He's wearing furry ears and a wooly gray sweater. He's turned so you can see his taped-on tail. I've drawn whiskers on his cheeks. His face is captured midgrowl, his hands held up like claws. I look at it now and think, *What a mess*. My son as a wolf. My daughter as an innocent. And the story, in the end, is really about some random woodsman who saves the day.

How we build our cautionary tales is, in and of itself, a cautionary tale.

It comes up again and again, this idea that trans women want access to private all-women's spaces like bathrooms and locker rooms in order to be wolves. It's an absurd claim. Men, so desperate to rape a woman, will dress as a woman in order to get into a women's bathroom? If you know anything about men, you know that they don't need girls' bathrooms and locker rooms in order to be violent to other men, boys, women, and girls. They can do this almost anywhere at any time. They don't need a ruse. They can take on their ordinary roles—as bosses or senators or priests or cops or stepfathers or a friend of the family or boyfriends or husbands. If a place exists, a woman has been raped there.

I will be frank with you, and I will be careful about the construction of my cautionary tales. And I will tell you the truth.

A woman's body isn't considered to be her own, not in the way a man's body is. Black bodies aren't considered to be their own, not the same way as white bodies are. Disabled bodies aren't considered to be their own, not in the same way able bodies are. Big bodies aren't considered to be their own, not in the same way thinner bodies are . . .

And a trans person's body is definitely not considered to be their own.

Your body is your own.

I'd say that in the cautionary tale of *Little Red Ridinghood*, you are, if anyone, a Little Red who can take care of herself. I'd offer you the ax, but you're not the ax type. And I've lost confidence in the allegory.

I prefer the truth. Your life has been an experience of claiming your body as your own. I want you to understand the power of that and carry it with you wherever you go.

33

THE SUPERINTENDENT ARRANGED FOR a follow-up meeting in February.

We went in confident. The last meeting had gone relatively well. And I stood by my work. The pandemic was looming, but it was far away. We had no idea what was to come. The superintendent was friendly enough, but a little more distracted. The youth pastor was invited back. I was glad to see him. He'd stumbled some in the last meeting, sure, but I was still hopeful about his perspective from the younger generation.

It was the four of us, seated in the same arrangement.

This time, however, there wasn't much warm-up banter. The superintendent drove to the point. "We won't have a place for your daughter in the foreseeable future." He mentioned the name of the high school that I'd attended, but after some quick questions, it was clear that this was a diocese-wide stance.

It was one of those moments when you actually stop moving, except for your eyes. What is this instinct to freeze? If I stopped moving, could I pause time and find my footing? Your dad did too. His body went rigid. We were quiet for a beat, just trying to process the complete about-face.

At first, I just didn't believe that it was a ban. I said, "But if she were to attend...." And I launched into the plans they would have for you. I sputtered about uniforms, bathrooms, and haircuts. These were arguments I knew well.

He mentioned a gender-neutral bathroom, but again, this was hypothetical—not really an offer.

I still took it as one. "Have you seen *Hidden Figures*?"

"Yes!" he said, happily. "I have!" He seemed to have fond memories of the film.

"You remember how the Black women had to run to the colored-only bathrooms and how it cut into their ability to get work done?"

"Yes. I do. Kevin Costner..."

"Well, the suggestion of a gender-neutral bathroom—which would probably be in the nurse's office?—is one bathroom in a sprawling three-story building in a schedule that includes five-minute breaks between classes. It's segregation. It's a 1950s policy reenacting separate but equal, which wasn't equal at all."

My arguments were moot. "Your daughter deserves to be happy, and she should go to a school where she can be herself." Meaning, not here.

I pivoted to a legal standpoint. "There's really only one line that needs to be highlighted in the entire Vatican document. They state that they defer to medical professionals. We know that the American Academy of Pediatrics and the American Medical Association have standards of care and best practices. If I were a lawyer, I would've highlighted that sentence sent it back to you and that would be the end of the conversation from my perspective."

My perspective didn't matter. I wasn't a lawyer. The Vatican's statement wasn't a legal document.

He complimented my response. "You should send it to the Vatican directly." Again, it was clear that my response held no water *here*, and we were both well aware that the Vatican really didn't care what I had to say on the matter. It was a clever if disingenuous suggestion.

He gestured to the youth pastor and explained that he'd been the one to point the superintendent to the policies of the National Catholic Bioethics Center in Philadelphia. He spoke to the youth pastor. "You'd say they lean . . . conservative, wouldn't you?"

The youth pastor said, "Yes, I'd say that."

This was also disingenuous. They don't *lean* conservative. They're *intensely* conservative. And there was no need for the youth pastor's confirmation of this fact. It was the only moment that felt . . . forced, as if we were suddenly watching a little piece of theater.

This center was where the youth pastor decided to dig in and do research. It was a very bad sign. The youth pastor wasn't here to help our cause. He was against us more than the superintendent was. Was he the one who changed the superintendent's mind? Was this why everything had changed between meetings?

It was Jeff who turned the conversation back to faith. "But she's a child of God," he said. "Don't you have to take in and educate children of God?"

This surprised the superintendent, and he launched into a speech that was so profoundly foreign to me that I still don't know what to do with it. "It's not for me to say who is or is not a child of God," he began. "Some people argue that murderers, for example, aren't children of God. . . ."

Our eyes met. I don't know what expression I had on my face—shock, horror, complete confusion? But he must have read it as dangerous. He moved away quickly. "We're not here to talk about all the ills of society."

No, I thought, *just this ill of society? Is that how you see my daughter?*

We're all children of God. I didn't know what *transubstantiation* was as a kid, but I knew this. Everyone knew this. It's the bumper-sticker, bite-sized, t-shirt motto version of Catholicism. Even murderers and rapists and those who cover up so that rapists can continue to commit rape. That's the hard truth. That is what we take on. It is a requirement of our faith.

As if he'd left this thought about whether you're a child of God or not ajar, like an opened box in some dank basement, he would drift back to it, now and then, during our conversation. "It's not for me to say who is or isn't a child of God."

I kept refocusing on the Vatican document. It was all I had. I told him that I'd given it to my father along with my response because I'd wanted a lawyer's take. "My father told me what he saw—a document filled with homophobia and transphobia. But I told him, 'No you're looking at the wrong parts. There is love in this document. There's enough love to work with—respecting other people's humanity.' " I was trying to call a foul. The superintendent was changing the rules, as I'd imagined them. I ignored the Vatican's bigotry to meet him while trusting his good intentions. And yet he was allowed to pretend that those good intentions had never really existed. He was allowed to ignore my good faith efforts to meet him where he was. He was allowed to backtrack completely.

"Look," he said, "I'm sure your daughter is lovely and fine, but—"

Those words, *lovely and fine*, were a slap. "My daughter isn't lovely and fine," I said, sharply.

"Okay," he backed off, laughing a little, "maybe she's a typical teenage girl—." He was going to continue on with his point, but I stopped him again.

"My daughter isn't lovely and fine. She is amazing. And if she walked into this room, she would change your mind," I said. Here, my tone shifted. I spoke slowly but with great conviction. "She would change you."

I sometimes cry when I'm furious, and this was one of those times. I'm assuming that it's an evolutionary trait. When you hit a certain level of anger, you might be more likely to survive if you can't physically keep talking.

The superintendent handed me a box of tissues.

For a moment, no one spoke.

Then your father stepped in. "Sometimes people misinterpret Carolyn's tears. They think she's sad, but that's not it." He didn't mention anger, but maybe it served as a fair warning. What your father said next was crucial. "Our kid will be fine, but not everybody has a mother like hers, someone who'd actually go and talk to that Catholic ethics group you mentioned. But the people you're really harming are those who don't have other options and who have to go through Catholic schools not as themselves. Those are the kids who might not make it to college. Those are the kids who might not make it at all."

It was the perfect reminder. If they thought we were here just for our own sake, they were wrong.

Jeff's speech bought me time. I'd found my voice, but it was hoarse and very light. I didn't look up. I twisted the tissue in my hands. I spoke very slowly. "It's your loss because all those students and all of those teachers will never get to see our daughter live her life as an example of living authentically as your true self. They'll hear the story of Jesus having to come out as his true self and how people didn't believe him and how some needed to put their hands in his wounds. Some needed his flesh as proof of who he was. This isn't about my daughter's flesh. It's about her soul."

With that, we got up to go. We were still well-mannered, Jeff thanking them for their time, pushing in our chairs.

But there was one last moment. Just before the door was opened to take us back to the reception area, the superintendent tried to release himself from responsibility. He said with kind conviction, "I want you to know that I'm not rejecting your daughter. That's not what happened here. It's not me." He was just following orders?

I called him by his first name and then said, "That is exactly what you're doing. Maybe they put you in that position, and if so, I am sorry that they did that to you. I am very sorry for you."

And I meant it.

We walked out.

I want to take a moment here to talk about love. Not maternal love—which, I hope, is infused into every page. But instead I want to take a moment to discuss my love for your father and his love for me.

It is rare that you are given a moment in a relationship—even one that spans decades—when you get to fight alongside each other so fiercely and unequivocally. There is no one else in the world I would have wanted with me in that room.

That office sits on the second floor. The stairs are long and carpeted. While descending them on our way out, my vision was blurry with tears. Your father was there beside me. He had my arm. We made it out of the front doors and around the building. Your father called me by my nickname. He stopped me. There was a light rain. "I can't believe what I just saw. That speech, my God. That speech." He was crying too.

"It was you who kept pulling us back to what was important," I said. "Without you . . ."

"I don't know what happened in there," he said.

He hugged me then. And we stood there, holding each other.

This was a gift. To see each other in this moment, to know that we could rely on each other in this way, when it was so personal, so pointed.

We got in the car. Your father drove. Together, we remembered everything we could about the meeting, as exactly as we could. We put it all back together, in order. Sometimes this is what love is—two people trying to remember everything they can, trying to put something back together for each other.

Sometimes love is two people trying to make sense of things. Maybe, in the end, this is what I'm doing here with all of these words on all of these pages—trying to make sense of things.

Maybe it's that simple.

I replayed the meeting over and over again.

Each time I went back to the superintendent questioning if you were a child of God and his mention of debates about murderers.

I'd roll out different answers. They often went like this: *Murderers? Huh.*

How about priests who've raped children? Are those priests children of God? What about the people who helped cover up the sexual abuse, allowing priests to continue to rape children for decades? What's their current child-of-God status?

How dare he insinuate that there is something wrong with you. I wanted to remind him that there is something very, very wrong with the Catholic Church.

I was also mad at myself. What blind optimism, what hubris. Had I actually thought my research, my little writing assignment, was going to move an institution?

Was the assignment a setup? Was it make-work? Was my failure predetermined?

Why had I taken it on? Vanity? Some schoolgirl can-do bullshit?

The superintendent didn't take me on argument for argument because he couldn't. He deferred to an organization without actually pointing to any policy. He couldn't take me on because he was wrong, scientifically and morally. And he knew it. And he knew that we knew it.

The Catholic Church taught me God's love and then, on top of that, to question and argue like a Jesuit at the height of Liberation Theology. He couldn't argue with me, but that's in large part due to my Catholic education. I am their own creation. Moreover, Catholicism teaches us to love each other unconditionally. And when they fail to do that, they fail utterly. There is no argument to defend it.

34

AFTER THE MEETING AT the diocese, I picked you up from school. I'd already discussed telling you about the meeting with your father, and we'd decided that this was something you should know. I tried to explain it, using a voice that was clear but not beaten down. "We met with the superintendent of the Catholic diocese today. It didn't go well. . . ." I dove into the conversation.

You interrupted. You had a question.

"What is it?"

"Can we swing by the Dollar Store? I want to see if they have stickers for my craft book."

"Okay, sure." I paused the story. "I think I should tell you these things. I don't think I should hide them. But do you want me to tell you these things?"

"Yes," you said. "I want to know."

By the time we got to the Dollar Store parking lot, I'd finished the story and explained that you had been essentially banned. I was now giving more context to help you process it.

You interrupted me again. "I want to braid my hair at night so that it doesn't get messy while I sleep."

"That was a pretty hard pivot." I looked at you through the rearview mirror. "You don't want to talk about this anymore, I take it."

"That's right," you said.

"Fair enough. But I'm going to want to circle back on it. Okay?"

"Sure."

That night, in the kitchen, after I'd talked to your dad about our conversation, I did circle back. The three of us were all cleaning up after dinner. "How do you feel now, about what happened?"

You thought for a moment and then said, "There's always someone who's going to try to stop you from living your best life," you said. "For me, that's a lot of people." You tilted your head a little and smirked. "It's from that movie *Little*," you said, "but I added my own take."

I didn't ask for any more elaboration. You'd taken what happened and were making something from it. You were shaping it.

That night, after you were asleep, I looked up the screenplay for *Little*. I found the lines. "There she is. You know her: the person who just can't let you live your best life."

What I love about the movie quote is that it teaches you to recognize the person who's about to take from you. *There she is.* It seems to say, *You know her before you even know that you know her.* No one is taking you by surprise. It's completely unlike the way your father and I had walked into that office earlier that day.

But your addition is heartbreaking. The person who's going to try to stop you from living *your* best life is a lot of people. It's true. The culture itself takes shape in all of these people with all of their disparate and unwieldy agendas, and they come at you. It's overwhelming, but you've taken control. You see them coming—*There she is*—and they won't take you by surprise. *You know her.* You have power in that seeing and knowing.

Also, the line has subtext: (1) You know what your best life is, and you're going for it. (2) This person is going to try to stop you. But they're not guaranteed to succeed. In fact, the line has an undercurrent of *I see you coming. I know you. Go ahead and try to stop me. I dare you.*

I don't really know how you're processing what the dioceses has done in banning you from their schools. I don't know how it exists within you. I worry. But I know that you have no interest in seeing yourself as a victim. At this point, that feels like a very healthy defense. What I love the most is the way you put the superintendent and the youth pastor and the diocese and the Catholic Church in their place.

How much space in your life do they deserve?

There's always someone who's going to try to stop you from living your best life. For me, that's a lot of people.

That's it.

Your dad told me about a conversation he had with a friend of ours. Your father was telling him that we weren't sure what to do, where you should go, how your high school education should work. He's a photographer who grew up in New York City. He said, "You can't pave the road for her!"

I looked at your father. Just stood there for a moment and looked at him.

And then I said, "Wait. Is there a way to pave the road? For this kid? Go back and ask him what that is."

His comment presumes there could be roads, pavement.

His comment presumes that I could go up in a helicopter and miraculously see the fast rivers and steep mountains, and I could chart an easier path and then pave it.

His comment presumes that I know the destination.

35

IT WAS AROUND THE same time as the dealings with the Catholic diocese. It was not a doctor we knew. It was a follow-up call. This doctor had made a mistake. The mistake had to do with your tongue. It was painful, but it would heal.

The doctor had a Russian accent. He had a medical degree and knew the difference between each and every heart valve, all the tendons of the hand, the functions of the brain.

He knew that you were transgender.

In his follow-up call, your father and I were answering questions. One question didn't make sense. "Is it shrinking?" he asked.

Was the wound shrinking? "It's healing nicely," I said. "It looks good."

"No," he said. "Is it shrinking?"

I answered again. There was no swelling. Was that what he meant?

"Fluids," he said, "are important. Is it . . . ?"

And then I knew what he was asking. He wasn't asking about the wound. He was talking about you. *It* was you.

The question wasn't: *Is it shrinking?* The question was: *Is it drinking?*

Was *it* (you) drinking.

In the intensity of the moment, your father and I were just so relieved to understand that the question was about your intake of fluids that we answered. "She's drinking well! She's good!"

But as soon as we hung up the phone, I knew what had happened.

I felt sick. Physically sick.

I cannot dwell here.

And I won't.

Just this. My fear when I first heard of the mistake—and Sophie's fear as soon as I told her—was that he might have caused harm to your body, consciously or unconsciously. Was it really an accident? Did he harbor some ill will? Did he think of you as less human than other children?

And my anxieties from our time in the South kicked in too. I didn't want to report it because I was scared to get on the doctor's radar.

I found a way to report it anonymously.

This is a horrific thing to have to write—that someone didn't just misgender you as *he*, which would be unsettling, but it could happen in a medical context where people move quickly, they're overwhelmed, charts aren't always updated . . .

But that wasn't the issue.

No. He used a pronoun that stripped you of your humanity.

But, look, your humanity was not stripped. You are here. You are luminous and whole and brimming with humanity.

No one can take your humanity. Just as no one can take away what makes you divine.

No one.

36

A FEW MONTHS AFTER the last meeting with the superintendent, I had a dream. I was in the gymnasium where I'd read at Sister's funeral, but it was now a cathedral. One of the elderly nuns who used a wheelchair in real life strode toward me. She took my hands, as she often did, and said, "Sister is here. It's very special. She's here with us. I'll bring you to her." It was special because she was dead, of course, but among us.

We didn't go far. But the nun we came to was not the sister who'd recently passed away, but my religion teacher who died a few years earlier. This nun was stout with a round pink face. Back in middle school, she didn't like it when the Book of Jeremiah made us sing, "Jeremiah was a bullfrog. . . ." But if you got her laughing, she would turn red and then flush a little bluish, like ice cream with berries mixed in it.

She pulled me to her, hugged me. I can remember the itchy wool of her habit. She talked about you. She told me that you were going to be okay. "She'll be fine. She will. Do you hear me?"

"Yes, I do. Thank you," I said, because this meant she'd be taking care of you from beyond. "Thank you so much."

"And Nina," she said, "Nina is okay too. She's here and she's alright now."

I didn't know who Nina was, but it was clear that I should, and that Nina was also trans. "Okay," I said. "Okay. That's good to hear."

She told me not to worry about you. She assured me that all would be well.

The dream ended.

I woke up feeling comforted by the dream. I felt taken care of, loved.

And I was also thinking about how insistent she'd been about Nina. I felt like I should know the name. Nina was with her. She was okay. Who was she?

I had breakfast and headed to my writing desk. But I couldn't shake what my religion teacher had said to me. For reasons I can't explain, I googled the dream. I've never done this before. Who would google a dream?

Well, me. On this day, I did.

I looked up: *Transgender woman Nina.* Just those three words.

A two-day-old headline appeared in my feed. A trans woman named Nina Pop had been murdered in St. Louis. Nina was a Black woman with delicate features and a beauty mark on one cheek. In her picture, she's radiant and very young, only twenty-eight. She was stabbed to death.

It jangled me. I called to your father.

When he appeared in my office, he said, "Are you okay?" He'd read the alarm in my voice.

I told him about the dream. My side of the family tends toward these kinds of encounters—signs, dreams, saints. Your father's side doesn't. And so I started rationalizing for him. "I could have seen the name on Twitter but not have registered it consciously. The name then might have sifted into my subconscious and reappeared from the mouth of my religion teacher in a dream."

"Maybe," he said. "But how did you feel while dreaming the dream?"

"I felt reassured," I said. Sister was telling me that she was watching over you. And she was also telling me that she was tending to the trans community—even in the worst of times, even in death.

"Hold onto that then," Jeff said. "You were reassured."

I called a friend of mine who is deeply Catholic. "Like it or not," she said, "you've been given a gift."

I accept the gift—of love, of protection, of comfort.

When I read about the murder of a trans woman, I'm terrified. It's my deepest fear.

So, maybe my subconscious was taking care of me in this moment. A deep unseeable part of who I am taking care of the conscious part of my self—the version that I walk around thinking I know and understand. Let's assume it's not about faith and God. Let's assume it's this so-called simpler, scientific explanation of the subconscious. How incredible is that so-called simple scientific explanation? What byzantine design made that possible? What weird flex of our DNA? What architectural precision and whimsy of the evolutionary process tweaked itself in just such a way that our brains do this for us—when we're sleeping, no less?

Or, again, maybe we remain connected with those who've passed, and they can give comfort to us in our dreams. Maybe they can watch over us.

Regardless, this was what I've decided. We tend to each other in ways that are seen and unseen, here and after. In the present moment and from memory. We also, in many ways seen and unseen, take care of ourselves.

In writing this dream about being reassured by a nun who's died, I am also acknowledging my own mortality. I'm writing it now because it's fresh and because I won't always be here. Isn't this what parents do every time they tell a story or give advice? They're pushing themselves into a future that they may well not have access to.

The Catholics have an entire ancient Church backing them. But I have a family. And I wouldn't ever make the mistake of underestimating a family. God sent his only son, not a stranger. The Church doesn't exist without family. The Church is part of the engine that fuels the sanctity of family, that gives it power and, in turn, uses that power.

The American family is presented as sacred. But that's not completely true.

When we were in crisis, we turned to an expert, someone who'd helped other people who were afraid of losing custody of their trans child—or who already had lost custody. She had a checklist. The questions on it were used to assess our risk of losing you. That was a checklist of privilege.

Are you white? Yes. . . . It started there. Every yes that I was able to utter increased our chances of being perceived as sacred. To put a finer point on that: of being perceived by a caseworker and a judge as sacred.

"Are you married?"

"Yes."

"Are you both straight?"

"Yes."

"Your husband is also the father of the child?"

"Yes."

"Do you have money—and by that I mean, if this becomes a legal situation, can you hire lawyers?"

"Yes."

For every yes, I imagined a no. I was haunted by what would have happened to us if we were Black or brown or poor or not married and gay, lesbian, transgender, or queer. . . . I was haunted by the stories I didn't know—of those who had to fight harder to keep their children or who ended up losing custody.

I already knew, in my bones, that our white American family is perceived as sacred. I didn't know that I knew it until that list, until I got to pile up a bunch of yeses.

Political campaigns revolve around the white, straight, cisgender, upwardly mobile able-bodied, Christian, American family.

For all of our talk about the individual, the American dream isn't really about the individual; it's about the next generation doing better than the one that came before. It is invoked like a spell.

In John Mulaney's comedy special *The Comeback Kid*, he talks about the biggest civil rights movement of his lifetime. "The rights of children have gone through the roof," he says. "I had no rights when I was a little kid. I remember, one time, I walked into a supermarket by myself, and I walked in through the double doors, and the woman behind the register just looked at me and she went, 'No!' And I went, 'All right.' And I turned around and left. That's how broken I was."

There was a shift in my lifetime. I noticed the swell of this movement in 1985 with the *Baby on Board* signs that people started putting in the back windows of their cars. When I was a child, we didn't have seat belts in cars. My father, whose father died as a result of a car accident, ordered the first available seat belts and installed them in our station wagon, by hand. By the time your dad and I had our first child, we weren't allowed to leave the hospital without a safety check on a properly installed backward-facing infant car seat.

When we were in the thick of raising kids, the term *helicopter parents* thudded in. My guess is that many of the women of my generation who got college educations started into ambitious careers, and then, often after the second child, decided to be stay-at-home moms. They'd suddenly gone from high-powered jobs to a more singular focus. The previous generations of women—no matter how high-powered, smart, and ambitious—often had so many kids that they simply couldn't helicopter each one.

Having a big family in the era of the helicopter mom was, from my perspective, fantastic. The other moms wanted to go to all the games and rehearsals. Since they were already going, could they drive one of our kids? Sure. They signed up to bring all the snacks. Literally, you could just bring a kind of crappy snack one time, and then, suddenly, you were demoted to cups or napkins. Golden.

A lot of things happened to empower parents. One of them was the twenty-four-hour news cycle, the sudden barrage of terrifying news stories being covered without end. The news rattled our trust and terrified us. That empowered parents to protect their children against institutions—like churches and schools and Big Tobacco and advertising and skinny Barbies. It's been effective.

And by "empowerd parents," I mean, once again, parenthood that's largely a sanctioned display of white privilege. The kinds of grievances that white parents can bring to the attention of a teacher or a coach or a principal are not perceived the same way as those brought to the fore by families of color or same-sex parents or disabled parents. Some fertility clinics won't work with mothers who are overweight. Folks who are LGBTQ+ are still fighting for their legal rights to be parents. Why are Native American mothers more than twice as likely to die in childbirth than white mothers? Why are Black mothers three to four times more likely to die in childbirth than white mothers? How are our motherly bodies cared for at the start of our pregnancies, throughout all three trimesters? How are our motherly bodies perceived when we enter those hospitals?

When I was in a difficult labor with your sister, Sophie, and the doctor was pushing a C-section, I asked questions, lots of them.

He was impatient and angry with me.

I was scared and panting through contractions. I apologized. "I'm sorry," I said. "Asking questions is just what I do. I was raised by a lawyer."

I hadn't meant it as a threat. I was actually trying to get on his good side. I was saying, *This isn't personal. I just like to know things.*

But that was a moment when I realized how that word, *lawyer*, changes everything.

"Oh, that's your dad?" My parents were waiting in the hall. They'd come in and out to check on me.

"Yes."

That obstetrician finally had all the time in the world for my questions. He talked me through all the options. Everything slowed down. He gave me more time to push. "As long as the baby isn't in distress," he said, "we have time."

So when I show my face and dress in my conservative clothes and am passionate about my child, I have a weapon. When my white husband of twenty-five years sits next to me and expresses his love for and pride in having a trans daughter, he has a weapon. When we talk about our grown children and our supportive relatives, we are invoking generations of family. When we show our educations—in how we speak or how we've done our research—we are doubling down on privilege. When we show our money—and we do this in ways both conscious and unconscious—we're saying, *You can't touch us.*

And when we talk about faith and God, our sanctity grows like a protective casing.

We know how powerful it feels, and we also know how quickly that casing balloons into a soap bubble and can be popped. This is who we are, and this is the strange and twisted power that our country doles out and strips away, while denying that any of these structures are in play.

To be aware of these things is to be aware that there are people without any of these protections, without any of this perceived sanctity.

And when they fight, that is where true strength can be found.

They fight without any armor whatsoever. That is actual courage. It scares the hell out of those in power because they are upending power and claiming it as their own.

I was a toddler when, in the spring of 1972, Jeanne Manford got a call from the hospital telling her that her son had been beaten up in New York City while handing out flyers at a political event called the Inner Circle Dinner. It was a comedic event hosted by City Hall reporters to roast local politicians. It was an annual thing, with more than 1,500 guests, and a lot of the jokes and skits were homophobic. Jeanne's son, Morty Manford, then in his early twenties, was protesting. The man who beat him up was Michael Maye, head of the Uniformed Firefighters' Association. Protesters stormed the stage, taking over the mic, shouting at the crowd. A fight broke out. It was vicious. Maye claimed that "the fact that they were gay never bothered me. I just didn't like them insulting the guests. Our wives were up in the balcony watching this."

Uh . . . the wives were sex-segregated in the balcony?

Maye was a former professional heavyweight boxer, a very good one. A father of four, two daughters and two sons, he was head of the firefighters' union during an era of great upheaval in the city. He was known as a tough negotiator with the habit of lighting matches during meetings—one match after the next. He claimed he wasn't homophobic, using his time as a bouncer at a gay bar as some kind of proof. But he opposed hiring gay men and lesbians as teachers and firefighters. He's made the *Advocate*'s list of biggest homophobes. Maye's beating of Morty Manford sparked outrage and demonstrations.

Jeanne, a teacher in Flushing, New York, wrote a letter to the *New York Post* accusing the police of doing nothing to protect her son from the beating. She referred to herself as the mother of a gay protester. That was a stunning act—simply admitting publicly that she had a gay son. This was in the era of sodomy laws and raids of gay bars. Homosexuality was still considered a mental illness by the American Psychiatric Association.

Jeanne, born in 1920 in Flushing, was Jewish. She was the third of five daughters. Her parents were Sadie Sobelman, a homemaker, and Charles Sobelman, a salesman. She'd lived through the Great Depression and World War II. She saw the photographs of the concentration camps, and of course, she knew Jews who'd survived the Holocaust. She must have had the ability to take the suffering she knew and apply it to the suffering she didn't know. It seems simple, this transference of empathy, but many people can't make the imaginative leap, no matter how obvious. Some people can make that leap but can't put it into action. She did both.

That summer, she and her husband, Jules Manford, marched with Morty in the New York Pride Parade, then called the Christopher Street Liberation Day March. They carried a sign that read "Parents of Gays Unite in Support of Our Children." They were met with an outpouring of love and gratitude. People screamed and cheered; they ran up and embraced them.

Afterward, Jeanne and Jules founded a group called Parents of Gays. Twenty people showed up for the first meeting in a Methodist church. That organization is now an institution in its own right, PFLAG (Parents, Families, and Friends of Lesbians and Gays). Jeanne was awarded the Medal of Honor by President Obama.

For several reasons that are far too complex for me to begin to unwind here, more families started supporting their LBGTQ+ children and brothers and sisters and cousins and aunts and uncles. Things changed quickly. When a minority gets connected with the majority, when we expand our definitions of family and friends and love and loyalty, no one has to stand alone.

I hear the voice of an older woman in my head, drinking mimosas with friends. "Judy," she says, "I've come to all of your kids' weddings. Each one of them has gotten a Belgian waffle maker from me. And now my daughter is getting married to her girlfriend, and you owe her a Belgian waffle maker."

No one has a right to a Belgian waffle maker. But everyone has the right to marry who they want. That simple right has happened in your lifetime.

The patriarchy in its various institutional forms with its sexual repression and rigidity around rules of gender was forcing mothers and fathers to hold back their love for their own children. And when that dam broke, there was a force of love that was tsunamic. It was unimaginable in its force because it had been invisible, hidden—that love had been closeted.

But that love was there all along, thronging in the chests of parents who denied it. That love was beating them from within.

Jeanne's son, Morty Manford, became an assistant New York State attorney general. Twenty years after that spring of 1972 when he was a kid in his early twenties, beat up for handing out flyers, he was sick from complications of AIDS. Jeanne tended to him through his illness and death.

What's become just a small detail in his story is that Morty and Mike Maye became friends. They would get together for coffee and pastries, to talk. Maye went on to testify in favor of gay rights on behalf of teamster president Barry Feinstein. When Mike heard of Morty's death, he was retired and living in Florida. "It threw me for a loop," he told Jane H. Lii, a reporter for the *New York Times*. "I visited his grave afterward. That damn disease!" In the article, Lii noted the crack in Maye's voice.

Jeanne said that the idea for PFLAG was that it would serve as "a bridge between the gay community and the heterosexual community." I see that bridge sometimes in my head. It is a living, breathing, human bridge.

37

RECENTLY, YOU DREAMED ABOUT a dress. You woke up and found me at my computer. You told me about it. In great detail, you explained its one enormous sleeve, so enormous that it became a train. It was gray with a blue interior. You'd already drawn it, and you showed me the picture.

"It's rare that you get to dream a dress in that much detail," I said. "You should probably make it."

You've made me rethink feminism and the display of femininity. I used to think that femininity was about wanting to attract boys. The simple reason is that I paid no attention to how I looked until I was attracted to boys. Suddenly, I was trying to curl my hair and put on makeup and think about my outfits. Then I realized that some of the energy I put into my appearance was really about competing with other girls my age—for the attention of boys but also as a display of power or affluence or my sense of taste. To assert myself, in a way.

But, for you, fashion has meant so much more. It's not about attracting boys or power plays among other girls. It's about self-expression. It's art.

It's such an obvious thing, and yet it was obfuscated by my own issues.

You love fashion—high fashion and street fashion and kawaii fashion and the art of fashion. You love Fashion Week and the annual red carpet at the Met Gala. When you were nine years old, your favorite movie was *The September Issue*, a documentary that centered on Anna Wintour, the longtime editor at *Vogue*.

Together, we watched a documentary about Diana Vreeland, a former editor of *Vogue*. In a clip, she's being interviewed by Dick Cavett on his talk show. Vreeland is a wild character, someone who seems to have truly invented herself.

Cavett, ever the provocateur, asks, "What does it matter how people look and how they dress?"

"I should think that it only matters to them," Diana Vreeland says. "I don't see that it matters to anyone else."

"Do I look alright?" Cavett says, one arm cocked on the back of his chair.

"You look great, and that matters to me," she says. "You look great!"

"I do?" He laughs a little, as if suddenly shy.

What I didn't understand was that even when people are defaulting to the expectations of what they believe they should wear according to their culture within the greater American culture, they're making choices. Again, I'm reminded of RuPaul's famous line, "We're all born naked, and the rest is drag." (And, note, *RuPaul's Drag Race* comes from a long tradition; drag balls in America date at least as far back as the 1800s. During the Harlem Renaissance, drag was celebrated, especially as a long-standing tradition in Black communities. The Sepia Greta Garbo was the drag name of a man named Louis Diggs, a Washingtonian who performed in the 1920s and '30s.)

What RuPaul is expressing here is the idea that as soon as any of us gets dressed, we're in drag of some kind, even if our point is to pass as "typical," as ordinary, or as above fashion or below it.

To watch someone grow up expressing themselves through fashion has been altering. Because it's not just that you're *expressing* yourself; you are *creating* a self. You are creating a person for the world to see and for the world to reflect back to you.

Again, all of us do this. You just do it better and with more intention and artistry.

Take your class photos, for example. The first few years, you were guaranteed the front row because you were always one of the shortest in your class. It's clear from your pose that the front row suits you. "You like the front row, don't you?" I asked after the first-grade photo arrived.

"You can see my whole outfit."

Then, one year, you were pushed to the second row. But there's a gap between the two kids in front of you so your whole outfit is still in view. I'd caught on by now. "Did you ask those two kids to move out of the way?" I asked.

"How else were people going to see what I'm wearing?"

A few years later, you're in the second row on the end, but the second row is seated with kids sitting cross-legged in front of you. You've obviously pushed your chair away from the group and turned ninety degrees so that, yes, we can see your ensemble.

This year, every student in your class wrote a picture book. In the lead-up to printing, your teacher asked you if you wanted to do an author photo.

You did. "First off," you said to me, "I'll need a backdrop and a fan. I want to be windblown."

Your picture book was about the environmental and human costs of fast fashion. It was a beautiful and spare book. I overheard your teacher talking to you about the finished product on the phone. "Do you have a photography studio in your house?" she said. "You have by far the best author photo."

In each class photo, you have a regal air, an ethereal dignity. You hold yourself differently than the other kids. One afternoon, at your weekly internship at a boutique in town, a chatty woman who worked as a character in renaissance fairs called you Elizabethan. It's true. You are regal.

At twelve, you dressed as Anna Wintour for Halloween, in a raw silk Ann Taylor dress found at a Goodwill that you altered to a perfect fit. You in your oversized sunglasses and your pearls and your clutch with a perfect bob and bangs were an icon. And, as usual, you had two more costumes: Regina George from *Mean Girls* and a superhero based on, well, yourself. You in superhero form, with a hand-sewn costume of a stretchy, shiny material.

It's not just about being seen but being embodied. I think about how important it is for transgender people to feel located within their bodies. I think of two trans men I know who were Division I college athletes before they transitioned. I think of another friend, a trans woman, who transitioned later in her life but, in her childhood, was a fantastic athlete and then became a somatic meditation guide. She'll tell you that she believes that being rooted in her body has saved her life. How important was it for these people to be so fully embodied? Did it help their transition? Is it coincidental that two of the most well-known transgender people in American history were a professional tennis player and an Olympic gold medalist in the decathlon?

One of the first things to be taken from a transgender child when they begin to transition is the sport they love. There are boys' teams and girls' teams, and the transgender child is often forced to choose between being outed or misgendered or seen for the person they do not see themselves to be or to give up the sport altogether. They often choose to give it up. At a crucial time for them to feel more empowered in their bodies, they're robbed of this fully embodied powerful self. Transgender kids are more likely to be anxious and depressed. What helps with anxiety and depression? Exercise.

If the child is disconnecting from the sensory world and their own body, and if they're having less access to sports—and therefore community and that feeling of being of use as well as the integration of their bodies—all at the same time, does this put transgender people at great risk? I think the answer is yes.

When I watch you dance and do gymnastics and pretend you're in fight scenes from *Buffy the Vampire Slayer*, I feel you stomping and kicking and cartwheeling and spinning yourself into your body. I see your power being repetitively drummed into your being.

Brilliant writer, producer, actress, and activist Jen Richards speaks to this. In the documentary *Disclosure*, she shares her experience of watching another documentary in which a father expresses his love for and pride in his transgender child. She says, "No one's looked at me that way. How could I look at me that way?"

Director and producer Nance Ford, the first openly trans man to be nominated for an Academy Award, puts it this way: "We cannot be a better society until we see that better society. I cannot be in the world until I see that I am in the world."

Take the documentary *Suited*, which tells the story behind Bindle & Keep, a fashion company that specializes in making clothes precisely fitted for trans bodies. I was struck by Rae Tutera, a queer/transgender-identified tailor and partner in the company. Rae said, "I had gotten really accustomed to being invisible. It was really hard for me to embrace myself." I thought of the word *embrace* and decided to take it literally. How do you hold yourself if you are invisible, if you are disembodied? We need to hold ourselves and to be held, not blindly, but fully embodied and accepted in that body.

Not just trans people.

All of us.

There's a particularly philosophical moment in the Vatican's document on gender. It goes like this: "The formation of one's identity is itself based on the principle of otherness, since it is precisely the direct encounter between another 'you' who is not me that enables me to recognize the essence of the 'I' who is me." (What? I know. A moment of existential philosophy.) On some level, they're talking about the formation of the self in relation to others; they're talking about gazing, about seeing and being seen for your true self, and loved, wholly. They know how crucial this is and yet they also seem to be unaware of the consequences for those who are denied this truthful, loving gaze between the self and the "you" who is not me.

When we look at a transgender child and we deny them an expression of their true identity, when we refuse to call them by the name and the pronouns that reflect who they truly are, we are refusing to see them. We are messing with their existence in the world.

In *A General Theory of Love*, it's made clear that "if a parent actively hates a child, if she affirmatively knows him in the punishing clarity of her fury—that child will fare better than one who languishes in the dim ether of emotional ignorance." If a parent doesn't see a child for who they are, they are negating the child's existence. If they see the child for who they are and hate that child's gender identity, at least that child is being seen. What's most dangerous is to ignore. In doing that, we are wearing away the child's sense of self.

Or maybe this is what other parents who use the word *mourning* mean. They mean this tidal feeling—a riptide, really, that makes you cry so suddenly—a sting behind the eyes and then tears and these heaving hearts thudding in their chests. They think that some truth has been altered. It hasn't. There's a human being standing in front of them; that person is the truth, their own truth. That is the truth that matters.

The woman who'd trained me to take calls from families of transgender kids explained to me that the parents will tell you they had no idea. "They'll say that the child was typical and never told them a thing. They'll swear that there were no clues," she said. "But the vast majority of the time when I've met the families on down the road and I've had the chance to hear the kids' side of the story, they tell it completely differently. They talk about all the things they did, the ways they dressed, the toys they loved—how obvious it all was. And they'll tell you how many times they explained it to their parents, in different ways at different ages. They went ignored."

I've met trans people who gave no indication, who tried very hard to hide that truth from everyone, including their families. I've met parents who said that their child clung to the gender they were assigned at birth.

But in cases where the two stories are at odds, maybe both the parents and the children are telling the truth. Human beings will refuse to see what they don't want to see. They'll refuse to know what they don't want to know.

Take the case of Mrs. Dodds laid out by Dr. V. S. Ramachandran in his book *Phantoms in the Brain*. Because of an injury to the right hemisphere of the brain due to a stroke, she was unaware that she was paralyzed on the left side of her body, with a diagnosis of "anosognosia." She'd report that she wasn't paralyzed, that both of her hands worked absolutely well. When asked to touch the doctor's nose using her left hand, she didn't move. But when asked if she was touching his nose, she was a little exasperated. Of course she was. When asked to clap her hands, her left hand did the motion of clapping. But it clapped air. In her mind, she'd clapped her hands.

There are complex neurological reasons behind the interplay between the left and right hemispheres of the brain that explain Mrs. Dodds's experience. But all of our brains do tricky things. Navigating our lives is a process that requires that our brains make these moves in little ways all day long. Some things fit with the story we need in order to survive, in order to feel safe. Other things don't. We focus on the things that do.

When I see a transgender child who hasn't been allowed to transition or who is at the very earliest stages of that process, I'm usually looking at someone who hasn't been seen. In most cases, they don't make much eye contact. They've learned not to. Why keep looking at people who reflect a distortion back to you? Their experience of being seen is a funhouse mirror, disorienting. Their voices are often so hushed they're barely heard. Sometimes they're awkward in their own bodies, hunched over to hide breasts or slouching in order to take up less space. Sometimes there are a bunch of diagnoses; the parents have been trying to unravel the mystery of this quiet child. But after transition, the child emerges. Usually, the previous diagnoses lighten or disappear completely. Where once there was a pale outline of a self, as hidden from our incorrect gaze as possible, now there's this beaming face, this brightness, a nearly phosphorescent shimmer of light. It's beautiful to watch.

What's also beautiful to watch? You in the mix of all of your cousins.

Everyone in the family knows you're trans, knows you're a girl, knows some of the story, more or less, that I've written down here about the South and why we left.

My brother and sister-in-law have five kids; four of them are daughters. They're all now in their twenties and early thirties, and from the moment you arrive at their house for family occasions, you are doted on. A bathrobe with your name monogrammed on it awaits. When their oldest daughter asks you what you want for breakfast, you say, "Poached eggs." And she looks up how to poach an egg. You have in-home spa days and hand-me-down gifties. You lounge with the cousins on the deck, drinking your fancy fresh-fruit smoothie, windblown and sunstruck. At a recent wedding, my brother made sure that you got to ride in the limo because—of course. You are not just seen. You are the baby, fussed over and adored.

My hope is that all of this sweet affection is what you become accustomed to.

You're now about to turn thirteen, the age when so many religions and cultures pause to allow the child to acknowledge who they are, who they want to be, and often when they affirm some idea of manhood or womanhood. (You are so poised and full of self.) You have your vast, rich interior life, your spot-on perception of the world, your way of seeing and knowing yourself and that world. Like all kids, you have things you want to do with your life. Today, those go something like: learn Japanese, perfect an Australian accent, make your own movies, design your own clothing line. . . . We all need to have our selves reflected back to us, on a very basic human level. But as much as you need to be seen for who you are, your relationship with fashion, specifically, goes beyond that. It goes inward. It is about knowing yourself. It is about vision and imagination. It is about these bright, vivid gifts of the eye, knowing what is transcendent and being drawn to it. It is about the beauty of what human beings can make, what they can spin from a dream into reality.

It's a glimpse of our own divinity—if you believe that we were made in God's image. He made us. He is our Creator. If we're made in his image, then we are creators too. It is an essential element of our creation to desire to create.

We make. And in so making, we make a self.

We bought the material for the dress you dreamed of. We went to the store where Sophie buys fabric for her wingback reupholstering projects. Your sleeve had to be a thick, stiff fabric to create the structured look you were after.

The sleeve now exists. It cuffs your elbow and flares out like a gray-blue lily.

Part V

PAST, PRESENT, AND FUTURE

38

HERE'S A GLIMPSE OF who your siblings are now.

Tate is twenty. The boy who loved soccer is now a college soccer player. In his college entrance essay, he mentioned the Montgomery Bus Boycott, Harvey Milk's boycott of a liquor store in the Castro, Trump's loss of non-profit galas at Mar-a-Lago after his support of neo-Nazis and the KKK in Charlottesville, and the NBA's threat to boycott in North Carolina after the state government passed the bathroom bill. "I want to make money to position myself to do right by others," Tate wrote in his essay. There are some inherent contradictions that he'll bump up against, but that's where it'll get interesting.

His girlfriend, also a college athlete who's played ice hockey and lacrosse, came to visit recently. Afterward, it dawned on me to ask if he'd told her that his little sister is transgender. You've always let your brothers and sister tell those they're close to.

"I never tell anyone until after they've met her," Tate said, and he checks with you first.

It's a beautiful rule. You exist first, fully your ebullient, funny self. This other piece of who you are comes later. It's only one piece.

As for Isaac—the boy who once wrote in his college essay, "It's not about being selfless but other-people-full"—he's grown up. He's twenty-three and finishing his degree, having moved from a college in Chicago to one in LA. He's studying film production and screenwriting. He spends a lot of his time creating characters, sometimes acting, but in either case, he's practicing the art of being other-people-full.

Sophie is now twenty-five. The girl who threw herself into art when she felt helpless and was grieving is now in graduate school, an artist. You've been one of her models. In one of her works, you stand with a proud chin, an imperious look, a smile. You're barefoot, wearing a skirt and a tank top, your belly button a shadow visible beneath it. The stretch of the tank top material is so perfectly rendered that you can tell that you've just taken a breath.

While we keep your identity protected, your father and I continue to do a lot within the community and for it. I dedicate a lot of my time to pushing for some law, fighting for some change. The Supreme Court's ruling hasn't yet created a change in our health insurance policy. So, I keep urging.

I stayed in touch with the superintendent for a while. I waited a long time before following up after our last meeting. I ended my email this way:

> *I disagree with the National Catholic Bioethics Center and was dismayed by some of the medically inaccurate information. But there's one thing I completely agree with: "Even when they have engaged in actions that have done irremediable harm, we must continue to accompany them and show them the love and compassion of Christ." When you said, at the start of the meeting, that you would not have a place for our daughter in the coming years, you were not living up to that duty to show her love and compassion in Christ. But I must acknowledge my own duty. I believe that your current policy will cause irremediable harm. It puts children's lives at risk. I believe that, one day, you might need me. And I want you to know that I am here to meet you with love and compassion in Christ.*

He wrote back. Although there was no change in policy, he was apologetic and thankful. It was not an ending.

I've stopped believing in endings.

And you.

As the first pandemic lockdown was put into place, you were about to turn thirteen. You'd been planning a dance party with all of your friends. That plan was scuttled. Now I was stumped. How was I going to make this birthday special?

I was looking out an upstairs bedroom window. It was afternoon. The backyard was awash in light. One tree, a tall magnolia, was heavy with blooms. The limbs were so weighted that some touched the ground.

I had an idea. What if we brought the beauty of that tree inside?

When it got dark, your father went out and trimmed the lowest limbs.

Some were long, some short. He laid them on the floor of the garage, which was filled with their perfume.

Later that night, once you were deeply asleep, I collected clippers, painter's tape, scissors, all of our metal water bottles, and vases.

I carried some of the flowering limbs into your room and taped them to a chair. This was one of the first chairs that Sophie had claimed, secondhand, but hadn't reupholstered. It has a tall back with wide arms and pink fabric. I made sure that each limb was situated in a water bottle that was also taped to the chair.

I then taped more limbs and their bottles to the banister, heading downstairs. I lined the stairs with little vases of individual blooms. And when I ran out of vases, I put the blooms in bowls of water, where they floated.

At the end of the stairs, I rolled out a piece of purple and violet batik cloth given to me by a Nigerian friend. I collected the flowers that had fallen to the garage floor and made a path of petals down the hallway, down the stairs, along the cloth.

I decorated another chair, making it into a throne of blooms that would arch over your head.

What I remember most clearly is that morning when, still sleepy, you followed the petals down the stairs and found your way to the flowering throne and sat down in it, the petals grazing the top of your head, that fine christening of pollen. A few of the magnolia's thick petals fell to the floor. They were so heavy, we could hear them tap against the wood.

What would the person who made the call to the Department of Children and Families think of you now? The knock at the door rarely crosses my mind these days, but when it does, it feels like it was inevitable. If not that person, that call, on that day, then someone else, something else, on some other day.

We moved as we needed to move and learned what we needed to learn, and what lies before us is unknowable. The future has always been unknowable. But right now, it feels more unknowable than ever before in my life, and that's the lesson before us. Accepting that unknowable future with a fuller understanding of its unknowableness.

For a time, early in the pandemic, your sister and brothers came back home.

Tate was the first. He set up in the basement. Isaac was next. He had an apartment in LA but didn't want to be holed up with his roommate for months on end. He got on a plane as numbers started spiking. Sophie showed up once it was clear that her studio was closed for good and her summer work had dried up. We were all suddenly back in the same house again. Zoom classes were going, room upon room. And when they weren't—and sometimes even when they were—we were loud and obnoxious and kept busy. Sophie hunted Facebook Marketplace for beaten-up wingbacks for around thirty bucks or less. One by one, she reupholstered them on the porch. The dining-room table was filled with earrings she'd made; you and Tate took over her marketing plans. We have two elder dogs, sweet and a little doddering. We took turns lifting the oldest one to stand, carrying her up and down steps. And because we were all here and had the energy, we adopted a dog. Sophie trained her. A Hula-Hoop was tied to the fencing around the garden because the dog turned out to be an excellent jumper. Sophie bonded with the dog so much that she took the dog with her when she headed back to her life. And we adopted another dog, an adorable tiny dog that can fit in a pocketbook but prefers not to. In the evenings, Tate taught Zoom soccer sessions to kids in Wisconsin from our driveway. You and Isaac worked on a film together. He curated all of our movie watch lists. You made your own short film, a comedic spy thriller starring our dogs. You've been learning to write with your left hand, perfecting your churro recipe, sewing dresses and curtains and dog outfits. We took walks together—various dogs, various kids, various conversations.

And sometimes, at dusk, we all got together and crossed the road and hopped the fence to tour the golf course at the country club that we don't belong to. Tate brought one of your dad's old spare clubs and teed off at random holes.

One time, we all froze in place as a herd of deer pounded across the grass to the neighborhood on the other side of the course. And it was clear. We were standing on the edge of something. Not just as a family, not just each of us as individuals, but all of us. The whole world. Maybe that edge is always there. Maybe that's part of what I've learned—how quickly things can change. In that moment, the edge felt so clear and manifest. It emerged, and we were on it.

39

THIS PAST FALL, YOUR dad and I were on a walk, and he said, "*We hold these truths to be self-evident.* That's how I see it now. She's a girl. It's self-evident." He was circling back to an earlier conversation we'd had about your decision not to tell people that you're trans and how that might change at some point. You talk about coming out from time to time—about who, among your friends, would have your back, who wouldn't get it, who'd be hostile, who'd make it about them, mainly the person who'd claim you had been deceiving them.

Jen Richards has this to say: "I kind of hate the idea of disclosure in the sense that it presupposes that there is something to disclose." You are a girl. "It reinforces their assumption that there is a secret that is hidden and that I have a responsibility to tell others and that presupposes that the other person might have some kind of issue or problem with what's to be disclosed. And that their feelings matter more than mine."

Meredith at five years old said, "Okay," but wanted to know what made her special; the conversation went back to her, which is absolutely delightful for a five-year-old, but it's where a lot of people remain. When the Catholic youth pastor made up in his imagination the teenaged boy for a hypothetical dating situation, he was worried about the boy, not you. If you tell your middle school friends, some will be wonderful. Some will find ways to make it about them. You have to see this coming and try to prepare for it.

"We used to worry that people would think we were lying or tricking them. But we're not even withholding the truth," your father said. "*We hold these truths to be self-evident.* She presents as a girl because she's a girl. Her journey just isn't the usual one."

Of course these truths are not always self-evident for everyone. Laverne Cox had to be out. She claimed her beauty. Some people simply have to fight hard for the right to have the truth of their identity respected. Everyone has an unalienable right to life, liberty, and the pursuit of happiness. I wonder if the drafters of the Declaration of Independence had any idea how radical happiness would turn out to be.

Joy is radical.

Your father and I believe you have an unalienable right to pursue joy, which rightfully includes being seen for who you are.

Not all parents are built this way. There is a process of acceptance among the parents of transgender kids, and it has stages—or at least this is what I've noticed. Someone can fly through the stages quickly or get stuck on one and never progress. Your father got hung up, momentarily, on the stage of self-blame and shame. "This is my weakness made manifest," he confessed early on. But, once said aloud, he got over it. I got hung up on fear and still sometimes do.

But there are some parents, especially fathers, who get stuck on a stage and withhold acceptance forever. Their children can be failing at school, depressed, anxious, anorexic, cutting themselves, self-medicating, and even knowing what their child needs from them, they won't progress to acceptance.

Their child can attempt suicide, and they won't progress.

Your father has met some of these men in workshops. (In fact, he's helped run workshops for fathers.) There's a moment in the stories these men tell when someone sat them down and asked them a question. It's a story told over and over in many forms.

This is the question: *Would you rather have a dead son or a living daughter?*

Or, depending on their child's gender identity: *Would you rather have a dead daughter or a living son?*

Usually, we're not talking about a child at all but about a teen or even an adult son or daughter.

This question said somberly and with conviction can work. But, my God, the people who have to be faced with that question in order to progress to acceptance are the saddest people I've ever met. They are so incredibly sad, ripped apart from within by their own love for their child, a love they deny themselves. A love that is longed for.

What's more common is mourning. The parents who become great advocates and dedicate themselves to transgender rights still often mourn. I see this as mourning a story they've created around the child, the mythology of who they are as mother and father, who they are as a family. And I see it as mourning the imagination of the future, the narrative they were preparing to step into. In this way, they're mourning their own sense of self—the story they tell of who they are. We are built by the stories we tell ourselves. Writing a new story isn't easy, especially if they know no transgender people, if they know no transgender futures for their child to walk into. They have to create an entire mythology. They might feel like they have to build a world.

They don't. There is a world full of brilliant transgender people doing brilliant things, of course. But parents don't often know it.

They have to connect with others in order to create an imagined future, to shore up the story of self and the one they imagined for their child. It's not easy or simple, mainly because they love the mythology they created; the stories they have to give up are beautiful, crafted in fine detail with the hand-stitched embroidery of their imaginations. Their sense of self is inextricably stitched into it. They are mourning who they thought they would be. They are suffering from some hope transferred onto the child, some dream deferred.

Your dad and I had things to overcome, but I wouldn't describe our process as anything close to mourning. From the earliest moments of your self-expression, you were so elegant—toddlers can, in fact, be elegant—and funny and completely yourself. We have this picture of you at five years old, and you look like a young Diane Sawyer in patent leather shoes about to command an interview with a despot. We loved the human being that you were and the one you were becoming. We never mourned some imagined version of you. You were young; the story was just taking shape. We were able to start building the new story.

How do I explain the emotion that I felt, that your father felt in those early days of your transition? I don't know that there's a word for it. It's not one bright emotion with a clear outline. It's an overwhelming confluence of emotions. It's love, yes. And fear. It's knowing that you are going to change us, profoundly, and that there will be more love and more fear. It's knowing that there will be pain that we can't imagine and can't brace for, knowing that you will endure pain that we can't imagine or brace for. Your father and I understand the distribution of a child's pain by now, how it multiplies violently inside of the parent when we can't make it stop. It's knowing that, with this pain, we'll know more joy. Or we'll understand it more deeply.

It's this feeling of intense pre-nostalgia. Nostalgia that looks forward not backward. What is the word for that? We are overtaken by what we know will come, not knowing its shape.

We were old(ish) parents by the time you were born. So we knew a lot about how a child changes your internal landscape—those tide pools of pain and joy and love and fear. But new parents know it too, sometimes unconsciously. We were all children once. Most of us saw our parents walk it, live it, mess it up, wade into it, and sometimes get dragged out to sea by pain and joy and love and fear.

You don't remember your transition—only that you were always a girl. You said it and we listened. Now imagine the transgender boy getting his first buzz cut, shopping in the boy's section for his first button-down and necktie. Imagine the transgender girl who's finally allowed to grow her hair out, clipping it back in a barrette, wearing her first blouse. Imagine all the children in between, picking and choosing this part and that part of their identity—masculine and feminine, the brilliant haze of it. Imagine how it must feel to have longed to hear the correct pronouns, the right name, and how it takes shape when it's sprung loose in the air around you. Imagine how the pain would ease.

Imagine a series of firsts: the words *my daughter*, the words *my son*, and all of the power that comes with them forming in a throat, moving through the mouth of a mother, a father; to be kissed by those words on the forehead; to be gazed at with true adoration as the person you are by those you love; how those words, those gazes help you feel like you're stepping into your own tingling skin—for the first time.

This is love. Don't forget it. Being seen for who you are. Being known, adored, pre-forgiven. It's love.

What the LGBTQ+ movement gets right is pride. Pride and joy.

In the South, the lawyer told us that we had to decide who would take the blame, we had to figure out how to express our shame or fear. In order to maintain the structure of men and manliness as the highest power, we had to deny all joy and all pride in you.

We agreed.

We were complicit.

We bowed our heads and handed over our binder and said, *Look at all of our concern. Look at all of our fear. Look at our shame.*

We gave them what they wanted. That was cowardice or that was manipulation in order to keep you. What is cowardice when you have so little power? We knew what we wanted and what we were willing to do to get it.

We wanted, above all, to keep you. (This still doesn't make what we did right.)

We gave them what was expected, what our culture demands.

How could I ever be in a position to talk about my fears of assimilation for you? How, after that, could I ever expect you to want to come out and attend to others' confusion and rage and perversion and hate? Even knowing there will be love.

You know what's maybe even worse? I'd do it again. I'd play the role. I'd put on my face powder and blush and gummy mascara and my conservative skirt and blazer, and I'd perform my concern and shame and fear.

I denied my joy. I denied my pride.

I don't know if that should disgust me or if that's just part of how I'm supposed to operate. As a woman, I've learned that I have to have a certain plasticity in order to make my way.

But I carry my disgust with me. I'll never get over my fear of someone taking you from me. Never. I want to wear the proud-parent-of-a-trans-kid t-shirt; I also know that I'd fold if it meant someone was really coming for you.

They always blame the mother.

(This mother was willing to beat them to it.)

But listen. Listen to me.

I am joyful. You are joy. You are living, breathing joy. I am so driven by my steam of pride for you, I'm a ship. Maybe a battleship.

I adore you. My adoration is drilled into these pages.

One day, maybe you'll tell me how to fight for you, and I'll do it. And your father will do it. And your sister and brothers and your big extended family and your queer family will do it too.

Meanwhile, every day, joy. Every day, no matter how sick the news, we pursue happiness. Because that act alone is radical. Like girlhood. Girlhood is radical—your girlhood and all girlhoods.

I'm rarely surprised these days by human brutality, the cruelty of policy and law, the bloody violence.

But joy? It still shocks me. Expressions of love and pride? These can stun me.

Joy is a kind of rebellion. Within that rebellion, a mother's pride can be a mutiny.

My love for you is riotous.